To the Kennedys –
with love,

Susy

STUDIES ON ETHNIC GROUPS IN CHINA

STEVAN HARRELL, EDITOR

D1714626

COMMUNIST MULTICULTURALISM

ETHNIC REVIVAL IN SOUTHWEST CHINA

SUSAN K. McCARTHY

UNIVERSITY OF WASHINGTON PRESS • SEATTLE AND LONDON

THIS PUBLICATION IS SUPPORTED IN PART
BY THE DONALD R. ELLEGOOD INTERNATIONAL
PUBLICATIONS ENDOWMENT.

University of Washington Press, P.O. Box 50096, Seattle, WA 98145 U.S.A.
www.washington.edu/uwpress

Library of Congress Cataloging-in-Publication Data
McCarthy, Susan K.
Communist multiculturalism : ethnic revival in southwest China /
Susan K. McCarthy. — 1st ed.
p. cm. — (Studies on ethnic groups in China)
Includes bibliographical references and index.
ISBN 978-0-295-98908-2 (hardback : alk. paper)
ISBN 978-0-295-98909-9 (pbk. : alk. paper)
1. Yunnan Sheng (China)—Ethnic relations.
2. Tai (Southeast Asian people)—China—Yunnan Sheng.
3. Bai (Chinese people)—China—Yunnan Sheng.
4. Hui (Chinese people)—China—Yunnan Sheng.
I. Title. II. Title: Ethnic revival in southwest China.
DS793.Y8M4 2009   305.800951'35—dc22   2008045990

CONTENTS

FOREWORD

Susan McCarthy's *Communist Multiculturalism*, the eleventh volume in the Studies on Ethnic Groups in China series, exemplifies in many ways the methods and the message that the series employs and delivers. If we want to understand ethnicity, ethnic groups, and ethnic relations in China, we cannot rely on the study of single groups or single time periods, nor can we use the methods and theories of single disciplines. Rather we need to address full-on the complexity of the Chinese nation and its component parts. This means not only context, but detail. We need to recognize that we can understand a group only in relation to others with whom the group interacts; we can understand a historical period only in the context of what happened before and after. And we have to recognize above all that no group is quite like any other group, that no group can stand for "minorities," and that no group's relationship with the state is quite like that of any other group. In short, we need to compare, and to compare the details. And to do this comparison effectively, we need to employ the methods of many disciplines, which is why our series has already included authors and contributors from history, anthropology, political science, literature, linguistics, and geography. But more significantly, all our authors employ concepts and methods from multiple disciplines in single books and chapters.

Communist Multiculturalism embodies this approach and philosophy. McCarthy spent two years in Yunnan, learning through intensive field research and everyday experience just how varied and complex China's ethnic groups and ethnic relations are. In her rich yet rigorous synthesis of her findings among the Dai, Bai, and Hui, she offers a detailed empirical demonstration of some of the most important aspects of ethnicity in China.

To begin with, ethnic groups are not the same. Not only do their cultures differ—a rather obvious point—but their ways of being ethnic differ as well. Dai are very different culturally from Han Chinese and other non-Theravada-Buddhist peoples, as well as being proud of their descent from the formerly independent polity of Sipsong Panna. They are what the Chinese ordinarily think a minority should be—different, but not separatist. The Bai, long subjects of various Han-ruled regimes, are much less different culturally but still take pride in their ethnic uniqueness. The Hui are even less different from the Han—they speak Chinese as their primary language and their major differences relate to their Islamic religion. But they have a reputation for being oppositional to the state and thus rather dangerous.

These different ways of being ethnic may be interesting in and of themselves, but, more important, they serve to point out important truths about relationships between minorities and the state that are otherwise easy to overlook. Difference, celebration of difference, revival of identity, ethnic pride—all may add up to separatism or ethnic conflict in some cases, but they do not need to. There are certainly separatist sentiments and organizations among China's best-known minority ethnic groups—the Tibetans and the Uyghurs—but separatism is unimportant or nonexistent among the groups McCarthy describes. They are all part of the Chinese polity and have made little or no attempt to separate themselves from it. But even counting out separatism, there are varying degrees and different modes of ethnic conflict. In recent years, Hui have had disputes with Han and other ethnic groups in Yunnan and elsewhere, but there has been no overt conflict, and in fact little contention, between Bai and their neighbors. Put succinctly, ethnic identity and nationalism are not synonymous, nor are ethnic conflict and ethnic separatism.

But we would be oversimplistic if we saw these differences merely as a range from conflict with the state to no conflict with the state. A third lesson emphasized in McCarthy's study is that the state can—and in fact is usually wise to—not only not suppress certain forms of ethnic revival and ethnic identity but actively encourage and support them, as it does with the Bai and Dai in particular. This can promote ethnic groups' support of the state and identification with the multiethnic nation. But still, this does not always work—many Hui, despite being loyal citizens of China, have frequent conflicts with other ethnic groups.

In short, the questions of ethnicity and nation-building in China are complex and cannot be reduced to a simple formula. Nor can they be understood through a single discipline, as McCarthy, a political scientist, shows when she combines theories and concepts mostly from her own discipline with methods drawn heavily from anthropology and with insights from history and the arts.

We are thus delighted to present *Communist Multiculturalism* to the reading public. It tells us many things we need to know if we are to understand today's multiethnic China.

STEVAN HARRELL
Seattle, March 2009

PREFACE

This book is the fruit of many years of thinking about questions of cultural identity in the Chinese context. It analyzes the politics of post-Mao cultural revival among three Chinese minority groups, the Dai, Bai, and Hui, and explores how minority cultural practice and identity reflect, refract, and challenge broader Chinese discourses of membership and national identity. It also considers the implications of the Dai, Bai, and Hui revival for common conceptions (and misconceptions) of culture, identity, and the nation.

My interest in the subject of Chinese minorities grew out of experiences teaching English in China in the late 1980s. During the year I spent in Yunnan, it was obvious that minority culture was undergoing a renaissance of sorts, following decades of enforced conformity. I wondered how minorities perceived this revival, and what it meant to them. I also wondered about the state's role in promoting it. What oversight did the Chinese Communist Party (CCP) and the People's Republic of China exercise over minorities' cultural activities? Did officials merely tolerate this revival, or did they participate in more active ways, and if so, why? Moreover, what did this ethnic and cultural ferment mean for the coherence and viability of the Chinese nation?

It was several years before I began to investigate these issues in a more systematic fashion. As a graduate student of political science in the mid-1990s, I found myself drawn to questions of culture and identity. These issues were particularly salient during that time of the Soviet Union's collapse, the genocide in Rwanda, and ethnic cleansing in the former Yugoslavia. These crises pointed to problems inherent in multiethnic, multinational states. In the media, such events were frequently described as the fruit of ancient hatreds or as stemming from failures of cultural and national integration. Another issue garnering attention during this period concerned civil society and its liberalizing potential. The collapse of communist and authoritarian governments from Czechoslovakia to Chile and from South Africa to the Soviet Union focused attention on the power of citizen-led associations to challenge repressive regimes. Some observers argue that autonomous social organizations—civil society, in other words—helped bring about the end of these regimes and establish the conditions for democracy. In China, the Communist Party was firmly in power, but events such as the 1989 Tiananmen student movement revealed the potential for grassroots institutions to mobilize public action.

This book is an effort to understand the nature and meaning of cultural revival among the Dai, Bai, and Hui. It traces these groups' efforts to resuscitate and expand traditional customs, religion, language, art, music, and community institutions. In doing so, it explores what, if anything, this revival says about "Chineseness" and membership in the Chinese nation-state. At the same time, it examines whether and how Chinese national identity and membership shape the minority revival. The book also considers what the revival says about changing state-society relations in China.

RESEARCH METHODS

The research for this book was carried out over a number of years, and consists of fieldwork conducted in Yunnan and analyses of published research and other documents. Publications include Chinese government reports, statistical yearbooks, county almanacs, academic books and journals, special interest magazines, websites of religious schools, memoirs, etc. During the fieldwork portions of my research, I conducted semistructured and open-ended interviews with members of the Dai, Bai, and Hui, and other *minzu* (ethnic groups), including the Han majority. Interviewees included peasants, laborers, academics, students, officials, entrepreneurs, retired cadres, monks, imams, teachers, shopkeepers, and even ex-royalty. Some of my respondents and informants were retired cadres who had fought with the People's Liberation Army against the Nationalists, while others were young men and women whose knowledge of the Mao years is limited.

Fieldwork was carried out in a number of locales, from October 1996 through October 1997, and again in the summer of 2002. During the first year of research, I spent about two months each in the prefectures of Dali and Xishuangbanna, with the interludes spent in Kunming. I also made subsequent two- or three-week trips to these prefectures toward the end of my stay. While in Dali and Xishuangbanna, I lived in guesthouses, occasionally staying in people's homes. I conducted interviews in the main cities of Dali and Jinghong, as well as in nearby counties, townships, and villages. Many of these trips were one to several days in length, though some were several days to a week in duration. I made multiple visits to a small number of sites. In Xishuangbanna, I was usually accompanied by a Dai guide (*peitong*) who also served as a translator, necessary since I do not speak Dai. In Dali, I was sometimes accompanied by a Bai guide, though on many occasions I was by myself, especially when going to Muslim communities. Local people I befriended also took it upon themselves to show me around and introduce me to their friends, family, and neighborhood. In Kunming, I spoke to people in the city and nearby counties. In the summer of 2002, I revisited almost all of these places, saw some of the same people, and also traveled to a Hui community in the Tibetan autonomous prefecture of Shangri-la.

My fieldwork experience initially encountered problems. It took four months to receive permission from the provincial Foreign Affairs Office and Educational Committee to conduct research, during which I forlornly drew up lists of possible career alternatives, since it seemed clear I would never get my Ph.D. In the end, it turned out that my application had been misplaced and thus was never submitted to the provincial agencies. When I resubmitted the proposal, I received approval in less than a week.

Another problem concerned my topic: I was told it was not possible to do field research on the Hui. For reasons I touch on in chapter 5, the Hui were deemed too sensitive and thus off-limits to foreign field research. I quickly rethought my project, originally a two-case study of the Dai and Hui, and decided to add the Bai as another case. The Bai are interesting in their own right, but the choice was partly strategic. There are many Hui in and around Dali Bai Autonomous Prefecture, and I reasoned that once I got approval to conduct research there, I would be able to move about freely (I was correct). There are also many Hui in Kunming, and I did not need permission to wander around the city talking to people. However, the limitations placed on me made it difficult to conduct formal interviews with the Hui, especially Hui officials. These constraints hampered my efforts to systematically collect data.

In the end, however, many of the most interesting comments, observations, and insights emerged not in formal interviews but in informal conversations that began once the tape recorder was turned off and my notebook put away. Helping me in all this was the friendliness and hospitality of the Chinese people, minority and Han alike. I hope that what follows does justice to their experiences, hopes, and ideals.

ACKNOWLEDGMENTS

This book was made possible by the support and inspiration of many people. The chain of events that produced it was set in motion over twenty years ago, at Whitman College. It was because of Whitman that I first went to China, thanks to the late David Deal's efforts in establishing the Whitman-in-China program. At Whitman I was inspired by several professors, particularly Tim Kaufman-Osborn, whose courses convinced me to major in politics and whom I blame for getting me into this racket. Friends I made during that first year in China have assisted me greatly with this project, especially Xiang Rong and Hu Junqiang.

The theoretical and sociological questions that underpin this book first germinated in a graduate seminar in Chinese politics I took during my first semester at Berkeley, taught by Elizabeth Perry. My final paper in that course was a research design on minority cultural revival in Yunnan, which shows that path dependence can sometimes be a good thing. Over the years Liz has given me extensive support (and much needed criticism); she insists on the highest standards from her students, and for that I am grateful. I am also indebted to Robert Price, Laura Stoker, and Tom Gold, who read drafts and provided helpful critiques of the first iteration of this project. Ernie Zirakzadeh also read sections of it and gave me insightful advice. I would never have survived fieldwork and the interminable writing process were it not for the amazing friends I made at Berkeley: Samantha Luks, Jon Marshall, Bronwyn Leebaw, John Cioffi, John Brady, Dean Mathiowetz, Nara Dillon, Robyn Eckhardt, and others. They kept me sane, sort of.

I am grateful to all the people in China who befriended and assisted me along the way. During my fieldwork I affiliated with Yunnan University, where I benefited from the guidance of Professors Lin Chaomin, Gao Fayuan, and the late Wang Zhusheng. Li Donghong of the Archeology Department was a font of knowledge on Dali and the Bai. In the field, many people guided me: Li Jiaquan, Ma Hao, Yü Bian, Ai Han'en, Ai Xiangzai, Zheng Peng, Xiao Wang, Ma Jinxiu, Ma Yuanfeng, Mi Jinye, Mi Jinhua, Ma Yuan, and Zhang Wenbo. I am fortunate to have met Zhao Cunxin and Dao Meiying, who welcomed me into their home for tea and conversation. I must give particular thanks to the many people who agreed to be interviewed or who struck up conversations with me, including the guys in the orchestra and students and teachers at the Yongjian women's mosque, the Dali Muslim Culture College, and the Xizhong primary school. In the United States, my research was greatly aided by the fantastic collection of materials at the Yenching Library at Harvard. Access to those materials was facilitated by the Fairbank Center for East Asian Research.

Financial support came from the MacArthur Foundation, which funded a colloquium on the politics of cultural identity at Berkeley that provided me with a fellowship; the Department of Political Science at Berkeley; and the Providence College Committee on Aid to Faculty Research. Fellow members of the Providence College political science department have enthusiastically championed my research and writing. In Providence I have benefited also from the friendship and encouragement of a number of people, especially Wendy Schiller, Laurie Naranch, Mark Swislocki, and Janet Sturgeon. Janet and our fellow Yunnan researchers, Sandra Hyde and Sara Davis, have given me great theoretical and practical advice over the years. Our paths overlapped in the field, and their work has greatly enriched my own.

Some parts of this book have been published previously in journals. Sections of chapters 3 and 5 first appeared in *Asian Ethnicity*, parts of chapters 3 and 4 in *China: An International Journal*, and portions of chapter 5 and the conclusion in *Religion, State and Society*.* I thank these journals

---

*Susan K. McCarthy, "Ethno-religious Mobilisation and Citizenship Discourse in the People's Republic of China," *Asian Ethnicity* 1 (2) (2000); "Gods of Wealth, Temples of Prosperity: Party-state Participation in the Minority Cultural Revival," *China: An International Journal* 2

for allowing me to use material included in these articles, and I am grateful to the insights of the editors and reviewers. I would also like to thank the two anonymous reviewers of this manuscript for their trenchant insights, thoughtful suggestions, and attention to detail.

Finally, I must offer special thanks to my family: my mother, Lila; my father, Ed; and my two older brothers, Gene and Jim. My penchant for jetting across the globe and spending long periods of time in areas with minimal plumbing has no doubt led them to wonder at times when and if I would get a normal life. I could not have done this had I not had their support every step of the way.

(1) (2004); and "If Allah Wills It: Integration, Isolation, and Muslim Authenticity in Yunnan Province in China," *Religion, State & Society* 33 (2) (2005).

COMMUNIST MULTICULTURALISM

Because of historical and racial considerations [the Chinese]
have no problem identifying those who belong to the
collective "we" and those who are the "they."

—LUCIEN PYE, "How China's Nationalism Was Shanghaied"

INTRODUCTION

This book is the result of a faux pas. It grew out of a gaffe committed several years before I embarked on my academic career. In the late 1980s, I spent a year teaching English at Yunnan University in the city of Kunming. Yunnan is China's most ethnically diverse province and is home to more than two dozen minority ethnic groups, called shaoshu minzu. In Yunnan I met many people who were members of minorities, some of them students in my classes or professors at the university. On one occasion I asked an acquaintance, in English, about her ethnic background. I knew she was a member of the Yi minority, but I didn't know if both of her parents were as well. "My mother is Yi," she said, "and my father is Han."

"Oh," I replied, without thinking, "so you are half-Yi, half-Chinese."

I sensed at once I had committed an offense. "No!" she snapped, "I am half-Yi, half-Han. I am all Chinese!"

Fortunately, my friend forgave my error; she knew English well enough to know that in the West, the term "Chinese" is frequently used as a synonym for Han. I was, for instance, learning to speak standard Chinese (Mandarin), which in Chinese is often called Hanyu, the spoken language of the Han. Yet as I reflected on my mistake, I wondered if it was purely a linguistic one. Was I just confusing terms, or did I harbor some unexamined assumptions about Chinese culture and national identity?

China is often assumed by outsiders to be a homogenous entity. Yet the Chinese are remarkably diverse in terms of language, customs, and religion. True, the Han comprise the vast majority of China's population, but they are themselves a varied lot and include subgroups that speak dozens of dialects and practice an array of social customs.[1] Moreover, the Han majority are just one of fifty-six officially recognized "nationalities," or *minzu*. The Chinese population also includes a number of so-called "peoples" (*ren*), or unofficial ethnic groups.

According to the Chinese government, this diversity is something to be celebrated. Official documents describe China as a multinational, multiethnic nation-state, one in which the so-called "nationality question" has been resolved. China is roughly 92 percent Han; together with the minorities, the Han constitute the great, multinational Chinese nation, the *Zhonghua minzu*. Pre-communist conceptions of China and Chinese identity may have been tainted by Han-centric bias, but officially these have been discarded in favor of a broad participatory notion of Chinese national membership. Because Chinese identity is supposedly not tied to any one racial or ethnic heritage, no group need feel excluded if its roots lie in some peripheral ethno-cultural stock.

In reality, of course, the matter is not so simple. Unrest among Uyghurs, Kirgiz, and Tibetans and interethnic violence among Han, Hui, Mongols, and others indicate that the nationality question has yet to be resolved. Complicating matters is the fact that Chinese national identity is a contested concept. The twentieth century was marked by repeated efforts on the part of intellectuals, reformers, and revolutionaries to rethink the meaning of what it is to be Chinese and to possess a Chinese identity— national, cultural, ethnic, or otherwise. Some of these thinkers eschewed ethno-cultural essentialism in favor of ostensibly neutral notions of Chinese identity, the most obvious being Maoist socialism. Others invoked a racial, quasi-kinship-based, Han-centric ideal in an effort to rescue a Chinese essence from the decrepitude of cultural tradition. Still others sought to meld Confucianism with ideals of social and political modernization.[2] The contradictions of these formulations and the conflicts they pose for minorities show that the nationality question is alive and kicking.

The viability of the nationality question is evident also in the minority cultural revival that began at the start of the post-Mao reform era. For the purpose of this discussion, cultural revival is the reviving for new generations and transmitting to them the beliefs, social forms, and material traits that had once characterized specific groups. Throughout China, temples, mosques, and churches have been rebuilt and restored. Bilingual education classes are expanding, arts and culture associations are surging in membership, and Chinese minorities are discovering their religious and ethnocultural roots. Among the groups participating in this revival are the Dai, Bai, and Hui of Yunnan—the subjects of this book.

This minority culture fever (*wenhua re*) raises important questions regarding identity, culture, and the nation—in China and elsewhere. First, how should we understand these efforts to promote minority culture and identity? What significance does the revival have for prevailing theories of the nation-state and national identity? Does minority revival compromise Chinese national cohesion, given that some aspects of it tap into crossnational memberships and identities? What does it tell us about Chinese national identity and the Chinese nation-state? What role has the state played in cultural resurgence, and how have state actions shaped it?

Several hypotheses can be advanced to explain and interpret this revival. First, it may be a form of separatist or proto-separatist behavior. If cultural revival is an indicator that minorities increasingly identify with non-Chinese collectivities and are organizing on the basis of these other identities, the revival may engender challenges to the Chinese state and its territorial integrity. There is evidence to support this hypothesis: during the 1990s, members of some *minzu* engaged in violent anti-state activities, and cultural and religious institutions at times served as bases of organization. Another hypothesis is that minority revival represents a kind of nonterritorial exit strategy.[3] By rebuilding and expanding cultural institutions, minorities are fostering a collective identity and existence outside the Han-centric mainstream, without engaging in actual secessionist politics. Scholars of contemporary China have noted that nonminority organizations and cultural practices enable participants to circumvent constraints on private and social behavior dictated by party-state norms. The Chinese healing art of *qigong* is one example. Anthropologist Nancy Chen argues that qigong has "reframed the very boundaries of public and private spheres, opening up different possibilities for the organization of daily life in time and space."[4] With regard to minorities, examples of cultural revival as a kind of quasi-separatist but nonterritorial exit strategy can be quite concrete. For instance, in many parts of the country the re-opening of religious schools affiliated with temples and mosques has sparked an exodus of minority students from the state school system. While the state tries to curtail institutions and activities that contravene its goals and interests, it generally regards these phenomena quite differently from overt challenges to its authority and territorial integrity.

A related hypothesis is that minority cultural revival is one element of an emerging Chinese civil society. In the wake of the Tiananmen pro-democracy movement of 1989, some scholars began using the concept of civil society to analyze popular protest and social movements in China.[5] They argued that post-Mao reforms, by decentralizing political and economic power, had facilitated the emergence of social organizations relatively free from state control. This sphere of association and organization, some argued, engendered critical discourse and the emergence of alternative identities that made anti-state resistance feasible, in both thought and action. The florescence of cultural, religious, and other organizations among minorities might be part of this more general civil society formation. Yet minority cultural activism has an added significance, insofar as it stems from ethno-cultural notions of collective selfhood that may be at odds with those propagated by the party-state. Dru Gladney has suggested that increased political protest by and organization among Hui Muslims is evidence of an emergent civil society and a Chinese public sphere. At the same time, he characterizes these actions in almost separatist terms, as part of a "new tide in ethnic nationalism and 'primordial politics' sweeping China."[6]

Minority cultural revival can also be seen as a critique of Chinese economic, social, and minority policies and of dominant notions of what it means to be Chinese. This argument is advanced in a number of contemporary analyses of Chinese minority identity and culture. In *Other Chinas*, Ralph Litzinger argues that Yao cultural and religious revival entails a repudiation of Maoist politics of class struggle and a search for new forms of what (borrowing from Foucault) he calls "'governmentality'—ways of governing at the local level that are legitimated through resuscitated cultural practice."[7] Revival as criticism and resistance is also a key theme of Erik Mueggler's *The Age of Wild Ghosts*, which examines life in an impoverished Yi community in northern Yunnan. Mueggler demonstrates that the return of traditional practices such as exorcism is bound up with a rejection of the state's efforts to control land, bodies, and behavior. Maris Gillette's *Between Mecca and Beijing* focuses on a different kind of challenge to the powers that be; her analysis of urban Hui Muslims in Xi'an shows how Hui aesthetic and religious expression opposes mainstream Chinese understandings of modernity by asserting alternative Islamic ones.

Still another hypothesis is that cultural resurgence ultimately serves state interests, sometimes at the expense of minorities' own goals. In other words, cultural revival may be not so much an assertion of minority identity and interest as it is a Han-centric tool for the advancement of the state's agenda. There are precedents that support this argument. Katherine Palmer Kaup shows how the creation of the Zhuang *minzu* in the 1950s helped the CCP consolidate its control over the province of Guangxi.[8] Louisa Schein and Dru Gladney demonstrate the ways in which the promotion of minority identities feeds an ongoing, Han-centric project of national identity construction.[9] Stevan Harrell, meanwhile, argues that the Chinese state's post-Mao concern for minority development echoes the "civilizing discourses" of earlier regimes, discourses that ultimately sought to bring diverse peoples under state control.[10] Although Ralph Litzinger highlights the ways in which Yao revival critiques modes of governance, he also shows how state approval of Yao ritual practice has generated new channels of surveillance and control.[11]

The research in this book supports a number of these hypotheses. Cultural and religious revival among the Dai, Bai, and Hui has made it possible for some members of these groups to establish modes of existence detached or separate from the larger social milieu in which they live. For instance, the version of Islam embraced by some Hui Muslims promotes identification with a global Sunni Islamic community and a concomitant turning away from non-Muslim culture and society. Other Yunnan Hui Muslims, however, view Islamic faith and practice in ways that celebrate their distinctly Chinese Islamic history. They counter what they see as self-defeating isolationism with an integrationist Islam they believe is more authentic, more traditional, and more in keeping with the precepts of their faith.

Dai, Bai, and Hui articulations of identity also express criticism of official policy. One manifestation of the Bai cultural revival is the valorization, in books, articles, exhibitions, and media productions, of Dali-area capitalists from a century ago—precisely the kinds of figures long vilified as bourgeois enemies of the people. This celebration of Bai (or proto-Bai) economic achievement reflects the national emphasis placed on the market, and on the idea that getting rich is glorious. Yet it also hints at dissatisfaction with socialist policies that some Bai believe rendered them poorer and more isolated than their forebears. The rediscovery of Bai capitalists' contributions to local and provincial development also challenges the stereotype of minorities as backward. The embrace of capitalist heroes is of a piece with other aspects of the Bai revival, such as the promotion of bilingual education and the celebration of their ancestors' contributions to the arts and music of the Tang dynasty. However, continuities between the Maoist socialist period and the policies of the present persist. Elements of the contemporary cultural revival entail rejections of Maoist policies, but others build on the policies, projects, and accomplishments of the Maoist era.

One noteworthy feature of the revival is the role of the state in nurturing and supporting it. This support takes the form of legal guarantees of minority autonomy and specific minority rights. China's Constitution of 1982 and the Law of Regional Ethnic Autonomy of 1984 guarantee, among other things, freedom of "normal" religion, so long as religious activities do not undermine stability and the social order. These laws also promise the right to self-government in minority regions, to the development of minority languages, and to autonomy in administering the finances of minority regions. The maintenance of these rights, however, is uneven. The state determines what "normal" religion is and whether religious activities are disruptive or threatening. Nevertheless, for a variety of reasons local and national officials often acknowledge these rights.

Yet Chinese officials do more than tolerate cultural resurgence. Han and minority officials at the central, provincial, and local levels are actively involved in promoting it, and they participate in it in unexpected ways. To a great extent the state's promotional efforts can be chalked up to its interest in expanding trade, tourism, and tax revenues. The commoditizing of minority culture, religion, and history is, in short, a development strategy. This does not mean that officials are necessarily concerned with historical accuracy, authenticity, or even reality. As Beth Notar shows in *Displacing Desire*, the packaging and marketing of minority culture are at times shaped by ideas that are fantastical, if not "preposterous."[12] State promotion of minority culture and history is also a legitimation strategy. National, provincial, and local governments use—and manipulate—cultural institutions to enhance their authority over and relationships with a diverse minority population. The state at times also involves itself in cultural and religious affairs in an effort to define tradition and identity in ways that support its own agenda. Its support for minority culture thus reflects the government's interest in maintaining power and control. Yet not all of the government's actions are control-driven or instrumental in promoting government agendas. This is apparent when the state is disaggregated and the interests and motivations of local minority officials are taken into account. Local officials who are themselves minorities can and do mobilize state resources to achieve minority-defined goals.[13]

The role played by officials in the revival underscores the evolving nature of state-society relations in contemporary China. These relations are often adversarial, as seen in government efforts to crack down on activities by

Falun Gong and Tibetan Buddhists, among others. However, interactions between the state and social groups can also be cooperative and mutually beneficial. Scholars such as Jonathan Unger, Anita Chan, Ken Foster, and others have shown how state-created business associations help entrepreneurs and business groups pursue their interests while facilitating the flow of information to officials, thereby enhancing government control.[14] These scholars have proposed concepts such as "socialist corporatism" and "incorporated associations" to capture the cooperative and reciprocal aspects of this relationship. While revealing instances of conflict between and within state and society, scholars draw attention to the interworking of these categories and the positive-sum quality of their interaction.

Another hypothesis drawn from observation has been overlooked or downplayed in much of the scholarship on Chinese minorities. For members of the three groups that are the focus of this study, cultural revival can be as much about being Chinese as it is about being minority. Many participants in this revival view their endeavors in terms of several discourses that relate directly to concepts of citizenship and Chinese national identity more generally, including the discourses on minority autonomy and on China's post-1949 modernization. Certain instances of minority cultural promotion are efforts to put teeth into the party-state's promises of autonomy, to modernize minority religion and culture, and to reject the stereotype of minorities as backwards and uncivilized. For many Chinese minorities, the modernization of minority culture is a means of asserting citizenship and membership in the national body politic.

The findings of this book dovetail somewhat with Gillette's study of urban Hui in the city of Xi'an. Gillette argues that consumption patterns and Islamic practice among the Xi'an Hui demonstrate that Hui Muslims have internalized state-sanctioned norms of modernization. At the same time, the Hui counter these Han-centric, state-led definitions of modernity with Islamic (or Islamicized) versions, a strategy Gillette interprets as counter-hegemonic. For these Hui—and for the rural Yunnan Hui of this study—Islam serves as an alternative "index of civilization" that allows Muslims to assert their distinctive religious identity while demonstrating their success in light of norms broadly accepted throughout China.[15] While this book reiterates many of Gillette's findings, for the Dai and Bai as well as for rural Yunnan Hui, it takes the argument further. Efforts to modernize minority culture while preserving distinctiveness are more than counter-hegemonic challenges to Han-centric national ideals. They are—or rather, can be—forms of citizenship practice.

This discussion of the relationship between minorities and the party-state or of the cultural revival does not imply that everything is rosy. For one thing, the Chinese government's commitment to cultural pluralism is limited and ambiguous. Official tolerance is trumped by the state's concern for stability and its commitment to a Han-centric vision of Chinese modernization. Furthermore, although the goals of those who champion minority culture frequently cohere with the ideals embedded in Chinese nationalism, the identity-based ferment analyzed in this book can and does hold counter-state or counter-hegemonic potential.

Minorities may link their cultural and religious endeavors to the norms of Chinese national discourse, but they are not uncritical of those norms, or of the policies in which they are enshrined. Rather, in positioning their activities in relation to economic development, minority autonomy, and even socialist modernization, minorities "wave the red flag to oppose the red flag": they deploy these methods to criticize the shortcomings of CCP policy and practice. Nevertheless, evidence that minority citizens accept these ideals suggests that, to paraphrase Tip O'Neill, all nationalisms are local. For the Dai, Bai, and Hui, being minority is, or can be, one way of being national.

CHINA'S MINORITIES

What often perplexes outside observers about Chinese minorities is the variation among minorities. Some minorities appear quite ethno-culturally distinct from the majority Han, while others are relatively indistinguishable from the Han or other groups among whom they live. Some groups are geographically concentrated, or stand out in terms of dress, religion, speech, and custom, and yet still lack any strong sense of themselves as a distinct ethnic group. Other minorities are widely dispersed and appear assimilated to dominant regional customs, but possess a cohesive ethno-cultural identity.

This complexity stems in part from the official Chinese understanding of the term "minzu" and the broad way it has been applied to ethno-cultural groups. In the 1950s, China's new communist regime embarked on a project of classifying the country's ethnic, cultural, and linguistic diversity and establishing which groups should be granted minority status. Teams of ethnographers, linguists, and historians were dispatched throughout the country to collect data on the language, customs, arts, folklore, religion, economic practices, and social structure of hundreds of self-identifying groups. As has been well documented elsewhere, the state's effort to sort through this material and identify particular minorities was informed, at least in theory, by Joseph Stalin's definition of a nation. Stalin delineated four criteria that had to be met for a group to achieve status as a nation (*narod*). A nation, he claimed, was "an historically evolved, stable community of people, based upon the common possession of four principal attributes, namely: a common language, a common territory, a common economic life, and a common psychological make-up manifesting itself in common special features of national culture."[16]

To be recognized as a *minzu*, a group had to demonstrate that it possessed these four attributes. Official Chinese understanding of who constituted a minority was also influenced by Marxist stage theory and the social evolutionary theory of Lewis Henry Morgan, which had also influenced Stalin.[17] Thus, while Chinese ethnographers tried to figure out which groups deserved minority status, they also sought to determine the stage of economic development to which these groups had progressed. A group's level of development depended on the possession or lack of a written language, kinship and political structures, religious organization, and the nature of the local economy. Thus the Akha and Wa, who practiced shifting cultivation (so-called "slash and burn" agriculture) and lacked a written script, were considered more backward than the Bai, who were sedentary wet-rice cultivators well integrated into the regional market economy of early twentieth-century Yunnan.[18] In actual practice, however, political expediency and matters of convenience generally won out over theoretical purity in the categorizing process.[19] The party-state's desire to avoid a bureaucratic nightmare also informed its decision to amalgamate over four hundred groups seeking recognition into fifty-five officially recognized minorities.

The Dai, Bai, and Hui exemplify this complexity of identity and practice. There is significant linguistic, religious, and cultural variation among them, and analysis of their post-Mao experiences provides a broad, comparative view of the minority cultural revival. These three groups also vary in their similarity to or difference from the majority Han, in their geographic cohesion or dispersion throughout Yunnan and China, in the degree to which they were socially and culturally integrated into Chinese society prior to 1949, and in subjective matters of self-identity. In both official and popular perception, the Dai, Bai, and Hui are also characterized according to their level of docility and quiescence or restiveness and rebelliousness, perceptions that seem to have become an index for government in determining how receptive they are to state-led, Han-centric civilizing projects. In other words, these three groups represent the variation that characterizes Chinese minorities as a whole.

Historically, Chinese thinking about ethno-cultural differences distinguished peoples by the degree to which they had adopted and adapted to traditional Chinese cultural practices. Those who measured up to Chinese standards of behavior, etiquette, and learning were considered civilized, or "cooked," while those whose folkways, customs, language, and actions were irredeemably foreign were viewed as barbarian, or "raw."[20] This raw versus cooked, barbarian versus civilized dichotomy established a continuum of difference and assimilation. A group's place on this continuum was determined not by blood or kinship-based notions of ethnicity but by its members' adherence to behavioral standards.

A continuum of assimilation and difference informs Chinese thinking about minorities, although the meanings of "integration" and "difference" have changed over time. The three cases examined in this study could be positioned along this continuum, with the rather "exotic" Dai at one end, the relatively integrated Hui at the other, and the Bai somewhere in between. Such a continuum, however, fails to capture the ambiguities of how minorities perceive themselves and are perceived by others in the wider society. It also fails to capture the fact that ethno-cultural distinctiveness can vary through time and circumstance; such distinctiveness can be a reaction to the experience of political and social alienation rather than its cause.

This continuum also overlooks other criteria by which minorities are judged in popular opinion, if not in policy. As mentioned above, minorities are distinguished according to how docile or rebellious they are or are perceived to be. The ideal of a "model minority"—an ideal type that is exotic, docile, and, as many scholars have shown, typically feminine—informs official, academic, and popular Chinese discourse.[21] As a corollary to the model minority ideal, there is also a type of pecking order or scale of authenticity in popular and even official discourse. The more culturally distinct (from the Han) a group is, the higher its place on that scale. Minorities whose customs differ little from the Han and who are well integrated into modern Chinese life thus deviate from the minority ideal. Groups that are highly acculturated to Han society and are also restive or rebellious are even more suspect. During my fieldwork, all sorts of people—academics, officials, taxi drivers, urbanites, peasants—expressed doubts about my case selection, usually to suggest that I drop the contentious, highly integrated Hui and examine instead the more exotic, impoverished, matrilineal Mosuo or the

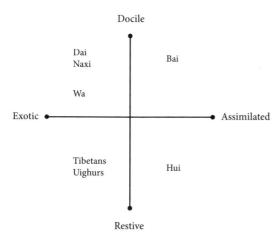

FIG. 1.1 Perceptions of variation among Chinese minorities

equally exotic and isolated Wa. My decision to study the Dai was met with universal approval.

This picture is complicated by the understandings of modernization that infuse much Chinese thinking about minorities and economic development. Exoticism is valorized, but so too is the embrace of a modernizing project that has assimilative consequences. Minorities are expected to be exotic, even quaint, but they are also expected to accept the assistance of the "elder brother" Han nationality along the path to modernity.

Rather than viewing minorities in terms of a continuum of assimilation and difference, it makes sense to situate them within a schema that includes two dimensions. Such a schema, as presented in Figure 1.1, indicates where the Dai, Bai, and Hui fit. The horizontal axis indicates the degree of cultural distinctiveness, ranging from "exotic" to "assimilated," they are perceived to demonstrate. The vertical axis indicates the nature of their responsiveness to state-led control, ranging from "docile" to "restive" (or rebellious). This way of characterizing minorities is not exact, and certainly is open to interpretation. For one thing, groups may vary over time in terms of how assimilated or quiescent they are or are perceived to be. The cultural revival itself has engendered assertions of minority uniqueness and a rejection of Han-centric conformity. It should be noted that characterizing a group as restive or docile in no way means that all members of that group are rebellious, troublemakers, separatists, passive, etc. These characterizations are generalizations of views—what Susan Blum refers to as cognitive prototypes of ethnic others—expressed in official and academic classificatory schemes as well as in statements by ordinary people.[22]

Of the three cases analyzed here, the Dai most closely approximate the minority ideal. Prior to their incorporation into the Chinese nation-state, the Dai of what is today called Xishuangbanna Prefecture constituted a fairly distinct political entity, whose linguistic, religious, and other cultural practices set them apart from mainstream Han society.[23] The Dai polity persisted several years after 1949, albeit in diminished form, due to CCP efforts to incorporate the region by co-opting the existing political and religious elite. The Dai, who number 1.3 million in Yunnan, are related to Tai peoples in Myanmar, Laos, and Northern Thailand, and their cultural revival has augmented their connections to some of these Tai groups.

The Bai are an intermediate case, and somewhat difficult to categorize. Although there are small communities of Bai in other provinces, the Bai reside almost entirely in Yunnan, mainly in the Dali Bai Autonomous Prefecture. With 1.6 million people, they are the second-largest minority in the province. The Bai speak a Tibeto-Burman language from which a written form was recently derived, and they are the descendants of various tribal and ethnic groups that held sway over Yunnan for over five centuries until the thirteenth-century Mongol conquest. They possess a number of cultural and religious practices that appear to be specific to them as an ethno-cultural entity.[24] In other words, the Bai evince many external markers of ethnic difference that justify their minority status. In terms of subjective matters of self-identity, however, the Bai are a bit of a paradox. Prior to and even after Liberation many Bai rejected the idea that they were a minority nationality. They called themselves not Bai but *minjia*, a term meaning "civilian households" that possesses no ethno-cultural connotation. They also emphasized their ancestral ties to eastern Han China and their cultural and economic accomplishments in a Confucian Chinese world. Even the "Bainess" of Bai cultural practices is somewhat murky. Past studies of *minjia* life portrayed them not as ethnics but as paragons of mainstream Chinese rural society.[25] For centuries the Bai have been well integrated in terms of culture, education, politics, and economics. Their contributions to Chinese culture and their cultural revival reflect this adaptation; they are proud of this history.

The Hui appear to be the most integrated of the three cases I examine. As the descendents of the historic latecomers to Yunnan who arrived with conquering Yuan, Ming, and Qing armies, many Hui appear indistinguishable from the Han or minority groups among whom they live. They share a language, an economy, and general cultural practices, although the degree of integration varies by region and even by settlement. Yet even where they appear mostly integrated or completely assimilated, the Hui possess a strong self-identity as a distinct ethno-religious collectivity. To an outsider acquainted with non-Muslim Chinese society there may be much that is familiar about the Hui, but they are, in Jonathan Lipman's formulation, "familiar strangers."[26] While many Hui live in communities that have undergone a significant religious revival, others neither practice Islam nor even adhere to prohibitions on the consumption of pork and alcohol. The Hui are both the smallest and the largest of the three groups examined here. Within Yunnan, they number over six hundred thousand, but nationwide the Hui number nearly 10 million. Yet many Hui scoff at the idea of the Hui as a separate *minzu*, seeing themselves instead as part of a more than 20-million strong Chinese Islamic entity some call the "Islamic nationality" (*Yisilan minzu*), a category not recognized by the Chinese government. The Hui are also the most "restive" of the three cases. Rightly or wrongly, they are viewed as the most prone of the three to be involved in ethnic conflict and criminal behavior and are regarded by many non-Muslims as troublemakers. Restive Hui are not, however, separatist rebels; interethnic and Hui-state conflicts usually arise out of local, specific grievances.

The characterization of the Hui as restive must be regarded critically. Thinking about minorities in terms of their responsiveness to the rules of Chinese society at large tends to obscure the historical and contemporary mistreatment of certain groups by successive Chinese regimes. The Hui are perceived as prone to rebellion because during the Qing and Communist regimes they were the targets of pogroms and persecutions.[27] Efforts to combat oppression have enhanced Hui cohesion and collective self-identity, and they are quick to defend themselves and their religion. There is a dynamic quality to Hui-state and Hui-Han interaction and conflict not captured in the diagram above, and both this dynamism and the history of anti-Hui persecution must be acknowledged.

The Dai, Bai, and Hui also differ from each other and the Han in terms of the contacts they possess with political and cultural collectivities beyond China's borders. Cultural resurgence among the Dai, for instance, has been facilitated by exchanges with Tai communities in neighboring Laos, Myanmar, and Thailand and has led to broader identification by Dai people with a greater Tai ethno-cultural milieu. Among the Hui, Muslim religious and educational activism is inspired and assisted by international Islamic organizations and the governments of Muslim nations. Since the Bai are found almost exclusively in Yunnan, their cultural activism has a more localized character. Yet this has not prevented Bai cultural and educational activists from looking beyond their locale—for instance, to international agencies like the United Nations—to promote their cause.

Located in the far southwest of China, on the borders of Myanmar, Laos, and Vietnam, Yunnan is the most ethnically and culturally diverse of China's provinces (fig. 1.2). The majority of China's fifty-five minorities are represented in the provincial population; the populations of twenty-four of these groups exceed four thousand. About one-third of Yunnan's 45 million residents are members of minority ethnic groups.[28] The diversity of the minority population and the province's historical isolation make it a fruitful test case for examining the relationship between national and minority identity.

Yunnan has long enjoyed, or endured, isolation from the heartland of Han China. Despite the spread of the silk trade into Yunnan as early as the second century B.C.E., the region was for centuries dominated by disparate tribal groups. From the eighth through the middle of the thirteenth centuries, successive Nanzhao and Dali kingdoms ruled much of Yunnan. These kingdoms participated in tributary relationships with the imperial courts of the Tang and Song dynasties. Cultural and technological contacts with the Chinese heartland increased, facilitating the adoption of Chinese writing and agricultural techniques. Yunnan's administrative and political independence ended with the Mongol conquest. In 1253, Kubilai Khan defeated the Dali kingdom and reorganized Yunnan as a province under the governorship of Sayyid ʿAjalls Shams al-Din, a Muslim from Bukhara in Central Asia. Under Mongol rule, that is, the Yuan dynasty, tens of thousands of Mongol, Chinese, and Muslim soldiers and civilian support personnel migrated to Yunnan and established settlements throughout the province. These settlement policies continued under the Ming (1368–1644) and Qing dynasties (1644–1911), accelerating the political and cultural integration of the province. The incorporation of Yunnan into imperial China, however, was not a one-way process. Chinese practices, norms, and institutions increasingly permeated Yunnan culture and society, but as C. Pat Giersch demonstrates, newcomers and their customs were often indigenized.[29] The province was and is today a cultural and political mélange.

Yunnan's character as peripheral to China's political, economic, and cultural core is a function of its topography and geographic location. The

FIG. 1.2 Yunnan and its neighbors

province is extremely mountainous, severely constraining the amount of land available for high-yield agriculture.[30] Until recent decades, the terrain made travel between Yunnan and the rest of China treacherous and time-consuming. Before 1966 no rail line linked Yunnan with the rest of China, although in the early 1900s, the French built a railroad connecting Kunming to Hanoi, in what was then French Indochina. Yunnan is also a border province and shares a boundary with Myanmar, Laos, and Vietnam. The province's peripheral status was mitigated somewhat during World War II, when thousands of American and Chinese troops were stationed in the province. During this period the Burma Road was constructed, the Flying Tigers flew supplies into the capital of Kunming, and major inland universities relocated from Japanese-occupied regions to the Yunnan countryside. Yet Yunnan was also one of the last areas of the country to be "liberated." The founding of the People's Republic was declared on October 1, 1949; Yunnan's liberation was accomplished half a year later in 1950.

Although Yunnan is increasingly tied into the global economy, a fact signified by the opening in 1999 of a Wal-Mart in Kunming, social problems continue to affect minorities and the province as a whole. The province copes with poverty, underdevelopment, illiteracy, and a growing AIDS problem. Yunnan is one of China's poorest provinces (table 1.1). In 2006, the per capita net rural income in Yunnan was ¥2,251 (approximately $281), just 70 percent of the already low average rural income in China of ¥3,255 ($408). Residents of cities and towns in Yunnan are considerably better off than those in rural areas; in 2006, net urban incomes averaged ¥10,070 ($1,259).[31] There are no figures on the number of minority poor, but the State Ethnic Affairs Commission estimates that minorities account for 40 percent of China's poor, despite comprising just 9 percent of the total population.[32] In Yunnan, as in other provinces, underdevelopment and poverty are aggravated by illiteracy and low levels of education.

Yunnan officials have been trying to expand the rural enterprise sector so as to increase incomes and the revenue base. The provincial government is seeking to refashion Yunnan as a gateway to Southeast Asia and to utilize its border location to economic advantage. Provincial officials have focused particular attention on the tobacco and cigarette, mining, tourism, and horticulture industries. Contraband markets and industries have mushroomed in tandem with officially sanctioned economic endeavors. Yunnan has also long been a major conduit for heroin trafficked from the Golden Triangle to the West. The province's border character is a decided advantage, or disadvantage, depending on one's perspective.

The peripheral character of the province and its peoples shapes cultural activism among the Dai, Bai, and Hui. Although concerns and interests specific to them motivate their endeavors, they are also responding to the disadvantages of residing in the geographic and cultural periphery. Minority entrepreneurs and officials are exploring how cultural institutions,

TABLE 1.1 Per Capita Rural and Urban Disposable
Incomes (in yuans) in Yunnan and China, 1980 and 2005

	1980	*2000*
Rural, Yunnan	148	2,042
Rural, all China	191	3,255
Urban, Yunnan	420	9,266
Urban, all China	478	10,493

SOURCES: *2006 Yunnan tongji nianjian,* 687, 754; National Bureau of Statistics of China, *2006 Zhongguo tongji nianjian,* http://www.stats .gov.cn/tjsj/ndsj/2006/indexch.htm (accessed May 27, 2007).

artifacts, and practices can contribute to economic development. While economic development is important, minorities think about development in more than just economic terms. For many, cultural revival means modernizing their cultures while preserving their identities.

Until recently, analyses of ethnicity and nationalism in the field of comparative politics mostly ignored questions regarding Chinese minorities. This neglect has stemmed in part from beliefs about Chinese homogeneity and exceptionalism. For good reason the Chinese were viewed as homogenous, despite significant regional diversity. Political science scholarship on contemporary China focused primarily on the big events of the twentieth century, such as imperial collapse, civil war, revolution, communism, and reform after Mao. Research on Chinese ethnic and religious groups was hampered for decades by restrictions on access and information. In the decades since 1978, however, scholarship on Chinese minorities has blossomed but few comparative political studies of Chinese minorities have been produced.[33] Moreover, Chinese minorities typically have been studied as minorities; their status as citizens and members of a Chinese national entity has been neglected, though recently that has begun to change.[34] While this book focuses on the experiences of the Dai, Bai, and Hui, it is about much more than that. It poses broader questions about culture, the nation, and the politics of national identity in China and elsewhere.

—1—

CULTURE, THE NATION, AND CHINESE
MINORITY IDENTITY

The story of the nation is often conceived of as a *Bildungsroman,* a narrative of self-journey and self-discovery. As the story is told in accounts of political nationalism or in academic theory, the development of the nation first entails the coming into consciousness of a national self and then the recognition and establishment of the nation's identity through relations and tribulations with others. If the journey is successful, the story ends with the integration of internal elements within a harmonious, well-ordered whole. The particulars of that journey vary from case to case. Some nations find what Homi Bhabha calls their "narrative of national unfolding" in anti-colonial revolution, and others in the gradual incorporation of culturally disparate elements via state-building and modernization, while still others claim their birth within the ignominy of defeat.[1] Whether depicted as conscious and politically willed, or in terms of evolutionary, "natural" development, the nation's struggle to emerge is believed to unite heterogeneous pre-national elements into a self-aware, autonomous, and sovereign entity.

Themes of narrative and the individual have figured prominently in nationalist thought and scholarship. This congruence between notions of personhood and models of the nation is not surprising, given that concepts such as autonomy, sovereignty, and will, not to mention the body politic, have their origins in Western thinking about the individual, the sovereign self. The very concept of national identity owes its existence in part to an Eriksonian notion of psychosocial identity drawn from psychoanalysis.[2] Theorists and nationalist leaders alike speak of nations following a course of development and maturation that often entails identity "crises." These crises, such as war, civil conflict, famine, invasion, and economic depression, challenge national integrity and require for their resolution a revised self-concept and stance toward other political actors.

For the nation, it is culture rather than a "personality" of selfhood to which the task of effecting unity and identity is delegated. That is, in romantic and modernist versions of the nation and some ostensibly postmodernist ones as well, something called "national culture" functions as the glue that holds the national unit together. Shared culture is viewed as a prerequisite to national consciousness and identity. It is the bedrock upon which the authority, legitimacy, and identity of the nation rests. This national culture may be modern and industrial; popular or developed as a defensive elite strategy; a residual feature of ancient collectivities; and genuine, imagined, or wholly constructed. Regardless of its nature, this shared culture is inseparable from the nation and its idea. Without the common symbols, myths, practices, and norms these express, the "we-consciousness" comprising national identity lacks any concrete basis—"imagined" though it may be.[3] In fact, without shared symbolic and cognitive reference points, no truly national identity can be generated. The invocation or creation of such a culture, therefore, is considered one of the central tasks facing would-be nation-builders. Paradoxically, shared culture is also seen as an indicator of national unity, as well as its cause, a notion whose circularity in no way hinders its appeal. National membership and identity are established, expressed, and maintained through adherence to certain specified cultural practices and ideals.

This account does not claim that successful nations are marked by the absence of nonnational cultural, civic, religious, or other political identities. As delineated in narratives of nationalisms and in much academic thinking, however, the process of national or nation-state development is expected to break down and absorb disparate sub-national or pre-national identities and communities, subsuming them within a coherent whole. To the extent that alternative, sub-national cultural identities persist, the nation is imperfectly formed, defective, or not yet complete. To extend the metaphor of the individual further, the persistence of alternative identities as rival spheres of authority and membership indicates schizophrenia, a failure ·of self-integration stemming from some genetic or environmental trauma.

There are a number of ways in which this shared culture may come into being. Nineteenth-century Romantic thinkers such as Fichte and Herder characterize the nation as the embodiment of a distinct national spirit or essence, one that achieves full expression when joined with the sovereign territorial-political entity of the state.[4] In the twentieth century, scholars began to explore the role of developmental, evolutionary processes in generating national culture. Proponents of this approach, mainly those working in the tradition (if it can be called that) of modernization theory, argue that large-scale processes of modernization and industrialization uproot residents of a territorial state by eroding traditional loci of membership such as the clan or tribe, thereby making individuals available for reintegration into the newly emergent nation. At the same time, these processes provide de-centered individuals with common experiences, educational homogeneity, and an interconnectedness that produced a sense of membership in a specific community. Because these transformations occur within the boundaries of the territorial state, the collective identity they engender is a national one.[5]

Though modernization theory as a whole has been widely criticized for its teleological assumptions and Western biases, the process model of national identity formation remains influential. Many of its assumptions underpin Ernest Gellner's influential *Nations and Nationalism*. Gellner pinpoints industrialization as the generative cause of national identity. He argues that the individuating and homogenizing processes of industrialization, combined with the spread of standardized education and literacy, endow citizens of the modern state with a common culture and shared self-image:

> When general social conditions make for standardized, homogeneous, centrally sustained high cultures, pervading entire populations and not just elite minorities, a situation arises in which well-defined educationally sanctioned and unified cultures constitute very nearly the only kind of unit with which men willingly and often ardently identify.[6]

The convergence of a standardized, industrial culture with the already delineated boundaries of the state prompts the emergence of nationalist consciousness and movements.

Other scholars emphasize the centrality of political leadership in creating cultural cohesion and the sense of "we-ness" on which national identity rests. Political elites, for example, can help forge cognitive and symbolic community among disparate individuals and groups. This approach derives from the theories of Max Weber, who highlighted the power of gifted, charismatic political leaders to create and bestow new cognitive and evaluative frameworks in times of cultural crisis. In doing so, the charismatic leader creates a new symbolic-cultural repertoire and identity with which individuals and groups can navigate experience.[7] Some analyses that draw on the Weberian approach emphasize the role of both processes and politics in national identity formation. Structural processes uproot people from their traditional memberships and identities, while political elites and parties recommit themselves within the emergent national entity.

Despite the significance of politics and processes, cultural homogeneity is the vehicle through which the nation is conceived and created, according to scholars emphasizing politics over process. Michael Hechter, for example, argues that boundary lines between ethnic and national groups result not from preexisting cultural identities or quasi-evolutionary processes, but from political institutions of control. Yet he also asserts that national cohesion requires cultural sameness to ensure that "individuals of a given nationality have certain values in common."[8] In the event that "micro-ecological variations" within territorial boundaries generate cultural differences, would-be nation-builders must work to overcome these.

This way of thinking about culture and the nation has an intuitive appeal that is enhanced by the fact that actual nation-builders stress the importance and role of shared culture. In China, after the CCP's ascent to power in 1949, for instance, cultural cohesion was of major concern to the communist leadership. It was not traditional culture the CCP sought to promote, which was after all something to be struggled against, but a new revolutionary culture expressed through conformity to socialist ethics and demonstrations of Maoist devotion. By wiring up every last mountain hamlet to a nationwide system of loudspeakers, establishing a single time zone, educating the masses, attacking feudal superstition, and promoting class struggle, the CCP demonstrated faith in the power of social communication and in the need to undermine traditional identities to build the new People's Republic.

Ultimately, however, the explanatory power of these models of nation and culture is limited. They assert or imply that shared identity is directly proportional to and dependent on a shared culture, and that the persistence of intra- or sub-national cultural difference compromises the integrity of the nation-state. In doing so, they encounter problems when trying to account for much nationalist phenomena in the contemporary world. These formulations fail to account for what is so crucial for nationalism and national identity: the mythmaking, the invention of tradition, the creation of what Prasenjit Duara calls "narratives of descent."[9] The framing of nationality in terms of cultural idiosyncrasy so often depends on the magnification of minute, even fictitious differences among people whose everyday lives are remarkable for their sameness. Much contemporary separatism and interethnic hostility spring from environments in which there is a wide "complementarity of social communication," to use Karl Deutsch's formulation.[10] Conversely, minute similarities are often emphasized by social actors seeking to create cohesion in the face of glaring differences.

Post-modern approaches to questions of cultural identity and membership are not immune to the problems of the models discussed so far. To a certain extent, they incorporate the same assumptions of identity and culture, although they typically valorize the fragmented and the particular rather than the national. While some contemporary analyses of globalization propose the emergence of supra- or transnational identities that explode nation-state boundaries, others predict the nation-state's implosion—the fragmentation of large national entities into micro-level ones. In the words of Zygmunt Bauman, "Exit the nation, enter the tribe."[11] The globalization of consumption and information has, argues Kenneth Gergen, "saturated" the self, spurring its fragmentation and fracturing national memberships and identities.[12] Many proponents of this view have been influenced by Foucault, Deleuze, and Guattari, theorists of the self who stress the constructed and contingent character of identity and who argue that the narrative unity of the self is an effect of power that obscures the fragmentary nature of actual experience.[13]

These post-modern approaches inform and enrich much contemporary scholarship on the post-Mao resurgence of localized cultural identities. Yet in valorizing particularity and viewing attempts at cultural or ideational integration as hegemonic effects of power, they run the risk of essentializing the difference and distinctiveness of minority identities and culture. Implicitly or explicitly, post-modern approaches rely on the same exclusionary model of culture and identity as does modernization theory, one that places the national in opposition to the minority. In doing so, the possibilities for syncretism and interpretation are underestimated. Certainly the political motives underlying these approaches tend to support the protection of distinct minority cultures and identities, and so are commendable. Yet post-modern approaches imply that particularistic, local-ized identities are sacrosanct, hermetically sealed constructs, incapable of being melded with national identities and values without being silenced or erased. Theoretical assumptions render post-modern scholars of cultural identity unable to account for how minorities may interpret the "national" in ways that expand its meaning and application.

One problem with these models of the nation and national identity for-mation is that they simply fail to explain certain features of minority cul-tural politics, in China and elsewhere. They furthermore hold pernicious implications for cultural minorities in general, for they are grounded on an assimilationist conceit—on the idea that sub-national, nondominant cultural identities and practices must be subsumed within an ultimately superior national identity if the nation is to achieve and maintain integ-rity. This conceit further entails that the promotion of minority identity and cultural practice must logically be viewed as subversive of the proj-ect of national identity formation. Cultural practices and institutions that promote identification with extra-national or transnational units are even more suspect, for they undermine the unity upon which national identity is based. In addition, state support for minority culture is, logically, irratio-nal self-sabotage.

These dilemmas are not simply academic. They infuse popular and offi-cial views, and thus the policies implemented to deal with minority and majority populations. The debate in the United States over multicultural-ism and its supposedly "Balkanizing" effects is one example of how theory, policy, and everyday life intersect.[14] Suspicion of cultural difference and the desire to eliminate that which will not conform motivated Serbian policy throughout the 1990s, and continues to hinder integration in the Balkan states. These ways of thinking about identity and the nation limit our ability to fully understand certain political and cultural phenomena. Alternative interpretations of cultural activism cannot be conceived, or if they can, they cannot be reconciled with existing theory. Disturbingly, the simple attribu-tion of ethnic strife to diversity or difference can lead to the blame for ethnic cleansing or religious violence being laid at the feet of its victims.

These dilemmas have led a number of theorists to propose alterna-tive ways of thinking about culture, minorities, and the nation-state. One approach has been to foreground the cultural and multicultural compo-nents of citizenship as opposed to its legal-political aspects.[15] Theorists such as Charles Taylor and Will Kymlicka, for instance, justify the pro-tection of cultural minorities in Western democracies in terms of liberal philosophy and practice. Both Taylor and Kymlicka argue that the protection of minorities and minority cultures logically follows from liberalism's basic tenets. For Taylor, minority rights and protections grow out of fundamental liberal values of tolerance and mutual respect.[16] Kymlicka, meanwhile, argues that liberalism's celebration of liberty itself necessitates such protections. Liberalism, he argues, expounds a notion of the good life in which individuals have the freedom to make rational, informed choices regarding their own lives. However, we cannot make rational, informed choices if we do not know who we are or what we want. Culture provides us with that knowledge, insofar as it constitutes our values and our very selves. Culture is the "context of choice"; it provides us "a range of meaningful options" and, in so doing, creates the preconditions for freedom.[17] For these reasons, we should recognize the contribution that minority cultures make to the achievement of shared political goals in liberal democratic states.

Unfortunately, Taylor's and Kymlicka's efforts to justify a space for minority cultural autonomy are hampered by a number of insufficiently examined issues. In considering which minority cultures deserve respect and protection, both theorists exclude the fragmentary and partial from their discussions. Taylor, for instance, dismisses from consideration any "partial cultural milieux within a society as well as short phases of a major culture."[18] Kymlicka argues that the liberal nation-state need not protect all cultures and cultural practices, since to do so would be impossible. Rather, he argues that only "societal cultures" deserve such treatment, because only these provide the "context of choice" that he claims makes liberal freedom possible. A societal culture is one that "provides its members with meaningful ways of life across the full range of human activities, including social, educational, religious, recreational, and economic life, encompassing both public and private spheres."[19] Fragments of cultures, "dying" cultures, religious minorities that are geographically and economically integrated into larger political communities, etc., are not Kymlicka's concern. Yet it is often those groups who do not meet his criteria that are most in need of political protections or are agitating for autonomy and separation.

Neither Taylor's nor Kymlicka's framework really help us think about some of the most vexing cases of cultural politics, including state-led efforts to suppress minorities and minority culture. Part of the problem lies in these theorists' mostly uncritical use of the models of nation and culture outlined above—models that turn cultural minorities into what Homi Bhabha calls "'foreign bodies,' in the midst of the nation."[20] Kymlicka states outright that he accepts the Gellnerian approach to the nation and national identity.[21] Even while trying to carve out a space for minority cultures justified in terms of liberal utility, the model he employs rests on assimilationist underpinnings.

As stated, these models of culture are predicated on the idea of culture as coherent, and as creating coherence in the body politic, whether it is a nation or an ethnic group. These models also imply that cultures are relatively discrete, distinct, and separate, as well as the property of differentiated social and political entities. But are they? Is culture coherent? Does culture create cohesion among those who share it and participate in it? Are cultures bounded entities, "owned" by their bearers? Certainly these assumptions are widespread, and their influence on our understanding of the nation, ethnicity, and other forms of political community is profound. As Akhil Gupta and James Ferguson argue,

> just as central as the concept of "culture" has been what we might call the concept of "cultures": the idea that a world of human differences is to be conceptualized as a diversity of separate societies, each with its own culture. It was this key conceptual move that made it possible . . . to begin speaking not only of culture but also of "a culture"—a separate, individuated cultural entity, typically associated with "a people," "a tribe," "a nation," and so forth.[22]

This conceptual move has shaped much social scientific research (and social science disciplines themselves) by making it "possible to bound the ethnographic object." One corollary of these assumptions is that communication across cultures—that is, among ostensibly bounded cultural groups—is difficult, even impossible. Because shared meanings cannot be produced, shared values cannot be created or assumed, except by accident. A shared identity is thus out of the question.

ALTERNATIVE MODELS OF CULTURE AND THE NATION

In place of a model of "culture as order," as Gupta and Ferguson put it, some recent scholarship underscores the partial and fragmentary aspects of identity and practice. Proponents of this view take aim at the idea of culture as societal glue, as the source, basis, and indicator of identity and cohesion. Rather than view cultures as coherent, bounded systems of meaning and value, these scholars instead stress the mutual interpenetration of cultures, their porosity rather than their purity.

One effort to rethink these issues centers on the notion of "hybridity," a concept that has garnered a great deal of attention in post-colonial political and cultural theory. Hybridity emphasizes that identities, knowledge systems, and cultures are heterogeneous mixtures of different elements, and are lived as such. Hybridity, however, is more than just another way of saying that cultures are syncretic—it is, or aims to be, counter-hegemonic. For Paul Gilroy the hybridity of black identity in Great Britain challenges hegemonic, racially "pure" (i.e., white) constructions of British national identity, as well as the very idea that identities are pure and absolute. In this reading hybridity destabilizes the exclusionary power-structures propped up by these assumptions.[23] Yet the concept is problematic in part because it may posit the very wholeness or system it aims to counter. As Terry Eagleton points out, "hybridization presupposes purity. Strictly speaking, one can only hybridize a culture which is pure."[24] It is also not a given that hybridity is inherently transgressive or subversive. Claims of hybridity may in fact gloss over questions of power, domination, and the ways in which some cultural institutions and discourses are backed by tremendous political, legal, and economic might while others are not.[25] Nevertheless, the point that cultures or discourses are less bounded and coherent than is often assumed is necessary and valuable.

The weaknesses of hybridity indicate the need for a closer look at the role of power, domination, and resistance in matters of cultural belief and practice. These issues animate the work of several scholars who take aim at the model of culture as societal glue. For example, Sherry Ortner's studies of Sherpa religion and Himalayan mountaineering highlight the asymmetries of power in cultural practice and their implications for shared meaning. Ortner emphasizes the variability of culture, by showing how cultural practices like ritual change over time, as practitioners negotiate shifts in the distribution of political and economic power. She also questions the extent to which shared meanings are either preconditions or the product of cultural practice. What Ortner finds is that the absence of shared meanings, the lack of agreement over the significance of symbols, can facilitate cooperation and cohesion. For instance, Ortner demonstrates how Sherpas have managed to get Western climbers to comply with the staging of certain religious rituals despite the Sherpas' subservient position to the mostly Western climbers, and despite the fact that these rituals criticize climber behavior. Furthermore, despite their joint participation, Sherpas and climbers view these rituals in quite different ways. For Sherpas, they are aimed at appeasing mountain gods for the sins the climbers—and their

Sherpa assistants—intend to commit. This indictment of mountaineering is not, however, apparent to the climbers. Instead, climbers value ritual participation for other reasons: it seems to appease the Sherpas and please the monks, which makes expeditions run more smoothly; it is politically correct and provides climbers a sense of cultural virtue; and superstitiously, it makes sense to play it safe. Climbers' ritual participation also satisfies an orientalist "yearning for solidarity and even identity with the Other," the exotic object of fascination, in this case Sherpas.[26]

Ortner's analysis pokes holes in the idea that shared cultural practices facilitate understanding and collective identity. Shared meanings are noticeably absent from the rituals she scrutinizes. In fact, insofar as Sherpa rituals criticize the whole climbing enterprise and its attendant violations, these rituals seem to require miscommunication and the absence of shared meaning. Transparency and undistorted social communication are neither established nor desired. Coherence of action (e.g., the act of climbing) is facilitated by Sherpa rituals, but it is a coherence that both expresses and criticizes power asymmetries and identity differences among the players.

While cultural identity and practice cannot be interpreted as the effects of power alone, Ortner's analysis shows that examining power struggles and differences can tell us about meaning in cultural practice—and meaning can tell us about power. Historian and anthropologist Nicholas Dirks pursues a related tack in his exploration of Hindu ritual in rural India.[27] Dirks' analysis is in a sense the converse of Ortner's. Where Ortner reveals how the absence of shared meaning may facilitate social cooperation, Dirks shows how agreement over the meaning of cultural practice can induce competition and conflict. Specifically, he demonstrates how shared norms and cohesive cultural identities, albeit identities shot through by factional and caste division, make ritual the site and focus of struggle.

The events under consideration in Dirks' study, annual festivals of the Hindu god Aiyanar, involve complex interactions and cooperation among different caste groups. A superficial reading of the festival suggests that it affirms and upholds existing hierarchical, unequal relations among castes. In other words, it appears to promote caste interdependence and to celebrate the status quo. Yet further investigation reveals the regularity with which festivals are disrupted, postponed, and cancelled because of conflicts over the right to stage festivals and in what fashion. A ritual event seen from one angle as system-affirming had in fact sparked years of competition and chaos as caste and village groups sought control of symbolic resources. Conflict ensued precisely because participants agreed on the ritual's meanings and symbolic value—the struggles were serious because everyone understood the stakes of the festival. Far from engendering social cohesion, shared meaning was at the heart of intergroup competition.

Dirks is sensitive to the difficulties in reading ritual for its counter-hegemonic implications. He cites Terry Eagleton, who points out that the public ritual that critiques power relations (e.g., carnival) is ultimately "a *licensed* affair . . . , a permissible rupture of hegemony, a contained popular blow-off as disturbing and relatively ineffectual as a revolutionary work of art."[28] Still, Dirks argues that social science has too often underscored the system-supporting effects of ritual, while underplaying "the social fact that ritual constitutes a tremendously important arena for the cultural construction of authority and the dramatic display of the social lineaments of power." "Ritual," he points out, "has always been a crucial site of struggle," precisely because of the "centrality of authority to the ritual process."[29]

To a certain extent, Ortner and Dirks are suggesting different things about cultural practice, its implications, and its effects. In the first example the subservient, economically dependent Sherpas use a variety of strategies to manipulate climbers into ritual cooperation. They do so without the latter having fully understood the nature and meaning of their participation. Ritual cooperation in turn facilitates practical cooperation during dangerous climbing expeditions. In the second case, a rural Indian religious event that seems to affirm caste identities and hierarchies in fact violates them and is itself the focus of conflict. Like Chinese Red Guard factions contending for control of revolutionary rhetoric, participants in these events fight to control religious symbols because they agree on their significance. Yet Ortner and Dirks are not so much taking opposite points of view as showing different ways in which culture and power, and culture and politics, interact. They undercut the notion that meanings and symbols are "possessed" by self-contained groups in any settled, established way, even though actors may struggle for possession. Their work also contests rigidly functionalist readings of culture that portray it as societal glue. Taken together, they show that while shared cultural identity is neither an inherent or necessary basis of cohesion, conflict and lack of cohesion do not indicate the absence of a shared identity.

Similar insights emerge in analyses of power, identity, and governance in the Chinese case, including Prasenjit Duara's *Culture, Power and the State*, an analysis of state-building and decline in the late Qing and Republican periods. In this work, Duara argues that the authority of the Qing state was affirmed and enhanced at the local level through what he calls the "cultural nexus of power." This cultural nexus was an interconnected web of lineage organizations, marriage networks, religious associations, irrigation societies, and other linkages comprised of symbolic as well as material resources. In Duara's account, these heterogeneous, overlapping, diverse organizations and practices augmented political cohesion and imperial legitimacy. Yet the cultural nexus was also a site of contest, competition, and the pursuit of local interests among local gentry, Taoist priests, village headmen, and other members of the local elite. In fact, competition helped legitimize authority. "The pursuit of these particular symbols by various groups," notes Duara, "enabled these symbols to provide a common framework of authority. More important, it did so even while very different, and sometimes conflicting, interests continued to be pursued."[30]

Duara's observations combine the insights of both Dirks and Ortner. On the one hand, during the late Qing shared cultural meanings sparked conflict and competition among the local elite, even as they fostered cooperation. On the other, the heterogeneity of institution, identity, and interest, rather than clear congruence between center and locality, enabled imperial authority to function. Like Dirks and Ortner, Duara also shows how cultural practitioners may turn to those outside the cultural group (e.g., the British Raj, the Qing state) in their drive to control symbolic practice, and they may borrow outside cultural elements to justify their actions regarding competitors. All three of these scholars stress the need to examine localized, marginal cultural practice and identity in light of broader power relations and entities, including states and nations.

HETEROGENEITY AND DIVERSITY IN THE CHINESE NATIONAL EXPERIENCE

The role of local, sub-national identities in the formation of larger social movements has long been the subject of research by scholars of Chinese politics and society. For example, in her analysis of labor-movement formation in Shanghai, Elizabeth Perry demonstrates the centrality of native-place ties and associations to working class activism. According to Perry, the persistence of regional, linguistic, and even cultural differences among Shanghai workers contributed to labor activism and labor movement formation. Thus, the erasure of difference was not a prerequisite for a working class movement. Instead the tenacity of differences added to the movement's vibrancy.[31] In an analogous vein, Bryna Goodman has shown how native-place identity and organization mediated the nationalist cause in Shanghai from the 1850s to the 1930s.[32] Referring to Goodman's work, R. Bin Wong argues that people in Shanghai "linked with others from their home districts into a new kind of native place organization to promote the community-transcending goal of a 'nation.'" The Chinese nation, Wong argues, may have been an abstraction, "but it was concretized on different spatial scales."[33]

The contemporary Chinese minority cultural revival is fertile ground for investigating how national or societal norms and identities are "concretized" in distinct, local ways. It raises questions regarding how sub-national identities and activities relate to central and national ones. For one thing, official party-state involvement in this resurgence presents interesting, even counterintuitive phenomena for investigation. Despite decades spent suppressing anything that smacked of tradition, government units in China now play the role of patron, curator, and consumer of minority culture and cultural institutions. The state now encourages minorities to develop their ostensibly unique cultural identities and codifies these in policy, education, history, and the arts. It even tolerates and promotes some cross-border, transnational religious, and cultural cooperation. Yet the minority case is neither unproblematic nor lacking in contradictions, including potentially irresolvable conflicts between imperatives of cultural promotion and social control and between modernization and cultural authenticity.

Minorities' participation in cultural revival stems from an array of motives and interests. To a great degree, cultural revival is an end in itself, a way of expressing meaning and membership. Yet much minority cultural activism, such as linguistic promotion and religious education, expresses claims derived from a Chinese political identity, a conception of minority membership in the Chinese national community. The cases of the Dai, Bai, and Hui thus show that sub-national cultural identities are not inherently at odds with national identity, nor are they necessarily eroded by state- and nation-building processes or replaced with a new national identity. Rather, such cultural identities mediate the nation-state-building process and can serve as the vehicle or framework through which the nation is experienced. As such, national identity can retain the distinctive cast of these cultural identities.

In a sense, the idea of the Chinese nation, and the values, norms, and goals this idea comprises, function in the manner of "master frames," as Snow and Benford call them: cognitive, normative, and interpretive schema that help social movement actors identify political challenges and mobilize support to tackle them.[34] Such master frames allow social actors to identify problems and issues, attribute them to specific causes, and mobilize individuals and groups to meet these challenges and find solutions through collective action. In the case of Chinese minority nationalities, certain ideals and values linked to Chinese national identity and membership—specifically, those of modernization, economic development, and minority autonomy—perform these functions. National ideals and values frame the challenges facing minorities and provide an interpretive schema through which their cultural endeavors are justified and understood.

Minorities' localized cultural activities can also function as a kind of citizenship practice. Citizenship has usually been understood as a legal-juridical concept, as a rights-bearing status or category. Yet citizenship can also be viewed in more participatory terms, as sets of behaviors and even rituals through which political membership is established and demonstrated. Sociologist Margaret Somers has proposed that citizenship be viewed as "a set of institutionally embedded social practices . . . contingent upon and constituted by networks of relationships and political idioms that stress membership and universal rights and duties in a national community."[35] She further argues that modern citizenship "is not in practice exclusively a national and universal institution. Rather, citizenship practices emerge from the articulation of national organization and universal rules with the particular and varying political cultures of local environments." In other words, citizenship norms and duties are mediated by local concerns, local institutions, and local cultural identities.

The application of the rights-laden concept of citizenship to Chinese politics is fraught with problems, given the lack of a tradition of rights in Chinese political thought or practice.[36] Yet the participatory, practice-based version of citizenship makes sense in the Chinese context. This version of the concept is appropriate, if not necessary, for understanding membership in a variety of nonliberal and revolutionary settings from late eighteenth century France to post-1949 China.[37] The Maoist understanding of political community, for instance, was nothing if not participatory—not to mention performative, as recurring spectacles of rectification and criticism made clear. The articulation of minority identity both embraces and contests the content of Chinese national identity, the limits of Chinese citizenship, and the privileges this membership bestows.

IDENTITY AND CULTURE
WITH (MINORITY) CHINESE CHARACTERISTICS

These contentions raise several interrelated questions. First, how should the words and behavior of Chinese minorities be interpreted? Do minorities' cultural endeavors really have anything at all to do with the Chinese nation and national identity? Is there a Chinese national identity? If so, what is it, and what aspects of it resonate with minorities in their pursuit of particular cultural identity-based agendas? Finally, are there ways in which conceptions of Chinese identity or the behavior of the state limit minority efforts to claim membership and its privileges?

It may be that this minority cultural resurgence has little or nothing to do with Chinese membership and identity, except to repudiate them. If so, the only relevance of Chinese political identity for the revival is as something for minorities to slough off, as they recover from the Maoist socialist interlude and get back to the business of being who they "really" are. Minority cultural ferment may also entail the unearthing of heretofore repressed "subaltern" voices. In other words, the revival is a form of resistance against hegemonic categorization (including ethnic and national categorization); its proponents seek to establish local collective identities free of the totalizing influence of Chinese socialist discourse and power. The explosion of minority-centric cultural activism in China perhaps indicates that the hegemonic edifice is beginning to crumble.

The idea of Chinese minorities as subalterns animates a number of influential recent studies. These works respond both to the remarkable post-Mao (re)discovery of minorities and their special characteristics by researchers, tour companies, and the party-state, and to an earlier generation of minority studies that framed the "nationalities question" in terms of assimilation and control.[38] This more recent research stresses the great variety of cultural practices and identities, and the multifarious ways in which the state is experienced at the local level. At the same time, they argue that minority cultural production expresses and enhances state dominance and Han-centric nationalist impulses.

This line of argument is exemplified by Louisa Schein's studies of cultural politics among the Miao.[39] Schein analyzes official practices and interactions among Han and Miao, as well as popular depictions and artistic representations. Melding Edward Said's notion of orientalism with Michael Hechter's concept of internal colonialism, Schein details how gendered and subservient depictions of minorities play out in experience, as feminized minorities (and minority females) are rendered products for official Han consumption. Where Said linked the Western orientalist impulse to capitalism and imperialism, Schein argues that Chinese "internal orientalism" derives from noncapitalist and even noneconomic forces. Yet like Said she argues that orientalism is productive: it consists not merely in the representation of how things are, but enacts and reproduces identities that maintain asymmetrical power relations.

Schein argues that this internal orientalism marginalizes minority nationalities to such a degree that they are essentially silenced. The fetish creation of a feminized, eroticized Miao subject, moreover, is inseparable from what Schein sees as a Han or Chinese national identity crisis. Chinese internal orientalism is carried out by a denatured, de-cultured, homogenous Han subject bereft of authenticity and meaning. For this Han subject, the minority "other" functions as a "surrogate and underground self" embodying qualities valued yet discarded by the subject responsible for its creation. As a result of this productive imagining, the minority nationality in some important ways ceases to exist, and a Han-generated, passive fetish object usurps its place.

A similar argument is advanced by Dru Gladney in his analysis of representations of minorities in popular art and culture (though not in his examinations of Chinese Muslim identity).[40] Gladney asserts that these representations help construct a sexualized, submissive, primitive, feminized minority object, which dialectically entails the construction of a Han-centric Chinese identity—the Chinese nation. The discourse of minority representations thus parallels a discourse of national identity that is both Han and Chinese; minority representations imply and even produce a dominant, active, advanced, masculine Han Chinese subject. Insofar as a Chinese national subject is established whose qualities oppose those of the feminized, submissive minority object, minorities are excluded from full membership in the imagined community that is the Chinese nation.

The implication here is that a minority cultural resurgence is deeply problematic—a trap that limits minorities to second-class status, or worse. Expressions of minority culture are inherently suspect, since minorities are assumed to speak only when they have the approval of their cultural and political superiors. As Stevan Harrell explains,

> as long as peripheral peoples agree, at least on the surface, to the terms of definition and scaling imposed by the civilizers, the civilizees will be granted a voice to speak to themselves and the world about the success of the project. In this sense, the answer to whether the subaltern can speak is that the subaltern can speak on the sufferance of the civilizer. Voice is granted on the provision that it will speak in favor of the project, or at least in the project's terms.[41]

A further implication is that it is a mistake to think that minorities are or desire to be full members of any Chinese national entity. What membership minorities do possess is neither meaningful nor self-generated, laden as it is with infantilizing, orientalizing effects. Minorities experience only a passive, mute, "othered" status in unequal relationship with a Han-dominated Chinese state.

Many other studies of minority cultural revival reject this characterization of minorities as mute and passive. Gladney's research of the Hui Muslim experience details the variety of self-generated Hui identities across China, as well as active, engaged, vocal Hui efforts to advance their interests. Similarly, Erik Mueggler's *The Age of Wild Ghosts* shows how members of the Yi nationality, despite their poverty and marginality, resist state power in their efforts to overcome past traumas inflicted by the Chinese state. In this work, Mueggler explores the "hidden transcripts" of Yi culture encapsulated in oral history, narrative, poetry, and song for what they reveal about Yi identity, memory, and experience under socialism. In particular, he demonstrates how revived Yi cultural practices challenge the totalizing effects of official policy and socialist identity construction.

In making his case, Mueggler draws on James Scott's distinction between the public and private transcripts of subordinate social groups.[42] According to Scott, subordinate groups are constrained and coerced into echoing the rhetoric of their oppressors. Yet they may also use that rhetoric to achieve subversive ends. Thus there exists a discrepancy between the public activities of marginalized social actors and what those actors say and do away from the gaze of power. Mueggler plumbs Yi funerary rituals, poetry, storytelling, and exorcism rites for what they reveal about the Yi experience under Maoism and the manner in which the Yi "imaginary" reflects and refracts the socialist party-state.

Mueggler demonstrates that for these minority residents of a poor, remote, mountain hamlet, much about the post-Mao era is hardly "post" at all. Systems of production and ownership have shifted from the collective to the household, and the utopian vision of Maoist socialism has faded. But for the Yi of his study, the past remains eternally present in the form of "wild ghosts," the troubled spirits of the thousands who died during the famine of the Great Leap Forward or who met equally traumatic and unnatural ends during the violence of the Cultural Revolution. In other words, the trauma of Maoist catastrophes continues to haunt contemporary Yi existence. Yi revival includes efforts to process and make sense of their experiences under socialism, and to exorcise these traumas.

The issue of trauma and responses to it are not the sole province of minority cultural practice. Studies by Patricia Thornton, Nancy Chen, and

Xu Jian on post-Mao *qigong* sects also highlight the link between popular Chinese spiritual and religious practices and efforts to overcome the psychic, political, and physical wounds of both past and present. Like the Yi with their exorcism, practitioners of *qigong* and Falun Gong wield these as anti-materialist critiques of Maoist-Marxist discourse and the science-and-economic-development ideology of the reform era.[43] Thus, in demonstrating how revived Yi cultural practices serve to process and resolve trauma, Mueggler's work points to ways in which the socio-political experiences of minorities overlap with those of Han Chinese. Yet the picture of the Yi that emerges is of an intensely marginalized, outsider minority whose cultural endeavors are ultimately ineffectual. Yi cultural revival may even be exacerbating their marginality insofar as resurgent practices inhibit their participation in market-oriented agrarian reforms. It seems accurate to characterize the Yi as marginal, but is their marginality a function of their minority culture and status, or of the crushing poverty and isolation that afflict many other communities, Han and minority alike?

There are very good reasons for framing the "nationalities question" in terms of marginality, subordination, and otherness. First, it makes sense given contemporary political matters, matters which themselves influence how the question gets raised. For example, the global prominence of the Tibet question and the sufferings of Tibetan people support the notion that Chinese identity is forcibly yet superficially imposed on minority peoples. Uyghur and Kirgiz separatist violence in Xinjiang and Beijing, which have received attention in the Western press, bolsters this view. The breakup of the Soviet Union and Yugoslavia further underscores the seeming primacy of sub-national ethnocultural identities and the shallowness and fragility of more inclusive, national ones. There are also good practical reasons for the consideration of minorities *as* minorities. China's opening to the West and the removal of travel restrictions to remote and previously closed areas of the country have allowed access to and promoted interest in disparate peoples about whom so little has hitherto been known.

There are other important reasons for focusing on minorities as minorities, and for assuming that cultural activism entails a rejection of a Chinese political or politico-cultural identity. The government insists that Chinese identity and membership is ethnically neutral, a citizenship rather than an ethno-cultural category. This is the reasoning behind the oft-stated claim that China is a "multiethnic, multinational" nation-state. But the category "Chinese" does have ethno-cultural components; it is, or can be, an ethno-cultural as well as a citizenship designation. To portray the state or nation as ethnically or culturally neutral is to misperceive or ignore these features of Chinese identity. One of the key insights of Schein, Mueggler, Gladney, and Harrell is that the ostensibly neutral, universalistic socialist state is imbued with Han-centric ideas and Han chauvinism. The multiethnic character of China is, for example, rendered suspect by many of the policies the state has pursued in the process of state-building, such as the use of targeted Han emigration to incorporate and pacify minority-inhabited areas such as Tibet and Xinjiang. Even Chinese applications of Marxist-Leninist doctrine have expressed elements of Han chauvinism. Seemingly neutral or universalistic ideologies of modernization and development, such as those that underpinned the policies of the Maoist and the post-Mao reform eras, can be used to justify one group's political, cultural, ethnic, or linguistic dominance of minority peoples.[44] To assume that Chinese identity and membership are ethnically neutral is to obscure how the values used to justify state policy rationalize and reinforce Han dominance.

The potential for incongruence between ethnic and national identity is apparent when the nation is considered as multidimensional. The "nation" conveys a sense of the people who comprise it, and on one level, nation is an aggregate body. It is, however, not merely equal to the sum of its parts; it has a wholeness and identity of its own. Yet the nation also functions as an idea that can be manipulated as a tool of state-building and as a mobilizing force. The nation's members can also turn the idea back upon the state as a weapon of critique, an idealized community by which to measure the success or failure of the regime entrusted with the nation's well-being. As an idea, the nation is manipulated and made resonant to its members through reference to cultural and historical, if not ethnic, markers. If the cultural, historical, and ethnic components of the nation conflict with the ethnic identity of its members, the legitimacy of the nation as an inclusive body is at risk. Furthermore, when ethnic identity links individuals to the culture, history, and ethnicity of a separate nation-state, their sense of membership within their nation of residence may be compromised.

The scholarship discussed above has raised important questions regarding the assimilationist underpinnings of an earlier generation of studies about Chinese *minzu*.[45] These approaches have much to say about the genesis and significance of the cultural activity and activism that this study documents. By detailing the reemergence (or emergence) of minority cultural practice, religious networks, and community bonds that are sometimes transnational in scope, this scholarship has also shown the strength and complexity of minority experiences in a socialist state often believed to have stamped out such difference. These studies are also a useful corrective to much of the social scientific literature on China that, because of practical concerns, sheer numbers, and theoretical bias, tends to privilege the experience of the Han. Moreover, minority cultural activism at times does involve the excavation of subaltern practices and collective identities interred by Maoist anti-traditionalism and social reorganization. The identities and institutions analyzed in this book can and do serve as a basis for resistance in thought and action against the state, its representatives, and its policies.

Yet to assume that minorities' use of official discourse is merely a public transcript concealing a hidden "true" one raises several questions. First, this distinction is based on Scott's analysis of the rhetoric of clearly subordinate groups, such as black slaves. The question of whether minority nationalities are genuinely subordinate is an open one: in many cases minorities enjoy preferential policies and regional political power despite (or because) of their numerical inferiority relative to the Han. Second, certain national ideals and goals enjoy a legitimacy not necessarily accorded the current political regime or its representatives. These ideals may in fact form the basis of the critique that minorities aim at discredited policies and officials.

Minorities' cultural endeavors cannot be assumed to be always and everywhere merely about minorities as minorities or to necessarily entail a repudiation of a Chinese political identity and membership. To argue thus is to essentialize minority cultural politics as simply anti-nation, separatist, and constitutive of ethnic nationalism. Such claims also presume minority identity to be morally and temporally primary to national identity—thereby falling prey to the same assumptions built into the models of nation and nationalism discussed in the first part of this chapter. Although minority cultural activism can involve resistance, it is erroneous to assume that it necessarily does so, or that all forms of resistance repudiate the ideals, values, and privileges of a Chinese political identity. On the contrary, resistance and criticism may embody such values and ideals and imply standards by which its critics judge the state and its representatives.

Fortunately, some scholars have begun to consider Chinese minorities not just as passive "others" or mute subalterns, but as critical subjects actively involved in the fashioning of their own histories and identities. For example, Litzinger demonstrates how Yao intellectuals and elites have used tradition to position a Yao subject favorably within a discourse of progress and civilization. Litzinger also confronts the question of how minorities are perceived, in scholarship as well as Chinese policy. He asks,

What happens when minorities are no longer seen as simply reacting to or always already resisting the Chinese state but rather as central agents in the cultural politics of the post-Mao nation? What might the anthropology of post-Mao nationalism look like if it refuses to find in the ethnic subject the perfected example of authenticity or resistance?[46]

Similarly, Gillette's work reveals how the urban Hui of Xi'an critically engage with national projects of modernization and development, and how they appropriate "modernity" as a norm and an ideal. Gillette's analysis of Hui consumption practices shows the extent to which Hui have absorbed the values and ideology of the post-Mao state. At the same time, they wield their interpretation of modernity as a critique of the Han people and the Han-dominated state, and as a justification of Hui beliefs and customs. Transnational Islam serves as a touchstone of legitimacy; by situating their own religious practices within the discourse and practice of global Islam, Hui counter Chinese and Han views of the Hui as a backward minority.[47]

MEANING AND PRACTICE OF CHINESE NATIONAL IDENTITY

These insights lead to another set of questions: What is Chinese identity? Of what does such an identity and membership consist? How do minorities' words and actions reveal a concern with their status as members in a national community? Answering these questions is a prerequisite for demonstrating how contemporary minority cultural activism taps into notions of national identity even as it enhances local and transnational minority self-conceptions. However, it is impossible—and conceptually dangerous—to pin down the components constituting Chinese identity. Such an attempt risks positing the very thing this chapter criticizes: the idea that Chinese national identity is a bounded, coherent entity comprising an equally bounded, coherent, and unique cultural core. As Rey Chow argues, "In the habitual obsession with 'Chineseness,' what we often encounter is a kind of cultural essentialism . . . that draws an imaginary boundary between China and the rest of the world."[48] Still, it is possible to illuminate recurring themes in ongoing debates concerning the meaning of being Chinese and the character of the Chinese nation. These issues have vexed Chinese intellectuals and Western scholars from the nineteenth century to the present. The eclipse of revolutionary Maoist socialism has again brought questions of Chinese culture and national identity to the fore.

China's disastrous and humiliating encounters with the nation-states of the West, beginning with the Opium Wars, made the question of what constitutes the Chinese nation a salient one to both Chinese and outside observers. One of the most influential analyses of the problem of Chinese nationalism was formulated by Joseph Levenson in his three-part study, *Confucian China and Its Modern Fate*. Levenson argues that prior to the Western incursion, Chinese identity was a cultural rather than a national one. Until the latter part of the nineteenth century, Levenson says, when the Chinese were forced to recognize the military and technological superiority of the West, the identifying aspects and the meaning of being Chinese were not tied to membership in an ethnic or quasi-ethnic collectivity known as the nation.[49] Rather, Chinese identity was a function of participation in the civilization and practices of China. China, Levenson argues, was not at this time a nation. Rather, it was a cultural collectivity whose boundaries were established by correct practice rather than territory or blood. As Myron Cohen explains, "[being] civilized, that is being Chinese, was nothing less than proper human behavior in accordance with cosmic principles."[50]

The criteria for membership in this culturalist entity were quite different from those generally ascribed to membership in a nation. One's behavior, one's adherence to principles and standards of etiquette and propriety, marked one as member or outsider, either civilized or barbarian. These principles and standards could be learned. While descent and kinship influenced opportunities to learn principles and standards, descent and kinship did not preclude or guarantee membership. As a result, so-called barbarians, those beyond the pale of Chinese civilization and territorial boundaries, could in theory be—and sometimes were—"educated up" to the status of civilized Chinese.[51] They could also rule. Since the standards of governance also rested on those culturalist principles and practices that could be learned, "legitimate rule was not limited to ethnic Chinese; aliens who accepted and exemplified Confucian norms might also rule."[52]

One corollary of Levenson's account is that Chinese culturalism could not survive the repeated humiliations at the hands of Western imperialist powers. The Western incursion struck at the roots of culturalism's presuppositions regarding the superiority of Confucian principles and practices. As James Townsend explains, Western imperialism "had only to demonstrate that its formidable military power carried an explicit challenge to the Chinese view of the world by agents who assumed their own cultural superiority."[53] Not only was Chinese cultural superiority undermined, the view of China as civilization par excellence was undercut by attacks that rendered it just one state among many, and a weak one at that.

A second corollary is that the demise of culturalism gave birth to Chinese nationalism. As long-established notions of Chinese identity and membership collapsed, political elites and intellectuals began considering what might take its place. Nationalism emerged as political leaders, intellectuals, and students tried to reconceptualize state, culture, and people, and began to think of China as a political entity within the international state system. Since foreign imperialism meant encounters with Western nationalisms, many Chinese came to view nationalism as a contributing factor in the West's power and technological capacity. The "logical outcome of the crisis," Townsend observes, "was rejection of culturalism and development of a nationalism that would provide a new basis for China's defense and regeneration."[54]

Not surprisingly, modernization—of government, society, economy, and culture—has been a trope of Chinese nationalism since its beginnings. The encounter with Western powers armed with technologically superior weaponry made traditional Chinese forms of learning and education suspect. Many Chinese nationalists repudiated traditional culture outright or called for its modification and the adoption and adaptation of Western learning. The student-led May Fourth Movement of 1919, for instance, a thoroughly nationalist protest against the annexation of Chinese territory by Japan, involved calls for the abandonment of Confucian education, its replacement with a curriculum based on Western science, and the creation of a "new culture" based on scientific learning.

Modernity, argues Leo Ou-fan Lee, became the "guiding ethos" of an emerging vision of China, a newly imagined Chinese national community.[55] Yet there was great regional, occupational, and even gendered variation in how this ethos was understood, expressed, and lived. In his analysis of urban civic boosterism in Republican Lanzhou, David Strand encapsulates the variety of ways of being modern, and being Chinese:

> Broad participation in China's development has long been more than a matter of state control or popular protest. One could become Chinese in the modern sense by joining a demonstration or a party, but also by training for a profession, opening a local museum, or marketing a local resource. These latter, more local and pluralistic enterprises should not be equated with democracy or a localism invariably hostile to national authority. But they do comprise sites

where social capital can be invested in ways that foster diversity, criticism, and a measure of autonomy.[56]

In other words, being Chinese and being modern have long been contested concepts, even if what they stood for was widely embraced. Those who both embraced and contested these ideals pursued a range of activities through which to demonstrate the modernity of themselves, their localities, and their nation.

It is easy to see official appeals to tradition and custom as bids for power and authority. Yet the manipulation of symbols of modernity and scientific progress can also serve those purposes. Although Chinese elites have appealed on many occasions to tradition, modernity has served as the touchstone of twentieth and twenty-first century political legitimation. Partly as a response to popular political currents, Chinese leaders have frequently attacked tradition as the source of all that stultified and retarded Chinese power and prestige, while valorizing modernity.

In the twentieth century, both the Nationalist and Communist leaders identified tradition as the counterweight pulling against the forward movement of modernizing strategies. The Nationalists led campaigns against popular religion and instituted assimilationist minority policies.[57] The Maoist socialist vision was shot through with ideals of modernity and progress. The promise of this vision to break through China's political, cultural, and technological stagnation accounted in great part for its appeal among intellectuals and the masses. Since the Republic was established in 1911, Prasenjit Duara argues, "the Chinese state has been caught up in a logic of 'modernizing legitimation' where its raison d'être has become the fulfillment of modern ideals."[58]

One of the noteworthy features of the Maoist vision, however, is that the charismatic and eschatological so often supplanted the scientific and technical in the pursuit of ostensibly modernizing ideals. Grand campaigns like the Great Leap Forward were marked by efforts to circumvent the laws of economics, agriculture, and even physics, and to overcome the limitations of the material world through voluntarist fervor. Voluntarism and revolutionary ardor indicated commitment, while plodding rational calculation and attention to technical feasibility were criticized as incrementalist and dangerously bourgeois. That projects such as the Great Leap and the Smash the Four Olds campaigns were driven by decidedly unscientific, irrational motives in no way undermines this point. Rather, the emotional, almost romantic adherence to ideals of modernization and modernity—and the concomitant revulsion toward the traditional, the superstitious, the "old"—underscore the centrality of modernization and technological progress as values, beliefs, and even ritual practices central to Chinese national identity and self-understanding.

The end of the Maoist era and the inauguration of Deng Xiaoping's reforms ushered in a welcome spirit of pragmatism and technically grounded experimentation. This pragmatism, this willingness to employ a variety of methods to achieve goals regardless of whether they are "white or black," has entailed a more tolerant, experimental, and less ideologically driven approach to matters of culture and local practice. The effects of this pragmatism on minorities, and the way it plays out in state-minority relations, are the subject of this book. The state is perfectly willing, however, to suppress religious and other cultural practices if they are deemed a threat. Minorities are as vulnerable as any other social group in Chinese society to the vicissitudes of a *fang–shou* cycle: the practice of letting go with one hand while tightening up with the other. The current period is different because the state's interests are framed not in terms of Marxist-Leninist-Maoist ideology but rather in more naked terms of order and control.

This reform-era pragmatism, with its emphasis on "expert" rather than "red," does not indicate the demise of values, nationalist or otherwise, in guiding Chinese policy. If anything, the ideal of modernization and the obsession with that goal have intensified as revolutionary socialism has fallen by the wayside. At times this concern with modernization emerges in the form of indictments against China's failure to adequately modernize, examples of what Geremie Barmé describes as a "tradition of self-loathing."[59] These self-indictments underscore the fact that to modernize, as to get rich, is glorious. Consequently, Chinese citizens are exhorted to do their part in modernizing themselves and their society. That modernizing impulse extends to agriculture, industry, markets, governance, family planning, education, social life, and thought and culture.

Chinese national identity (or Chineseness, for that matter) is neither uncomplicated nor definitively established. Some efforts to formulate a new Chinese nationalism have appealed outright to exclusionary ethnic and racial ideals and symbols, such as the dragon, the Yellow River, and the ostensible common descent of the Han people.[60] Even Deng Xiaoping's modernization-fixated regime resuscitated Confucianism in the mid-1980s to fill the void left by the demise of Marxist-Leninist-Maoist ideology after Mao.[61] Many of these nostalgic formulations are attempts to destroy tradition in order to save it. Appeals to distilled racial symbols may also be efforts to preserve an identity based on an abstract idea of tradition while dispensing with specific traditions that impede national objectives. Appeals to modernity and to culture are often part of the same package; nostalgia is harnessed while outmoded, archaic practices are abandoned in favor of efficacious, modern ones.

The preeminence of the modern ideal notwithstanding, Chinese ideologues, reformers, and intellectuals have regarded modernization warily. It is seen as destructive of much that is unique to China, and thus constitutive of national identity. Some appeals to tradition are explicitly hostile to modernization, or at least ambivalent toward it, as exemplified by the "search for roots" (*xungen*) movement in Chinese art and literature.[62] The *xungen* movement, Leo Ou-fan Lee writes, "typifies the defense of traditional Chinese culture by Chinese intellectuals as a whole. It is a new wave of 'culturalism' which permeates traditional thought in that it sees Chinese culture as the 'focus of loyalty' and the remedy for the country's ills."[63] Viewing modernization "as a threat to both its tradition and national identity," these *xungen* writers, filmmakers, and artists have sought "to bring out 'the Chinese essence' from local customs, rituals and folklore."[64] Despite these reversions to tradition, ideals of modernity and modernization are still paramount in Chinese society.

The modernizing impulse extends to minority nationalities. To a large degree, the "nationalities question" has been reframed in terms of the goal of modernization. Issues of order, stability, and central political control predominate in regions known for their restive minorities, such as Tibet and Xinjiang. But even here, these pressing matters are bound up with modernization, especially in the economic sense, insofar as economic change is viewed as a solution to the problems generating resentment and strife. The Chinese government is particularly concerned about growing economic disparities between the interior and western regions of the country, where most minorities live, and the wealthy provinces along the eastern and southeastern coast. Narrowing that gap by stepping up the pace of reform in minority areas is the primary response to this problem.

The socialist market economy is increasingly viewed as the answer to minority backwardness, and, ironically, as the means of furthering national integration. The socialist market economy is not without its problems, as illustrated by the regional disparities just mentioned. Yet many academics and officials view the market as capable of achieving what the Maoist socialist project tried but failed to achieve: completion of the task of nation-building. Numerous official and academic publications from the early 1990s onward describe how the market is breaking down local barriers and regional differences. According to these reports, the expansion of the socialist market links minority groups in a web of commodities exchange, thereby enhancing the interdependence and mutual reliance of the Chinese people. More often than not these publications cite *The Communist Manifesto* to demonstrate the market's unifying power. With the increasingly free flow of cheap commodities, the socialist market economy is breaking down all Chinese (minority) walls of cultural and geographic isolation, thereby drawing even the most backward *minzu* into contemporary Chinese civilization.

This emphasis on the modern has created a dilemma for Chinese minorities by engendering a new form of Chinese culturalism, or neo-culturalism. In Levenson's distinction between culturalism and nationalism in the development of a Chinese nation, the former refers to a mode of membership based on adherence to standards of civilized behavior. According to Levenson, the transition to nationalism involved the repudiation of many of these standards and a quest to replace them with a national identity. This quest entailed the elevation of modernity and modernization, of science and progress, as national ideals.

Indeed, Levenson's culturalism-to-nationalism thesis has come under criticism in recent years. For instance, Pamela Crossley's analysis of Manchu legitimation strategies contests the view that Qing adaptation of Chinese culture was unidirectional or indicative of sinicization.[65] These criticisms notwithstanding, culturalism persists, and, unlike the culturalism identified by Levenson, contemporary Chinese neo-culturalism is organized around demonstrations of modernity and modernization. The Chinese modernizing vision still entails standards of appropriate, civilized behavior to which Chinese citizens are expected to conform, but the good Chinese is a modernizing Chinese, the model worker a modern one, and technical progress is spoken of as a kind of revolutionary duty. The emphasis on behavioral standards, on adherence to civilized conduct, remains; what has changed is the content of those standards. That content is, or aims to be, modern.

Like other Chinese citizens, minorities are expected to work at modernizing themselves. The problem for minorities, however, is that a competing culturalist notion of what it means to be a minority also exists, a notion organized around authenticity, cultural integrity, and tradition. The minority stereotypes that Schein, Gladney, Harrell, and others dissect encapsulate both images and behavioral standards. As they point out, minorities are portrayed as and are expected to be backward, childlike, feminized primitives, in need of the developmental assistance of the elder brother Han. Some members of minority groups accept these depictions and the dependent relationship to the Han such depictions imply, while others acknowledge them but bemoan those who accept them. One senior Dai cadre I spoke with lamented the lack among the Dai of the "struggle spirit" (*fendou jingsheng*) necessary for economic development. In his view, Buddhist fatalism and the relatively easy life afforded by the fertile climate of Xishuangbanna had made the Dai complacent. For another Dai man working in tourism, this backwardness was not a problem: "We Dai have always relied on . . . the more advanced Han for their technical expertise."[66] Thus, while some members of minorities dislike these stereotypes, the view of the Han as the advanced elder brother *minzu* is a widely accepted notion, at times even a useful one.

These representations and stereotypes are not entirely negative, nor are they conditions from which minorities need to be extricated—although the drive to modernize would indicate otherwise. The sensual immediacy and proximity to both nature and culture widely attributed to minorities are admired qualities. Minorities are seen as repositories of authenticity, a vanishing commodity in a nation-state that has undergone remarkable change in the last half century, and which saw the destruction of many of its traditions during the Maoist era.

The incompatibility of competing neo-culturalisms presents unique difficulties for minorities, both in their efforts to claim full citizenship and membership and as members of the Chinese body politic. To the extent minorities modernize, they lose what makes them distinctive, which also constitutes the officially codified identity by which they are bestowed citizenship in the larger Chinese nation. To the extent they do not modernize, they are inferior citizens.

Much contemporary cultural activism of the Dai, Hui, and Bai is motivated by the desire to recover or reestablish traditions suppressed during the Maoist era. Yet the tactics of these groups in promoting religious, linguistic, artistic, and other cultural practices, and the ways they justify and conceive of their endeavors, suggest that they are trying to overcome competing neo-culturalist notions of membership and identity. Their activities are not based on simple nostalgia for a past long gone. Instead they evince a concern with economic, social, and cultural development that is filtered through the lens of minority identity and experience. The Chinese ideal of modernization, along with state guarantees of minority autonomy, are interpreted in ways specific to their concerns and used as justifications for their cultural activism.

Of course, justifying their actions in this manner is good symbolic politics. Minority cultural activists have good reasons for couching their cultural endeavors in terms sanctioned by the state and by official discourse. Situating their activities within a normalized discourse of economic development and nationality modernization is no doubt useful. Yet in interviews and conversations with people involved in linguistic promotion, religious education, and other activities, many demonstrated a genuine concern that their activities not be confused with superstitious and backward practices. Backwardness is the general approbation applied to minorities, and it is one that chafes. Revived, expanded, and updated cultural institutions and identities offer members of the Dai, Bai, and Hui means for combating this stereotype and the second-class citizenship it implies.

—2—

THE DAI, BAI, AND HUI
IN HISTORICAL PERSPECTIVE

The status of the Dai, Bai, and Hui as minority *minzu* is based on the idea that they exhibit unique configurations of cultural and religious characteristics. As official minorities they possess certain rights and privileges under Chinese law. Yet, are the Dai, Bai, and Hui distinct, bounded social entities? Do they see themselves in this way, and do others similarly recognize them as such? To what extent do state classifications dovetail with their self-perceptions? Might official categories imply boundaries or identities that in lived experience are blurred and porous?

These questions are not easy to address. Much of the historical and ethnographic material on Chinese minorities is the product of the socialist state and its scholars and reflects their assumptions and ideals. Chinese ethnologists, most of them Han, played a pivotal role in the classification process, and as Charles F. McKhann argues, "in framing the discourse on the 'nationalities question' . . . their freedom to do so was sharply circumscribed by the theoretical framework within which they were required to work."[1] Accounts of minority history and culture are consequently infused with Marxist and Maoist presuppositions about development and backwardness, class relations and exploitation, and the progression of history. These accounts also reflect the concerns of Chinese nationalism and national self-images. Popular and scholarly narratives about minorities may tell us as much about the Han and the Chinese state as they do about minority *minzu*. It is likely impossible to extract a history of minorities unencumbered by socialist and nationalist assumptions.

Despite this dilemma, this chapter seeks to explain something of who the Dai, Bai, and Hui are and who they were historically, especially in the period prior to the Socialist era. This effort to situate these groups in history relies extensively on materials produced by the national and local government units of People's Republic of China and by Chinese scholars. In doing so, this account no doubt fails to "rescue" the histories of the Dai, Bai, and Hui from the Chinese socialist nation-state; consequently, this account reflects many of the assumptions about ethnicity, development, and culture present in Chinese nationality theory and policy.[2] In considering the Dai, Bai, and Hui as distinct *minzu*, this analysis already commits itself to many of these assumptions. Nevertheless, this material conveys some of the early history of these groups' societies prior to the founding of the PRC, and more of their recent experiences in the Maoist era.

THE DAI

Of the three cases that are the focus of my research, the Dai most closely approximate the minority ideal. The Dai are a Tai-speaking group, linguistically and culturally linked to Tai Lüe peoples in Laos, Myanmar, and northern Thailand.[3] They are the third largest minority in Yunnan, and reside primarily in the south and southwest. About one-quarter of all Dai reside in the Xishuangbanna Dai Autonomous Prefecture, located in the southernmost part of Yunnan along the borders of Laos and Myanmar. It is this group of Dai and this prefecture of Xishuangbanna that are examined here.

Contemporary Xishuangbanna is roughly coterminous with Sipsongpanna, a self-governing principality established in the twelfth century. Historically, Sipsongpanna was one of several Tai political entities that existed in Laos, Burma (now Myanmar), and northern Thailand.[4] Today, Tai communities are still found in all these places as well as in parts of northern Vietnam and the Assam region of India. In contemporary Thailand, Sipsongpanna is viewed as a sort of motherland of the modern Thai people, as the source from which they came. Not surprisingly, people from Thailand make up a significant proportion of non-mainland Chinese tourists and investors in the prefecture.

Politically and socially, the Sipsongpanna Tai (henceforth the Dai) diverged considerably from the wider Chinese society and culture. Dai society was organized along highly stratified, castelike lines. Sipsongpanna was governed by a monarch, the *zhaopianling*. Below him were aristocratic officials who comprised the political leadership, followed by *zhaomeng*, quasi-feudal lords or princes who controlled the various districts or *meng* into which Sipsongpanna was divided. Commoner villages were made up either of *daimeng*, ordinary folk descended from the original Tai settlers in the region, or of the household slaves of the monarch and nobility. All lands belonged to the *zhaopianling*, although within their districts *zhaomeng* wielded considerable authority. The monarch's lands were allocated to villages and individual households to be farmed and managed, though such holdings could not be bought or sold. A small number of peasants were freeholders who controlled their own property but were the political subjects of the *zhaopianling*.[5]

The social and political hierarchy of Sipsongpanna was reinforced and legitimated by Theravada Buddhism. Although there is no consensus about when Buddhism arrived in the region, it is generally acknowledged that Theravada practices were widespread by the fourteenth century. Nearly every village had its own temple, which served as the educational, social, and, of course, religious center of activity. Like the villages in which they were situated, temples were part of a broader religious and political network, and hierarchical relations among temples of differing rank mirrored the political structure of Sipsongpanna. Buddhism also endowed the Dai with a script. Written Dai is the language of sutras and scriptures. This script is employed in the religious context by other *minzu* such as the Bulang, who also practice Theravada Buddhism, although their spoken language differs from Dai. Although Buddhism is central to Dai life and culture, certain animist practices persisted, and over time melded with Theravada beliefs and practices.

While Sipsongpanna enjoyed relative autonomy throughout the centuries, that autonomy waxed and waned according to the power and interests of Burmese, Siamese, and imperial Chinese regimes. Chinese imperial records indicate a long history of tributary relations between Sipsongpanna and the Imperial Court.[6] This relationship intensified during the Yuan dynasty, when Yunnan was "pacified" and brought under direct imperial administrative control. The main town of Cheli (today called Jinghong) served as a garrison post for imperial troops on their forays into Burma. During the Ming and Qing dynasties, Sipsongpanna was increasingly drawn into the imperial Chinese orbit as a result of reforms aimed at reducing the power of local chieftains (*tusi*) throughout southwest China.

These reforms codified local power-holders' subordinate position relative to the emperor and were attempts to "civilize" the chieftains and their families through education.[7] Yet Chinese imperial control over Sipsongpanna was not definitive. Records reveal incidents of Sipsongpanna elites defecting to or joining with Burma in conflicts with the imperial state.

Following the overthrow of the Qing dynasty in 1911, Chiang Kai-shek's Nationalists made further encroachments on Sipsongpanna's autonomy and independence. Sipsongpanna's internal district boundaries were amalgamated and reorganized as counties so as to undercut the power of the *zhaomeng*. At this time Sipsongpanna was also being gradually incorporated into the wider Chinese world via trade and commerce. Cheli became an important stopping point for traders headed to Burma and points south. Sipsongpanna was also developed as a prime tea-growing region. A few Dai capitalists emerged during this period, but most tea plantation owners and managers were Han, Hui Muslim, or Bai.[8]

Despite the erosion of its independence, Sipsongpanna on the eve of Liberation was still an isolated, relatively autonomous place. In linguistic, religious, and ethnic terms, its distinctiveness from the rest of China was notable; geographically, its isolation was striking. Yunnan itself is geographically somewhat isolated from the rest of China. In the early twentieth century travelers journeying from Kunming to Shanghai or Beijing would typically head south to Vietnam, and then continue by boat along the southeast China coast, instead of going overland through central China. Travel between provinces was no easier. In 1950, the journey from Kunming to Sipsongpanna took roughly a month due to mountainous terrain, poor roads, and the threat of banditry.[9] Today this trip takes less than a day by car; by plane, it takes just over half an hour.

Xishuangbanna under Socialism

The Chinese Communist Party has a well-deserved reputation for having run roughshod over pre-1949 religious and cultural institutions in its rise to power. Throughout most of China, the Communists built their support among the poor peasantry, galvanizing the dispossessed against a landed gentry that drew its authority from property and tradition. This assault on the feudal order reached its height during Land Reform in the early 1950s, when people received their official class labels and property was confiscated and reallocated accordingly. In the drive to radicalize the peasantry, the CCP also exposed the inequalities at the heart of "feudal superstition," such as religion and other cultural practices, and the political-economic arrangements with which they were entwined. In most areas, religious personages, cultural notables, richer landowners, and gentry suffered grave persecution, even death, at the hands of the party and a mobilized peasantry.

Among the exceptions to this practice was a large subset of the minority nationality population, including the Dai. The decision to go easy on certain minorities was justified according to Marxist and Morganian stage theories of development.[10] Groups that had reached a stage of socio-economic development similar to that achieved by the Han were treated like the Han—radically. Those who were deemed to be at an earlier stage of development underwent "peaceful, consultative" (*heping xieshang*) land reform. Thus, among "backward" groups stuck in stages of slave society, primitive communism, or, like the Dai, feudal manorialism (*fengjian lingzhu zhuyi*), the party refrained for a time from carrying out the divisive and extractive policies of land reform. Many preexisting cultural and political structures were left intact and even subsumed into the party-state structure.

Strategic concerns shaped this approach. In some cases the party had struck political bargains with minority chieftains to ensure their support against the Nationalists. The Communists also felt that a nonassimilative program was necessary to win the trust of minority peoples, allowing the Communists to distinguish their own program from the assimilationist policies of the Nationalists. Working with established political elites also facilitated the control and integration of diverse peoples.

The party's treatment of Dai culture and political elites in the early 1950s reflects these strategic concerns.[11] Cadres used certain features of Dai life—not always in accordance with official policy—to smooth the transition to socialism. Elements of Dai culture served as shortcuts in the state-building project by providing a framework according to which Chinese socialism could be made intelligible and legitimate to the local population. Whole sections of the Dai aristocracy were absorbed into the local party-state apparatus. The case of Zhao Cunxin is emblematic. Before 1949, Zhao, a member of the Dai royalty, had held the position of *zhaojingha*, an adviser to the monarch and liaison to the world outside Sipsongpanna. When Xishuangbanna was officially established as a Dai Autonomous Prefecture in 1954, Zhao was appointed head of the prefecture (*zhouzhang*), a position he held for forty years. Many *zhaomeng* and other aristocrats retained significant influence in prefectural and county government affairs.[12] The CCP's absorption of the pre-1949 minority elite was not limited to Xishuangbanna; this policy was used throughout minority regions in Yunnan, Sichuan, Guangxi, and other provinces. In Xishuangbanna, the policy worked especially well because of Zhao Cunxin's support for the Communist Party. Zhao had joined the underground Communist Party in 1947 and helped fight retreating Nationalist forces.[13] The Communists were thus in the position of having won over one of the most powerful and esteemed political elites in the area.

Zhao's conversion to socialism might be dismissed as savvy politics on the part of a calculating local chieftain. Written memoirs and interviews with Zhao, however, suggest a dedicated believer. At the time he joined the Party, the Nationalist presence in Xishuangbanna was substantial. The area had been under Nationalist control since 1913, and Communist operations were clandestine and fraught with danger. Zhao was one of only a handful of Dai elites to join forces with the party at this time, as many other elites were collaborating with the Nationalists. Zhao sums up his reasons for joining the Communist Party:

> The Nationalists were very corrupt. They were not interested in the livelihood of Dai people. They took money and land from Dai peasants, but did not do anything to improve their health or economic situation. The Communists I met seemed honest and trustworthy, and had plans to develop Xishuangbanna's economy, build schools and hospitals, and deal with problems like malaria. In my opinion, there was no real choice to be made, so I joined the party.[14]

As one of the most influential members of the royalty, and as someone with extensive knowledge of local conditions, Zhao was instrumental in helping the People's Liberation Army (PLA) infiltrate the area and drive remnants of the Nationalist Army into Burma. He personally guided a division of the PLA's Ninth Route Army across the Lancang River, and was later injured in a battle on the Ganlanba plain.[15] Older residents of Ganlanba still speak reverently of Zhao's role in the fighting.

Upon its victory in 1950 the Party "forgave" the errors of many Dai elites who had supported the Nationalists. Collaborators who had fled over the Burmese and Lao borders were encouraged to return and promised positions in the new party-state apparatus. "Minority autonomy" was the rallying cry during this period of velvet glove treatment of wayward Dai elites; the Party knew that without their support and connections to Dai commoners, its job would be more difficult.

The challenge facing the CCP in Xishuangbanna was one of integrating a culturally cohesive, yet highly stratified, devoutly Buddhist society into the

new socialist order. Cadres attempting to preach a message of socialist egal-
itarianism were up against castelike social distinctions that shaped settlement patterns, labor practices, and cultural taboos. Yet aspects of Dai village
life related to status inequalities assisted the party's efforts to establish its
presence. Though the ultimate aim was to impart a post-feudal, revolutionary socialist culture, cadres used elements of traditional society to habituate
the Dai population to the goals and ideals of the new socialist order.

Two of the institutions that cadres found useful were *huoxi* and *heizhao*,
quasi-feudal communal responsibility systems which had dictated the
allocation of symbolic, political, and productive labor among and within
villages.[16] Such labor included communal village labor as well as corvée
in service of the *zhaomeng* or *zhaopianling*. Under the *huoxi* system, each
village within a particular district (*meng*) was responsible for performing
specific tasks and services. One village might be responsible for providing
food, clothing, and other necessities to the local *zhaomeng*. Other villages
built and repaired roads, maintained boats and ferry service across the
Lancang River, or provided cooking services for the royal palace. Some of
the responsibilities were rather idiosyncratic; one village was responsible
for raising the *zhaopianling*'s peacocks and elephants, while others blew
trumpets during royal processions or made implements for use in religious
ceremonies. One village was charged with the task of peeling very thin
strips of bark for the *zhaopianling* to use as toilet paper.[17]

Other kinds of labor responsibilities were allocated under the *heizhao*
system, usually among residents of a particular village or district. Assignments were allocated on a rotating basis; an individual would be assigned
a task for five to fifteen days, depending on the nature of the work. The
allocation method varied, but was typically egalitarian, even democratic.
In some villages the headman might make all decisions; in others, selection
by lot determined the division of tasks.

During the first half of the 1950s, CCP cadres sometimes made use of
heizhao and *huoxi*. On several occasions when boats were needed to move
materials up and down the Lancang, cadres mobilized boat-building villages rather than assemble a random group of peasants to construct them.
One benefit of this strategy was that there was no need to pay for the boats
or for road-building crews, horses, kindling, construction materials, cooks,
etc.; Dai people performed these duties out of customary obligation.[18]

In the short term, *heizhao* and *huoxi* were convenient means for mobilizing labor, building infrastructure, moving goods, and addressing material necessities. These traditional systems may also have helped naturalize

the transition to socialism, by allowing the CCP to organize Dai society through familiar practices. Yet the reliance on these institutions had political and ideological costs. Conceptual confusion arose from cadres' use of traditional responsibility systems to explain and anchor CCP policies in Dai terms. Cadre reports from this period complain of Dai peasants describing the Party in terms remarkably similar to those used to describe the former ruling elite. Where the Dai once were the subjects of the *zhaopianling*, they now owed their loyalty to the "*zhao gongchan*" ("King Communists").[19] To the contemporary reader, this characterization seems particularly appropriate, given later Maoist megalomania. At the time, however, the subjection and stratification implied by this phrase did not square with the Party's stated commitment to the mass line.

The exploitation of traditional intra-village labor allocation systems also caused headaches, even while helping solve practical problems. For example, when assigned to positions in work units, government posts, and mass organizations, some Dai peasants would carry out their responsibilities for only five to fifteen days—the typical timeframe for *heizhao* assignments—then quit working, return to their villages, and await reassignment. Moreover, under *heizhao* one was allowed to find and pay substitutes to perform assigned tasks. It was not unusual for cadres to discover that Dai representatives at meetings in Jinghong and Kunming were not who they were supposed to be, but rather a friend, neighbor, or cousin paid to take someone's place. On hearing that cadres had been at their jobs continuously for a year or more—an extreme length of time given *heizhao* custom—many villagers expressed their sympathy for these cadres' subjugation to what was clearly a cruel feudal master. More problematically, these practices were accompanied by new forms and avenues of exploitation. For instance, members of the aristocracy in Menghai County on whom high party positions and salaries had been bestowed continued to demand corvée from their former subjects as late as 1955.[20]

As the national tide turned increasingly leftward in the mid-1950s, the melding of Party policies with a Dai worldview became further suspect and a matter of concern. Although practical matters of securing the border and establishing basic organization occupied the party during roughly the first five years after Liberation, it should be remembered that the CCP's goals were not merely social and economic but cultural and even spiritual. The incorporation of socialist theory and practice within the traditional, "feudal" worldview of the Dai complicated the propagation of a Chinese Communist worldview.

Officials were particularly alarmed at the continued florescence of Theravada Buddhism. Despite the party's apparent success in establishing a solid institutional base in Xishuangbanna, the persistence of Buddhism and other religious practices indicated that the ideological and cultural transformations sought by the CCP were failing to materialize. Ethnographic reports show that religious activity actually increased in the early 1950s. Ironically, this was the result of Communist success. The founding of the PRC and the party's state-building efforts had improved the lives of many in Xishuangbanna. Consequently, temple offerings proliferated as people sought to demonstrate gratitude for their good fortune and ensure its continuation. For the Dai, Liberation had resulted in the "three betters": better food, better clothes, and better temple offerings.[21]

During the high tide of collectivization in the mid-1950s, officials were still proceeding somewhat cautiously in many minority areas. In Xishuangbanna the modified, "consultative" version of land reform was not completed until 1956; large-scale collectivization could not take place where the reallocation of land and other property had not yet occurred. Those in favor of gradual change argued that since border minorities historically lacked private property, commodities markets, and capitalism, socialist change was unlikely to unfold according to the schedule followed in more developed areas. The collectives that were established differed markedly from those in Han-dominated regions. They were generally smaller, comprised of fifteen to twenty households rather than the one to three hundred households per typical collective. Many Dai were allowed to retain draft animals and small private plots.[22] Local cadres were exhorted to refrain from assigning households from different *minzu* to the same collective, to avoid misunderstandings. Despite the increasingly radical character of the movement at the national level, cadres were instructed to avoid fomenting intra-minority class conflict. Above all, cadres were expected to tailor work teams and management to the abilities of local minority cadres and the receptivity of the people.

However, this commitment to "consultative" change did not survive the first decade of the PRC. The decisive end to caution and experimentation came with the campaign against "local nationalism," the form the Anti-Rightist campaign of 1957 took in minority regions. Those minority and Han cadres who had promoted the consultative approach endured public criticism sessions and were sent away for rectification and political study. This leftward shift also entailed a second land reform in Xishuangbanna, deemed necessary since the earlier consultative form had left too much power in the hands of pre-Liberation elites.[23] Among the Dai, land reform was especially complicated. Prior to Liberation all property had belonged to the *zhaopianling*, so identifying landlords was difficult. Moreover, despite the castelike stratification of Dai society, the communal character of land and labor had created a fairly egalitarian standard of living among non-elites. The imperative to divide and label classes led to some creative and egregious solutions. For example, many who had served as village head-men prior to Liberation were denounced as landlords. Yet the position of headman was a nonhereditary, rotating one, often assigned by democratic or consensus methods. Moreover, village heads controlled no more prop-erty than other villagers, yet assumed greater responsibilities to the district *zhaomeng*. Landlord and rich peasant labels were also applied to families who possessed more gold and silver jewelry than others, even though these items did not translate easily into practical material wealth.[24]

Except for brief interludes, from the start of the Great Leap Forward until the end of the Maoist era the Xishuangbanna Dai and other minorities were subject to the uniform, "cut of one knife" policies applied to all Chinese. Showing respect for minorities' special characteristics was repudiated as "local nationalism" and bourgeois. The Great Leap Forward and the Cultural Revolution were profoundly disruptive and destructive for Dai and other residents of Xishuangbanna. During and immediately after the Great Leap, food shortages were severe, and many local people fled to Laos and Burma.

Xishuangbanna's remoteness did not protect it from the chaos and fac-tional strife of the Cultural Revolution. The issue of Dai participation in the Cultural Revolution is complex. This complexity results in part from cultural stereotypes about the Dai, in particular the widespread charac-terization of them as "docile." Perhaps owing to this stereotype, many Xishuangbanna officials downplay the extent of Dai involvement in this movement. A number of officials interviewed claimed that conflict in Xishuangbanna was instigated by "*neidiren*" or "*waidiren*," terms that mean "insider" and "outsider" respectively, but which refer to the same entity: people from the interior of China, or from outside Xishuangbanna and the land of the Dai. Many of the participants in factional fighting were indeed among the thousands of mostly Han settlers and sent-down youth who had come to the area to work on the rubber and tea plantations of the state-run farms. Interviews with Dai villagers, however, suggest that many participated in Cultural Revolution struggles.[25] For better or worse, by the end of the Maoist era, Dai culture and society had been profoundly trans-formed by Maoist socialism.

THE BAI

While the Xishuangbanna Dai constituted a fairly distinct cultural, linguistic, economic, and political entity, and were thus obvious candidates for classification as *minzu*, the situation of the Bai prior to 1949 is quite different. One of the difficulties that arise when speaking of Bai cultural resurgence concerns the very "Bai-ness" of the Bai. The term "Bai," which means "white," derives from the historical usage of the terms *bai* (white) and *wu* (black) to distinguish among various Yunnan ethnic and tribal groups.[26] Yet prior to the mid-1950s, Bai people rarely if ever referred to themselves as such, or even considered themselves as ethnic. Instead, Bai called themselves *minjia*, a Chinese term that has been translated as "common people" or "civilian households."[27]

Several mid-twentieth-century studies of Dali life and society emphasize the Chineseness of the *minjia*. One of these, Francis L. K. Hsu's *Under the Ancestor's Shadow*, portrays its subjects as paragons of the Confucian Chinese order. His subjects' concerns with filial piety and ancestor worship, and the way those concerns played out in their social behavior, are characterized by Hsu as emblematic of a Chinese way of life. The "shadow" cast by ancestors over the actions and self-conceptions of West Town's residents typified rural social organization and cultural practice throughout China. In Hsu's interpretation, the *minjia* people "would be seriously offended" if their Chinese origins were denied.[28] In *The Tower of Five Glories*, C. P. Fitzgerald echoes many of Hsu's findings, emphasizing the strength of Confucian and Chinese folk traditions, values, and ideals among the *minjia*. However, whereas Hsu avoids the issue of the ethnic status of the *minjia* people, Fitzgerald raises it if only to reveal its tenuous character. Fitzgerald considered the *minjia* to be a distinct ethnic group, mainly on the basis of their language, but if they possessed any sense of minority or ethnic identity, it was a weak one.[29] The *minjia* subjects Fitzgerald discusses seemed embarrassed to be considered as ethnic, downplaying or dismissing the idea.

Neither of these studies use the term "Bai" to refer to the *minjia* people of the Dali region. Both studies show the degree to which *minjia* were acculturated to mainstream Chinese life and society. Together, Hsu's and Fitzgerald's studies suggest that in terms of both objective, "external" aspects of ethnicity and subjective ones based on self-identity, the *minjia* people could be viewed as "strongly" Chinese and only a minority in a minimal, "weak" way, certainly not constituting any social entity called the "Bai." The fact that their spoken language differed from standard Chinese was relatively unimportant, because Chinese people throughout China spoke (and continue to speak) a number of mutually unintelligible dialects.

The minority classification project of the 1950s, however, greatly relied on external markers of uniqueness in demarcating minorities from the Han and from each other. In post-1949 Chinese scholarship on the Bai, one phenomenon typically cited as "proof" of Bai distinctiveness is *benzhu* worship. *Benzhu* worship is a decentralized, village-specific polytheistic set of practices organized around the worship of local tutelary gods and protector spirits. It is often portrayed as a distinctive and distinguishing aspect of Bai culture, unique to them as a people. It is even described as their "national [or nationality] religion."[30] In terms of Stalin's criteria of nationhood, *benzhu* worship is proof that the Bai possess a unique and shared psychological make-up, as manifest in distinct cultural practices. Yet the notion that *benzhu* demonstrates Bai distinctiveness is problematic. First, the Bai do not practice *benzhu* exclusively; they are as fervent in Buddhist and Daoist practice as they are in the worship of their local tutelary gods, and some Bai are Catholic or Protestant. While *benzhu* may be the most ancient of the religions they practice, there is no evidence that it stands in a hierarchically primary relation to either Buddhism or Daoism.[31] Second, although *benzhu* worship originated in the Dali region, it resembles folk religious practices found in other parts of China. Much like the worship of tutelary, protector gods elsewhere, *benzhu* practice sometimes parallels irrigation societies where hierarchical, intra-village relations concerning water rights are symbolically reproduced.[32]

The *benzhu* religion underscores not so much Bai distinctiveness as their syncretism. It demonstrates a willingness to adapt and meld complex, even contradictory symbolic practice. *Benzhu* originated in the worship of spirits embodied in the natural world, such as trees, streams, rocks, and rivers, but over time it incorporated deities from other religions and figures from myth and history. There are *benzhu* temples dedicated to Guanyin and other staples of Chinese folk religion, and it is not uncommon to find *benzhu* temples adjacent to those of other faiths. There are also *benzhu* temples dedicated to Kubilai Khan, who defeated the Dali kingdom and incorporated Yunnan into the Chinese empire; to Nanzhao kings; and to statesmen and scholars of various dynastic periods. In one village there is a temple dedicated to both Kubilai Khan and Duan Xingzhi, the last ruler of the Dali kingdom who surrendered to the Mongols (figs. 2.1, 2.2). Another village worships a Han dynasty official who allegedly introduced their ancestors to the art of carpet weaving, their most important cottage

FIG. 2.1 Statue of Kubilai Khan in a *benzhu* temple, Xizhou, Dali. Kubilai's invading Mongol armies defeated the Dali kingdom in 1253. Photographed in 2002.

FIG. 2.2 Statue of Duan Xingzhi, *benzhu* temple, Xizhou, Dali. Duan was the last king of the Dali kingdom. After surrendering to the Mongols, Duan was made a marshal in the Yuan army and continued to govern the Dali region. This statue of Duan stands at the foot of the one of Kubilai depicted in Fig. 2.1. Photographed in 2002.

industry.[33] Half-jokingly, I asked a Bai archeologist if there were any *ben-zhu* temples dedicated to Chairman Mao. "Not yet," he responded seriously, "but maybe in a hundred years or so."[34]

Bai syncretism and the weakness of their *minzu* consciousness (*minzu yishi*) notwithstanding, phenomena like *benzhu* worship were enough to win minority status for the Bai. However, the classification of the *minjia* as Bai was met with some local resistance. In ethnographic work conducted in the 1980s, David Y. H. Wu found that many older people in the Dali region still referred to themselves as *minjia*.[35] Wu also noted that until 1983, a self-described group of *minjia* in Hunan was denied Bai minority status because they were deemed too assimilated to Han culture, a fact which further complicates the issue of Bai identity.[36] The tenuousness of Bai identity raises several questions. Why, for instance, has there been so much confusion over the "authenticity" of the Bai as a minority nationality? What significance does the syncretism of the *minjia* have for the contemporary resurgence of Bai culture and articulations of Bai identity? Does this resurgence entail an "invention of tradition?"

The confusion over Bai identity and culture stems in part from Chinese minority policy and its theoretical justifications. In terms of many of the relevant criteria, as Hsu, Fitzgerald, and Wu suggest, the Bai, or *minjia*—though distinct enough to justify their classification as minority *minzu*—were highly acculturated to Chinese, and thus Han, forms of agriculture, language, religion, and social customs. Since Han ways served as the standard and were by definition "advanced," the Bai too were seen as such, at least relatively. This acculturation stems from geographic, economic, and political factors. Despite their isolation and independence from the rest of China, the Erhai and Dianchi plains of Yunnan were never completely cut off from Chinese political and cultural influence. During the Eastern and Western Han dynasties, the southern Silk Road brought textiles and other products from central China through Yunnan and into Burma and India to the West. Historical records indicate the existence of a classical Confucian school in Dali County as early as 85 C.E. During the period of the Nanzhao and Dali kingdoms (738–1253), the ruling elite, which maintained a tributary relationship with the Tang and Song courts while enjoying de facto independence, imported noted scholars to teach them Chinese writing and Confucian classics.[37] These elite also adapted Chinese characters to fit the spoken tongue, and produced literature and written records of their deeds and histories. The Mongol invasion of the mid-thirteenth century and the consequent founding of the Yuan dynasty entailed the further expansion of classically Chinese cultural practices and institutions.

Acculturation was at times achieved by force. During the tenth century, Nanzhao rulers carried out attacks on the city of Chengdu in Sichuan and parts of Guangxi, bringing back tens of thousands of Chinese captives in the process.[38] The regional dominance of Nanzhao and Dali, moreover, translated into control of the fertile plains of Yunnan. This control of the flatlands facilitated the development of sedentary wet-rice cultivation and multicrop agriculture—hallmarks of ostensibly "Han" Chinese economic practice. Most significant in the acculturation of the peoples of the Erhai plateau, however, was the settlement of soldiers, traders, and ordinary peasants from central and eastern China that began with the Mongol conquest and accelerated under the Ming and Qing. These settlers opened up uncultivated land, intermarried with aboriginal and tribal peoples of the region, and helped effect the integration of Yunnan into the broader Chinese culture and civilization.

Bai political, economic, and cultural preeminence is not only a feature of the distant past. During the nineteenth and early twentieth centuries, *minjia* were prominent in Yunnan's political and economic elite. Two *minjia* trading companies, the Heqing and Xizhou groups (*bang*), dominated Yunnan commerce and long-distance trade during this period. These two *bang*, along with the Hui Tengchong *bang*, established powerful commercial firms whose networks spread to Shanghai, Hong Kong, Bangkok, and beyond.[39] One of the interesting features of the post-Mao Bai cultural revival has been a rediscovery of these *minjia* capitalists. A spate of recent publications on the Bai celebrate these capitalists—until recently vilified as enemies of the people—as early proponents of "minority nationality economics" (*minzu jingji*).[40]

In a way, the question of why the Bai are so advanced is misplaced. It is not that the Bai are somehow inherently inclined toward such acculturation. Rather, the Bai of today are the products or descendents of the "winners" of indigenous political struggles in Yunnan and of the later Yuan, Ming, and Qing conquerors who settled the region and intermarried with its inhabitants. This relative advancement and cultural integration of the Erhai region had important implications for the Bai in the early years of the People's Republic. For one thing, the CCP did not need to start from scratch to establish an education system as it did in places like Xishuangbanna. After 1949, the Party reorganized and expanded existing schools under new administration and with the new socialist curriculum. In general, the

Bai did not present to the same degree the kinds of linguistic and cultural obstacles to state-building as did other linguistic, ethnic, and tribal groups.

The history of Bai integration within China played out in the implementation of Maoist policies. Like the Dai, until 1958 and the beginnings of the Great Leap Forward, most minority nationalities in Yunnan were subject to "peaceful, consultative" land reform policies and practices that minimized the pace and extent of socialist transformation and left many traditional elites in power. The Bai, however, were not subject to these modified policies. Land reform and collectivization among the Bai are noteworthy only for being unremarkable. The experiences of most Bai were in fact utterly "normal," if such a word can be applied to the Maoist era's radical experiments. The counties of Dali underwent land reform in the early 1950s; mutual aid teams were introduced in 1953 and 1954, and over the next three years collectivization intensified. With the advent of the Great Leap Forward, nearly the entire Dali population was reorganized into People's Communes. It was not until the start of the reform era that the Bai's "special characteristics" were again allowed to flourish.

THE HUI

Folk histories and archeological evidence suggest a Muslim presence in Yunnan as early as the ninth century C.E.[41] Both Dali and Kunming were stops on the southern Silk Route, and Middle Eastern traders may have passed through Yunnan on their way to the Tang capital of Chang'an.[42] Yet it was Kubilai Khan's conquest of Yunnan in 1253 that brought the first waves of permanent Muslim settlers to Yunnan. Although the Yuan dynasty was founded and ruled by the Mongols, the very first governor of Yunnan, Sayyid 'Ajall Shams ad-Din, was a Muslim of Central Asian descent. Sayyid, or Saidianchi Shansiding in Chinese, was from Bukhara and, according to his family history, a thirty-first generation direct descendant of the prophet Mohammed.[43] Because the Mongols had a long-standing practice of incorporating conquered armies rather than annihilating them, Saidianchi attained a high position in the Mongol army. Many of those soldiers who fought under him were Muslim.

On his appointment as Yunnan's first provincial governor, Saidianchi implemented the *tunken* policy, a land settlement program that stimulated the in-migration of thousands of soldiers and civilian support personnel to Yunnan from elsewhere in China. *Tunken* was aimed at cementing Yuan power; toward this end, these soldier-settlers opened up vast tracts of uncultivated land for agricultural production.[44] This policy was aimed at controlling and subduing as much of the province and its inhabitants as possible; as a result of this, the pattern of settlement under Saidianchi's rule was greatly dispersed. Contemporary Hui communities reflect these settlement patterns: Yunnan Muslims are widely scattered, and reside in all but two remote counties.

Saidianchi brought Islam as well as Muslims to Yunnan. Historical records mention his accomplishments in establishing mosques, including twelve in the capital of Kunming.[45] Yet as Morris Rossabi points out, Saidianchi did not impose Islam on the Yunnan populace. Owing to Kubilai's own interest in Confucianism and Chinese cultural practice, Saidianchi is best known for the more "orthodox" policies and measures carried out during his tenure, and he is celebrated as a Confucian civilizer.[46] Saidianchi introduced Chinese marital and funeral customs, established Confucian schools, expanded the imperial examination system, and transferred the provincial capital from Taihe in Dali to Kunming, where it is today.[47] He promoted agriculture, lowered the tax burden on the populace, and ordered the repair and expansion of flood control and irrigation systems around Lake Dian near the new provincial capital, many of which functioned well into the twentieth century.[48] Although efforts to co-opt tribal leaders did not reach the level they did under the Ming, Saidianchi made some inroads in that direction. The first Yuan governor-general fits neatly into the pantheon of benevolent Confucian administrators and reformers. Following Saidianchi's death after just six years of governing Yunnan, Kubilai Khan decreed that his policies and plans would continue in perpetuity. In 1297 he was posthumously awarded the title Prince of Xianyang.[49]

So successful was Saidianchi in cementing Yuan rule that his sons also rose to prominent military and political positions. Nasr al-Din, the eldest, held high rank in the Mongol-Muslim army that conquered Yunnan and succeeded his father as governor of Yunnan.[50] Accounts of the history of Muslims in Yunnan praise Nasr al-Din's success in pacifying indigenous tribal peoples and enlisting them into the army. Nasr al-Din is further lauded for having developed the economy, "eradicated superstition, and improved the backward customs of every region."[51] Saidianchi's other sons also attained political prominence in Yunnan, Guangdong, and Jiangxi. This illustrious family history is a source of pride to Hui people in contemporary Yunnan, many of whom trace their ancestry directly back to Saidianchi.[52]

Continuation of Saidianchi's benevolent policies was not an option, unfortunately, for the short-lived Yuan dynasty; in 1368, it was overthrown and replaced by the Ming. Under the Ming, however, Muslims continued to play a prominent role in the military and in the governance of Yunnan. Four of Ming founder Zhu Yuanzhang's top generals and military advisers—Chang Yuchun, Hu Dahai, Lan Yu, and Mu Ying—were Muslims from Anhui and Jiangsu in eastern China.[53] Lan Yu and Mu Ying served as assistants to Fu Youde, commander of the Yunnan expeditionary forces that brought Yunnan under Ming control.[54] Mu Ying, an adopted son of the first Ming emperor, played a particularly key role in establishing Ming control over Yunnan in the mid-fourteenth century. Under his leadership the influx of Muslim as well as non-Muslim Chinese from the eastern Chinese heartland increased dramatically. A large proportion of Yunnan mosques were built during the early Ming, mainly during the reign of Zhu Yuanzhang, who for a time displayed tolerance toward Islam. The Ming period is also viewed as the high tide of *"Hanhua"* ("Hanification" or sinicization) in Yunnan. The policies of Mu Ying and others were largely responsible for "Han" Chinese culture permeating Yunnan life and society more thoroughly than ever.[55]

The roster of accomplished Yunnan Muslims includes adventurous as well as ordinary Hui people. The eunuch Zheng He, China's greatest Chinese seafarer, who led maritime expeditions to Arabia and the eastern coast of Africa in the early fifteenth century, was born to a Muslim family near Kunming.[56] During the Ming and into the Qing, Yunnan Muslims began playing an important role in the spread and development of markets, long-distance trade, mining, and handicrafts, even though the vast majority of Hui were peasants. Yunnan Muslims also flourished culturally and intellectually. During the late Ming and through the Qing, Hui scholars and teachers developed a uniquely Chinese approach to Islam, one that used Confucian precepts and thought to explain Islamic philosophy, ethics, and law. This effort was driven to a large degree by political exigencies, specifically the need to render Islam coherent, and thus palatable, to the Ming and Qing courts. The attempt to reconcile two schools of thought was no easy task, due to fundamental contradictions between their basic principles. On the one hand, Islam stipulates the supremacy of Allah and the equality of all human beings before him. The Chinese Confucian worldview, on the other hand, posits a hierarchical social, political, and moral scheme in which the emperor, as the Son of Heaven and possessing divine characteristics, is venerated. Yet the reconciliation worked both ways; Yunnanese Islamic scholars borrowed from the neo-Confucians to deepen proofs and arguments for the existence of Allah and the truths of Islam.[57] Many of these scholars and religious leaders held imperial degrees or military rank.[58]

Under the Qing (1644–1911), the social and political position of the Hui greatly deteriorated, in part because of Manchu control over the military and political apparatus. Unlike the Ming and Yuan rulers, the Manchu made little room for Muslim leadership. The decline in relations with both the imperial state and the Han partly resulted from—and fueled—Hui support for Ming restoration. The slogan "oppose the Qing, restore the Ming" (*fan Qing fu Ming*) was widely propagated among Yunnan Muslims. Ming restoration societies sprung up throughout the province, and some Hui changed their surnames to Ming in a not-so-subtle protest against Manchu rule.

The later Qing dynasty is remembered today for its anti-Muslim massacres and repression and for Muslim revolt. The persecution of Muslims reached its nadir during the nineteenth century. In Yunnan, a series of Han-Hui ethnic riots and massacres of Hui took place beginning in the early 1800s. Many of these originated in petty, individual conflicts, such as a failure to pay debts, fistfights among individuals, etc., or from economic competition, but later escalated into larger group conflicts and even massacres.[59] Unfortunately for Hui involved in these conflicts, local and provincial Qing officials followed a divide-and-conquer strategy of "assist the Han, suppress the Hui" (*zhu Han mie Hui*), and publicly advocated a "destroy the Hui" (*mie Hui*) policy. Qing magistrates and military units in Yunnan backed and even participated in the massacre of Muslims at the hands of Han. Not surprisingly, efforts to seek redress through local and even Imperial Beijing venues were ignored, or used as justification to step up anti-Muslim attacks.[60]

The most famous response to this persecution was the Dali-based uprising known as the Panthay Rebellion, led by Du Wenxiu, which lasted from 1856 to 1873. Du, a Muslim, had traveled to the Qing court in Beijing to protest the slaughter of fellow Muslims following ethnic riots in his native Tengyue (now Tengchong), in western Yunnan. His petition was received, but his request for redress was denied.[61] In the face of this, Du spent several years organizing and mobilizing the resentful locals, who were predominantly Muslim, in Menghua County (now Weishan). Backed by a network of Muslims and *Gelaohui* secret society members—like Du himself, many Muslims were also members of the secret society—Du led an attack on Qing administrative and military units in Dali.[62] They succeeded, and what originated in a search for justice and redress grew into a province-wide secessionist uprising. From 1856 through 1873, Du and his armies controlled a wide swath of central and western Yunnan and parts of neighboring Sichuan Province. Though roughly contemporaneous with the Taiping

Rebellion, Du's revolt had little in common with that religiously motivated uprising. Rather, this rebellion on the edge of the empire was a revolt against Qing persecution and injustice.

At the height of their power, the rebels controlled roughly half of Yunnan Province, including the outskirts of the capital in Kunming. The rebellion's longevity was in part a reflection of the fact that Qing soldiers were embroiled in trying to suppress a host of other uprisings throughout China. The most notable of these was the Taiping Rebellion, whose size and proximity to the seat of Imperial power made it a more immediate threat.[63] Once the Taipings were quashed in 1864, Qing armies turned their might on the Panthay rebels, eventually defeating them with the help of Ma Rulong, a turncoat Muslim who had originally fought on the side of the rebels. The defeat ushered in a period of anti-Muslim repression far harsher than that which had inspired the uprising.[64] Muslims throughout Yunnan were slaughtered, lands were confiscated, and many Hui tried to pass as Han or Bai by abandoning identifiable surnames such as Ma, shaving their beards, and eating pork.

Today, the Panthay Rebellion is hailed as a valiant precursor to the people's revolution of the twentieth century. The main figures and events of the uprising are celebrated in numerous books and magazine articles, and a museum chronicling the rebellion now stands on the site of Du's military and political headquarters in Dali. Although its origins lay in Hui efforts to seek justice and redress, the rebellion involved coordination and cooperation among many different ethnic groups in Yunnan. It is characterized as an exemplar of *minzu* unity, a multiethnic people's struggle against a corrupt, decrepit, feudal Qing empire that fomented ethnic strife as a way of maintaining control. But for the lack of a vanguard party, the hagiography of Du implies, the rebellion might have succeeded.

One ironic outcome of the failure of the rebellion was the expansion of Hui involvement in commerce and trade. The confiscation of Hui lands after this and other Muslim revolts meant that few Hui families or communities could support themselves by farming alone, and many turned to trade. Hui came to dominate the long-distance transport industry, running horse and mule caravans (*mabang*) into Tibet and Sichuan and south into Burma, Vietnam, Laos, and Thailand. Using these extensive networks and connections, the Hui, like the Bai, established prosperous commercial firms, some of which had branches as far away as Hong Kong, Shanghai, and Vietnam. During the late nineteenth century, their role in handicrafts and cottage industry also expanded. Hui in the Tonghai region of central

Yunnan, for example, became famous for their metallurgy, particularly for gun and knife manufacturing that continued into the 1950s and beyond. Thus, despite persecution, many Yunnan Hui continued to prosper.

The latter half of the nineteenth century also witnessed important developments in Yunnanese Islam. During this period one of the most venerated Yunnan Islamic scholars of the late Qing, Ma Dexin, translated and printed the first Chinese Koran using woodblock technology. Ma also translated a number of Arabic works into Chinese and wrote a series of Chinese texts on Islam. He was also active in the Panthay Rebellion and helped organize a contemporaneous uprising of Muslims in central Yunnan that joined with the Dali-based revolt.

The list of illustrious Yunnan Muslim personages of the time spanning the late Qing, Republican, and early Socialist periods is as long and varied as that of previous eras. It includes capitalist entrepreneurs, Beijing and Yunnan opera singers, teachers, scholars, literary figures, newspaper publishers, and heroes of the Revolution.[65] Such achievements do not imply that all Yunnan Muslims were engaged in equally benevolent, service-oriented activities. Contemporary Chinese histories of the Yunnan Hui seem to have difficulty dealing with the "traitor" Ma Rulong, bandits, local tyrants, opium smugglers, and Yunnan Muslims who helped suppress revolts in China's northwest. It is difficult to find more than oblique references to such figures. Yet the fact of their existence highlights the degree to which Hui participated in and were integrated into Yunnan culture, economy, and society. The picture is of a flourishing though at times beleaguered Muslim community linked in important ways with the greater Islamic world, yet fully invested in, and inseparable from, the Chinese social, political, and economic order.

The lives of most ordinary Yunnan Muslims did not differ significantly from other groups, especially the Han, among whom they lived. The leaders of this dispersed and extensive Muslim community aspired to Confucian and Chinese ideals of benevolence, community service, prosperity, respect for ancestors, and defense of the motherland. While a history of persecution and resistance informs the contemporary Hui cultural revival, so too do their ancestors' economic, cultural, political, and military accomplishments. The particulars of the Hui revival, and those of the Dai and Bai, are the focus of the next three chapters.

—3—

DHARMA AND DEVELOPMENT AMONG

THE XISHUANGBANNA DAI

In the spring of 1997, the villagers of Manchunman, in the Xishuangbanna Dai Autonomous Prefecture, celebrated the dedication of the recently rebuilt local Buddhist temple with an elaborate festival. Manchunman is situated on the banks of the Lancang (Mekong) River in Menghan Township, roughly twenty miles southeast of Jinghong, the prefectural capital. The original temple, damaged by time, termites, and Cultural Revolution conflict, had recently been renovated with funds from a variety of sources: the Xishuangbanna Buddhist Association, private citizens, tourist revenues, and prominent politicians from Thailand. The festival to dedicate the rebuilt structure was held in May and took place over several days. The festivities included musical performances, banquets, temple offerings, and the chanting of Buddhist sutras. On one day, villagers and political elites gathered in the temple to make offerings and request blessings from the abbot. Among those present were the mayor of Jinghong, the head of the prefecture, and a representative from the Thai consulate in Kunming. The consul had donated ¥225,800 for the reconstruction effort, while the president of the Thai Senate had given ¥198,888.[1] Also present was Dao Meiying, a former princess, member of the pre-1949 Sipsongpanna royal family, and wife of the retired prefectural head. During the several hours of offerings and sutra chanting, the temple overflowed with celebrants.

Following a noontime banquet, the dignitaries moved to the banks of the Lancang River to watch a rocket festival. Hundreds of spectators who had come for the event, most of them other Dai people from villages across the township, joined the dignitaries. Rocket festivals are held in Tai communities throughout Southeast Asia; the launching of rockets is believed to ensure abundant rains. This particular event entailed competitions among teams of men from villages throughout Menghan. Teams launched rockets in groups of two or three; teams whose rockets flew highest won cash prizes from the visiting dignitaries. The bestowing of prizes was as much a sight as the rocket-launching. After each heat, the winning team chanted and slowly danced its way from the launching platform to the reviewing stand, surrounded the seated dignitaries, and lifted them in their chairs up in the air. The dignitaries—including the consular representative, the mayor, and the prefectural head—were held aloft for several minutes, until each produced thick wads of ¥100 notes as prizes for the winning team.

These events illustrate how, in contemporary China, the party-state has repudiated the anti-religion, anti-tradition bent of Maoist socialism. Despite noteworthy exceptions like Falun Gong, the Chinese leadership tolerates the resurgence of much religious and cultural practice among Chinese minorities and among the Han. Yet what is striking about the events depicted above is that officials not only tolerated them, they participated as central and essential players as well. In the absence of their participation, the Manchunman festivals, though entertaining and important in their own right, would have lacked the significance they possessed.

This kind of state participation is not unusual. In Xishuangbanna, Dai culture and religion are conspicuously promoted by the party-state. Officials see the maintenance and propagation of traditional culture—or some facsimile thereof—as integral to their duties. Cadres pay public homage to traditional institutions by welcoming the Dai New Year at theatrical and musical events, accompanying members of the former royal family to dragon boat races, funding a variety of music, arts, and dance troupes, and participating in ceremonies like the one above. Officials even encourage cross-national Dai-Tai identification and interaction. How is it that the state has become patron and curator of, even participant in, Dai cultural practices? What local or national motives are at work in these public spectacles? Furthermore, how do minority cadres and ordinary Dai people regard state-sanctioned cultural endeavors?

Underpinning official support for Dai culture is the idea that it can serve the developmental goals of the Chinese party-state, nationally as well as in

Xishuangbanna. For officials, Dai culture possesses "instrumental" significance—it is an instrument or tool that can be deployed in the service of various ends. Dai cultural resurgence has been a boon for the tourist industry in
Xishuangbanna; tradition and revenues are tightly intertwined. The ostensibly friendly historical relationship between the Chinese empire and Tai
kingdoms is played up to attract foreign investment. Cultural and religious
ceremonies also serve as conduits through which the party-state asserts its
authority and legitimacy. The state makes a great show of its support for Dai
cultural distinctiveness, but it expects Dai compliance in return.

Yet this instrumentalist view of culture does not explain the Dai revival
as a whole. Officials' role in the revival is more than an effort to buy off the
support of minorities, entice tourists, or lure foreign investors. The state
has adopted a kind of caretaker relationship toward Dai cultural practice,
and the preservation of Dai culture is viewed as an end in itself. Among the
Dai, including religious leaders, intellectuals, cultural activists, ordinary
people, and officials, participation in the revival springs from a genuine
desire to reestablish practices through which Dai identity is expressed and
maintained. Such practices also express Tai identity, that is, Dai membership within the broader, cross-national "imagined community" of Tai peoples in Laos, Myanmar, and Thailand.[2]

Yet aspects of the revival also reflect and refract values and ideals related
to Chinese national identity and membership. Promotion of and participation in Dai cultural endeavors can be, at times, ways of being Chinese.
This becomes apparent when Dai revival is seen in the context of broader
societal efforts to rework Chinese identity that occur in light of national
imperatives of economic and cultural modernization. Cultural activists
and participants, however, do not accept uncritically the way these goals
of reworking identity and achieving modernization are defined. Instead,
cultural practice is a means through which identities, norms, and membership are negotiated and contested.

CULTURE AND MODERNIZATION IN XISHUANGBANNA

The Dai, who number over 1.3 million, are the third largest minority group
in Yunnan. Slightly more than one-quarter of the Yunnan Dai live in the
Xishuangbanna Dai Autonomous Prefecture. Another 29 percent reside in
Dehong, a Dai and Jingpo autonomous prefecture several hundred miles
away in western Yunnan. Dai also reside in the districts of Honghe, Simao,
and Lincang, which border or lie between the two autonomous prefectures.

TABLE 3.1 Composition of Xishuangbanna Population, 1956–2005

	1956	*1982*	*2000*	*2005*	*% in 1956*	*% in 2005*
Dai	128,700	225,485	298,004	358,930	50	34
Han	17,905	185,894	289,100	255,294	7	24
Hani	46,514	129,198	169,974	205,501	18	20
Lahu	16,203	33,336	52,530	59,118	6	6
Bulang	19,368	27,664	37,440	46,642	7	4
Yi	6,365	16,495	45,939	52,926	2	5
Jinuo	5,491	12,405	18,786	25,316	2	2
Other	18,099	15,972	81,618	45,873	7	4
Total	258,645	646,449	993,391	1,049,600	100	100

SOURCES: *2006 Yunnan tongji nianjian*, 712–15; *Xishuangbanna guotu jingji kaocha baogao*, 141; *Yunnan sheng 1990 nian renkou pucha ziliao*, 41–52.

In Xishuangbanna, the Dai comprise 34 percent of the population (table 3.1). Though it is a Dai autonomous prefecture, Xishuangbanna is ethnically diverse with forty-four nationalities living within it. The figure is misleading, however, since many of the groups identified, such as Koreans, Tibetans and Uyghurs, are represented by only a handful of individuals and their families who migrated to the prefecture in search of economic opportunity. Long-established minorities include the Hani, Yi, Lahu, Bulang, Jinuo, Yao, and Miao. Xishuangbanna is also home to over four thousand Hui, descendents of Muslims from north-central Yunnan who fled south to escape Qing persecution in the nineteenth century.[3]

The Han are the second largest group in Xishuangbanna. In 2005 there were 255,294 Han living in the prefecture, comprising roughly 24 percent of the population. In 1949 only about five thousand Han resided in the region. Their numbers grew dramatically in the 1950s, when thousands of people from interior provinces settled on rubber plantations created by the State Farm Bureau. During the late 1960s, these farms received an infusion of "sent-down youth" from all over the country. Dai and other minorities also work and live on the farms, but most hail from elsewhere in Yunnan and other provinces. In the reform era, the Han population again surged as economic opportunities drew new waves of settlers from all over China. By 2000, there were nearly as many Han in the prefecture as Dai. In the last several years their numbers have declined, partly due to de-collectivization of some of the state farms (fig. 3.1).

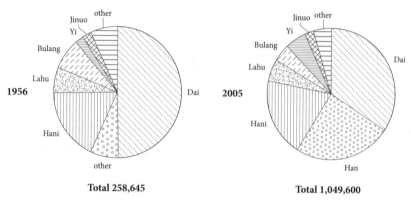

1956
Dai
Hani
Lahu
Bulang
Yi
Jinuo
other
other

Total 258,645

2005
Dai
Hani
Han
Lahu
Bulang
Yi
Jinuo
other

Total 1,049,600

FIG. 3.1 Demographic change in Xishuangbanna, 1956 and 2005

XISHUANGBANNA UNDER REFORM

The policies of the Mao years severely damaged the economy and society of Xishuangbanna. Post-1978 reforms have improved the situation considerably. The Chinese government resurrected its policy of respecting minorities' "special characteristics," or at least those the state believes do not encourage ethnic or religious strife. As a model minority with a reputation for being docile (*wenshun*), the Dai's special characteristics are vigorously promoted. Local and provincial governments showcase Dai art, customs, dance, architecture, textiles, and music. The state funds numerous Dai dance troupes at the prefectural, provincial, and national level; many of these are featured on state-run television programs throughout the year. Jinghong is home to a Nationalities' Culture Park (*minzu wenhua gongyuan*), although the city is something of a nationalities' culture park in its own right. Throughout the prefecture, miniature "Dai culture villages" have been erected next to the actual villages that manage them. In these culture villages, which are attempts to capitalize on Xishuangbanna's tourist boom, young women bathe conspicuously in the Lancang at scheduled times, and the annual water-splashing festival is celebrated daily. Even the Farm Bureau has jumped on board. In an ironic twist on the theme of internal colonialism, several state farm branches have diversified into the tourism and hospitality industries, and some are exporting "Dai flavor" (*Daizu fengwei*) to the more industrialized areas of eastern China.[4]

Much of this cultural promotion has a top-down, state- or business-led character to it, and is driven by economic concerns. Much of it can also be dismissed as ersatz. However, a genuine desire to reinstate traditions and cus-

FIG. 3.2 An active Buddhist temple, Menghai County

toms is also sparking cultural resurgence. The most visible example of this is the renaissance of Theravada Buddhism (fig. 3.2). With few exceptions, Dai are Theravada Buddhists. Buddhism has long been central to Dai life, and it continues to shape what it means to be Dai to a considerable degree.

In 1950, there were 574 active temples in Xishuangbanna, staffed by more than nine hundred full-time monks and more than five thousand young novices. Religion continued to flourish several years after the founding of the PRC, a result of the CCP's decision to respect minorities' cultural practices and work with and through preexisting minority elites. As is the case throughout China, the leftward lurch of the late 1950s severely curtailed religious activities in Xishuangbanna. During the Great Leap, Buddhist statues and other religious objects were melted down for the metal they contained. Temples were turned into meeting halls and granaries, and monks were persecuted as rightists. Policies toward religion relaxed for a few years after the Great Leap, but the Cultural Revolution put an end to this modest revival. At its height all temples in Xishuangbanna had shut and only one elderly abbot remained, the rest having fled over the border or been defrocked.[5]

Following the inauguration of reforms in 1978, Buddhist institutions recovered fairly quickly. In 1981, roughly one-fifth of the temples in Xishuangbanna had been renovated or rebuilt, and twenty-three monks were

TABLE 3.2 The Fall and Rise of Buddhist Institutions in Xishuangbanna, 1950–2005

	1950	1965	1970	1981	1994	2005
Temples	574	103	51	128	502	563
Monks	6,470	815	1	640	4,927	6,000

SOURCES: Mi Yunguang, "Shangzuobu Fojiao," 121; China Sangha Metta, "2007 Foguang Zhi Jia gong-zuo jihua"; *1997 XBNJ*, 212–11.

in residence, teaching more than six hundred novices. By the mid-1990s, Theravada Buddhism had recovered almost to its pre-Great Leap levels (table 3.2). Today, there are 577 temples and over 4,500 monks through-out the prefecture.[6] A number of these monks are returnees from Laos and Myanmar who fled Xishuangbanna during radical Maoist campaigns. Also among their number are younger monks from Laos, the Shan State of Myanmar, and northern Thailand.

Cross-border and regional networks are important to the Buddhist revival. Today, many Dai make pilgrimages to reliquaries, temples, and other religious sites in neighboring countries. Many are devotees of influ-ential Buddhist leaders from these countries and travel long distances to festivals organized in their honor. One of these is Khruba Bunchum, a charismatic Thai monk whose picture is displayed in homes throughout Xishuangbanna. Khruba Bunchum has visited Xishuangbanna on several occasions, and draws thousands of Dai faithful to events in Laos and the Shan State.[7]

The party-state mostly welcomes the Buddhist revival in Xishuangbanna. Yet certain practices, such as the education provided by Buddhist monas-teries, vex local officials in their efforts to implement various policies. Tra-ditionally, a large proportion of Dai boys and men would spend a period of time as monks, even if they did not enter the monastery permanently. On the eve of Liberation, one-third of the male population had spent some time in the monastery, at least temporarily.[8] This training served a variety of practical and symbolic purposes. Temples were the only place where Dai men could learn the written Tai language, the script in which religious texts are written. Temple education also included mathematics, literature, and history. Becoming a monk was also an opportunity for merit-making and a rite of passage for Dai males. Today, young novices around the ages of seven to fifteen are a common sight at village temples throughout the prefecture (figs. 3.3, 3.4). Temple education focuses on religious texts, the

FIG. 3.3 Novices studying the Dai script, temple school, Menghai County. Many Dai boys from the ages of about eight through their teens spend several years in the temple as novice monks. During this time they study and practice Buddhism and learn to read and write the Dai language.

FIG. 3.4 Novice monks, Menghai County. The majority of novices return to regular society after a few years in the temple, but some stay on to become monks permanently.

Dai script, and the ideals and philosophy of Theravada Buddhism. Girls and women are still excluded from temple education.

What concerns local officials is that the resurgence of Buddhist education has coincided with a drop in elementary and middle school enrollment rates throughout the prefecture. In Menghai, one of the three counties that comprise the prefecture, official statistics show that the primary school enrollment rate had been as high as 98 percent in 1975, but by 1982 it had dropped to 67 percent.[9] In Xishuangbanna as a whole, overall enrollment rates dropped from about 92 percent in 1975 to 85 percent in 1986.[10]

These figures should be regarded skeptically. The study fails to mention that drop-out rates were extremely high during the Cultural Revolution; not much "educating" was accomplished due to the political turmoil of the period. Moreover, economic reforms were a prime culprit in the decline of enrollment. As is true throughout China, the implementation of the household responsibility system after 1979 created unforeseen side effects. Peasant families, newly reliant on household labor after decades of collectivized farming, pulled their children out of school and put them to work. In Xishuangbanna, however, economic incentives were not the only cause of disruptions in education. Historically, religious education in Xishuangbanna was much more widespread than it was among Dai communities in Dehong, the Dai and Jingpo autonomous prefecture in western Yunnan. In the reform era, the resurgence of religious education has been considerably less extensive in Dehong as well.[11] Yet while the primary school enrollment rate in Dehong initially fell after 1979, by the mid-1980s it was over 96 percent.[12] Moreover, while enrollment and retention rates in Xishuangbanna lagged behind provincial rates throughout the 1990s, among novice monks they were particularly bad. In 1995, 67 percent of novices were in school in Xishuangbanna, compared to 92 percent of all school-aged children in the Dehong prefecture.

Rather than simply crack down on temple schools, officials have sought cooperation from high-ranking monks. A variety of strategies have been tried: special classes for novices in temples; requiring abbots to personally deliver novices to elementary schools each day; and segregating school classes by sex so that novices will not have to attend classes with girls. Officials have accommodated the religious calendar by, for instance, providing novices with tutors during holidays when their presence in temple is required. County branches of the Education Bureau have also penalized or rewarded teachers for attendance rates in their classes. In what appears to be an effort to capitalize on local interest in and respect for Thai Buddhism, a handful of Thai monks have been brought into the prefecture to teach English at several of the largest temples. This tactic is also aimed at stemming the tide of adolescent monks who leave Xishuangbanna to study in Thailand, Laos, and the Shan State.[13]

Results, however, have been mixed. Many senior monks, who are responsible for the religious education of novices, are unconcerned about whether or not their charges receive a state education. Some are simply indifferent to overall goals of modernization and economic development; they believe that their chief obligation is to the moral and spiritual development of the faithful. As one monk explained, "Whether or not this area develops is of no concern to me. I don't oppose development, but I don't promote it either. My purpose is to help the people live morally, in accordance with Buddhist principles."[14]

This quintessentially Buddhist detachment suggests that certain Dai cultural values do in fact conflict with the state's interest in integration, ethnic unity, and educational modernization. In *Lessons in Being Chinese*, a study of Dai and Naxi education, Mette Hansen notes the drop in school enrollment rates following the re-opening of Buddhist temples in Xishuangbanna and explains:

> The Chinese government and its civilizing envoys have not been able to spread and popularize Chinese education efficiently among the Tai in Sipsong Panna. One important reason is that most Tai fail to see any significant economic or social advantage in spending money on school education. Another reason is that the content and form of state education is in direct opposition to the traditional Tai Buddhist education of monks and to Tai values in general. . . . The few Tai who pass through the school system need to alienate themselves from their cultural heritage (their religion, language, and history, in particular) in order to be successful. . . . For most Tai, Chinese education has little direct bearing on their ethnic identity and cultural practices simply because they do not participate in it.[15]

The rejection of state schooling in favor of temple education thus signifies an assertion of Dai values and identity against those that are specifically Chinese.

The disparities between Xishuangbanna and Dehong, and between ordinary students and novices, suggest that Buddhist temple schools are seen by many Dai people as a viable alternative to a state education, and that traditional Dai values trump modern Chinese ones. However, although Hansen's interpretation has merit, the opposition of Dai values to Chinese education is overstated. For one thing, Hansen's interviews with female Dai students indicate that many Dai do in fact view a state education as necessary and valuable. Furthermore, this seeming repudiation of state education needs to be put in context. The reopening of temples occurred shortly after the end of the Cultural Revolution, when educational institutions expanded greatly but instruction consisted of little more than "unceasing criticism sessions."[16] Education in Xishuangbanna was in shambles during the more radical periods of the Maoist era, and there were few qualified teachers.[17] Values and cultural identity have no doubt led some Dai families to send their sons to temple rather than state schools, but the appalling condition of state schools needs to be taken into account. Those who choose temple schools are selecting an educational institution that has existed for centuries and that historically has offered real value and utility for Dai people, benefits state schools in the 1960s and 1970s mostly failed to provide.

The drop in school enrollment rates that occurred in the 1980s was not unique to the Dai. As in other Han and minority Chinese communities, the main culprits behind the drop were economic opportunities and constraints and the belief that a state-provided education is not so much opposed to cultural values as it is lacking in application to rural life. A former middle-school English teacher, himself a Dai, described the resistance he got from his rural students. "What's the point of learning English?" one student asked him. "Am I going to speak it to the cattle while plowing the fields?"

UNDERDEVELOPMENT AND THE SCAPEGOAT OF CULTURE

These educational dilemmas demonstrate that, despite its contribution to the economic development of the region, Dai culture has not always been viewed positively by the predominantly Han party-state. Through much of the first decade of reform, Chinese officials and academics were deeply skeptical about the compatibility of Dai values, traits, and customs with modernization and market socialism. Granted, the region was economically underdeveloped: local officials were slow to implement policies aimed at creating a market economy, and Dai households were slow to adopt them. The paddy fields of Xishuangbanna, however, are highly productive, and the climate allows two and even three plantings per year. Moreover, Xishuangbanna has a much more favorable land-to-person ratio than Yunnan as a whole; in theory Dai peasants should have been able to easily satisfy local rice consumption needs while devoting surplus fields to cash crops. Yet Dai households in the early and mid-1980s continued to devote far more land than necessary to cultivating rice, instead of pursuing a more "rational" and lucrative strategy of diversification.[18]

The so-called backwardness of the Dai economy could be seen in other ways. Although traditionally Dai households raised pigs, the prefecture as a whole was unable to fulfill its annual pork consumption needs in the early 1980s, necessitating the import of over one thousand tons of pork annually. Xishuangbanna also lacked any significant presence of manufacturing and other industry, and heavy industry was practically nonexistent. What industry did exist was limited to mining and the processing of primary products such as tea, sugar, rubber, and fruit. Furthermore, most manufacturing activities were confined to the Han-dominated state farms, which were essentially enclaves with little impact on the surrounding countryside. In the early 1980s, Dai peasant incomes were 73 percent below the provincial average.

How, officials wondered, could this backwardness and this failure to exploit market opportunities be explained? In trying to isolate the causes of backwardness, many officials and researchers blamed the traditional values and practices of the Dai. Buddhism was identified as a key part of the problem; its emphasis on detachment seemed incompatible with the acquisitive striving that drives a market economy. "Rice culture"—a distinctive Dai worldview that elevates rice to sacrosanct status—was also cited as a reason for continued emphasis on subsistence farming at the expense of more profitable ventures. This "rice culture" (*duomi wenhua*) includes not just rice cultivation but, as scholar Tan Leshan argues, "closely linked, mutually reinforcing forms of social life" that underscore the extent to which "people and nature are united."[19] Any transformation of the local economy would thus first require an overhaul of the Dai worldview and the practices that embodied it.

Lacking in this analysis is any consideration of the role of Maoist political and economic policies in maintaining, if not generating, backwardness. For instance, the region's industrial underdevelopment reflects the fact that it was neglected by Maoist industrialization programs. What little industrialization did take place was quasi-colonial in nature, located not in Dai villages or communes but on state farms. The persistence of a subsistence ethic among Dai peasants, along with the particular emphasis on rice cultivation, was likely a response to the food insecurity resulting from successive disastrous policies. During the Great Leap Forward and the "Learn from Dazhai" campaign, Xishuangbanna peasants were forced on several occasions to pull up entire fields of glutinous rice. Glutinous rice is a staple of the local diet; however, it is a lower-yielding crop than the "normal," longer grained varieties that are the foundation of Chinese agriculture. Dai cultivation of glutinous rice violated the drive to make grain—i.e., the longer grained varieties—the centerpiece of the rural economy. Naturally the destruction of glutinous rice crops exacerbated already dire food shortages in the prefecture. In the early 1980s, these crises would have been fresh in people's minds.

To a great extent, the cultural revival has empowered minorities. The reestablishment of traditional institutions enables them to pursue modes of life and citizenship that challenge limiting stereotypes and official classifications. Yet the post-Mao cultural turn also has the potential to disempower minorities in so far as it encourages a shifting of blame. Minority culture may serve as a convenient scapegoat for policy failures, a catch-all explanation for why China's more peripheral peoples remain underdeveloped. Party-state policies are absolved in the effort to explain the backwardness of minority regions; minority culture is implicated in their stead.

Today, many officials remain skeptical of the compatibility of Dai beliefs and customs with China's overall developmental goals. Even Dai officials express concern that cultural and religious values may inhibit the economic development of Xishuangbanna. Their ambivalence stems in part from certain Chinese conceptions of what it means to be advanced—of what constitutes proper, modern beliefs, and behavior. One official in the Minority Work Department expressed the view that Buddhism, a constituent part of Dai identity, was backward. "Of course I'm Buddhist," he laughed when asked about his beliefs, "I'm Dai! But I'm not very devout, because I am educated. If I had never gone to school I might still be a practicing Buddhist, but because I am educated, I do not believe in such things."[20] Similar views are expressed by Zheng Peng, a vice chairman of the Xishuangbanna Chinese People's Political Consultative Conference (CPPCC), member of the pre-1949 Dai royal family, and author of numerous books in Chinese about Xishuangbanna and Dai life. Zheng states that Buddhism had retarded the modernization of the Dai people because it encouraged passive acceptance of the status quo and discouraged worldly striving. Dai people, he explains, were inclined to be satisfied with what they had, and consequently they lacked "struggle spirit."[21] Despite these reservations, most Dai officials support the religious revival, and do so publicly.

REFORM AND ECONOMIC TRANSFORMATION

The alleged cultural backwardness of the Dai and Xishuangbanna notwithstanding, the region has experienced a remarkable economic transformation. Today, Xishuangbanna is held up as a model of "minority nationality economics" (*minzu jingji*), an example of what can be achieved when the special characteristics of minorities are harnessed to China's developmental project. The growing presence of investors, business people, and tourists from Shanghai, Thailand, Hong Kong, and beyond underscores how this formerly isolated frontier outpost has been drawn into transnational political and economic linkages.

The location of Jinghong along the banks of the Lancang River, known outside China as the Mekong, is a major factor in its transformation from remote idyll into commercial gateway to Southeast Asia. Over the last decade, trade between China and Southeast Asia has grown considerably.[22] China is one of six participating countries in the Greater Mekong Subregion (GMS) economic cooperation program, initiated in 1992 under the auspices of the Asian Development Bank (ADB). The GMS program aims to facilitate trade and transport among member states, which include Laos, Myanmar, Cambodia, Vietnam, and Thailand. Since the program's launch, over one hundred cooperative projects have been implemented. These are aimed at improving roads, bridges, and ports; removing physical obstacles to Mekong river transport; standardizing customs and immigrations procedures; increasing electrical power generating capacity and transfer; and harmonizing water resource management. Between 1992 and 2005 the ADB approved $1.4 billion in loans and $2.2 billion in co-financing for GMS initiatives.[23] A key focus of the GMS is the development of a north-south corridor that stretches from Kunming through Xishuangbanna all the way to Bangkok.

Xishuangbanna is a prime beneficiary of this activity. The opening of the Lancang River to cargo and passenger traffic has turned the city of Jinghong into an increasingly busy (albeit small) international port. In 1995, Mekong transport between Jinghong and Chiang Saen, in Thailand, was nonexistent. Today, boats ferry goods and passengers the 213 miles (344 km) between these two ports, and two-way trade between Jinghong and Chiang Saen grew from $101 million in 2003 to $162 million in the first nine months of 2005.[24] The volume of commercial freight from Thailand entering China through the port of Jinghong grew tenfold between 1995 and 2003, and a new Jinghong port facility is in the works.[25]

Xishuangbanna's economy has also been transformed by the growth in township and village enterprises (TVEs). From 1985 to 2000, TVE earnings increased 225 times over.[26] During the 1990s, Xishuangbanna outpaced most other prefectures in Yunnan in terms of TVE revenue growth.[27] Much of the growth in the TVE sector results from the expansion of the rubber industry. Xishuangbanna is one of only a couple of places in China where natural latex is cultivated and processed. Historically, rubber cultivation was limited to the state farms. In 1963, with assistance from the farms, some Dai communes began converting fields and forests into rubber stands. This trend accelerated in the 1980s following the implementation of reforms. The area dedicated to "civilian-managed" (*minying*) rubber stands grew from approximately 4,500 hectares in 1981 to over 78,000 hectares in 2005. *Minying* rubber cultivation occurs in thirty of thirty-seven rural townships in Xishuangbanna and involves more than 97,000 households and over 277,000 people, roughly 46 percent of the rural population. In 2004, *minying* rubber production accounted for almost 20 percent of agricultural output value in the prefecture, and taxes from rubber cultivation comprised 13 percent of public finance revenues.[28] Rubber cultivation is labor-intensive; some Dai farmers supplement household labor by hiring workers from the state farms, many of them Han.[29]

Despite problems in these sectors in recent years, overall the local economy has continued to grow. Total gross domestic product in the prefecture grew from ¥1.16 billion in 1990 to ¥7.9 billion in 2005. The benefits of this growth have gone to rural communities as well as more industrialized towns. Whereas rural incomes lagged behind provincial averages throughout much of the 1980s, from the 1990s to the present they have surpassed the Yunnan average. Clearly, the traditional Dai worldview has not stunted economic modernization.[30]

Economic growth has contributed to the expansion of public revenues. In the early 1980s before the start of the tourist boom, Xishuangbanna ranked in the bottom third of all Yunnan prefectures and municipal districts with regard to tax revenues per capita. By the mid-1990s prefectural revenues outpaced the provincial median by a margin of 1.6 to 1, and through 2003 Xishuangbanna ranked third among all prefectures and districts in Yunnan, trailing only Kunming and Yuxi, the two most industrialized regions of the province.[31] However, falling rubber prices and weaknesses in the tourist industry have hurt revenues, and recently the prefecture's revenue ranking has slipped.[32] Xishuangbanna continues to depend on central and provincial subsidies to fund public expenditures.

Perhaps no phenomenon is more responsible for the transformation of Xishuangbanna than tourism, a pillar of the local economy. Canny marketing and packaging of Dai culture along with the tropical, unspoiled reputation of the region have drawn millions of Chinese and foreign tourists to the prefecture.[33] Growth in tourism is particularly important to local officials because it generates foreign exchange. Tourism has also diversified the economy by spurring growth in services such as transportation and hospitality. In other words, tourism has helped modernize the economy by helping it break out of the mono-cultural tendencies of the early 1980s. In 1990 agriculture accounted for 60 percent of all economic output, while services, 26 percent. In 2003, agriculture accounted for 38 percent, while the share of the local economy comprising services had increased to 45 percent. Industrial output has remained steady at around 17 percent of total output.[34]

Xishuangbanna was opened to foreign tourists in 1982; since then tourism has mushroomed into a billion-yuan industry. In the last few years that sector has weakened somewhat. One of the main culprits in this decline is the expansion of tourism in other parts of Yunnan, especially Lijiang and Shangri-la County in the northwest. These have become hot spots for ethnic tourism in Yunnan, and many travelers now bypass Xishuangbanna in favor of these areas. Development itself is a problem: Xishuangbanna has garnered a reputation in recent years as being too modern and overbuilt.[35] Local officials and businesspeople fear that growth is eroding the area's exotic, bucolic charm, the very quality that made growth possible.

The chief of the tourism bureau in Menghai County articulated this concern in a conversation. In a region where one third of all revenues derive from tourism, the position of tourism bureau chief is an important one, even at the county level, and can be a stepping stone to higher prefectural and even provincial political office. During an outing to an ancient Buddhist pagoda, we (the bureau chief, myself, and two township officials) drove past a Dai village comprised of wood-shingled stilt houses along with several boxy, plain, two-storey concrete and white tile structures. These nondescript houses, built in a style common throughout Asia and the developing world, stood in stark contrast to the picturesque wooden stilt homes that account for much of Xishuangbanna's aesthetic appeal. The bureau chief exclaimed,

> Look at that! These people are getting rich and building modern, Han-style houses. Our prefecture has developed very quickly in the last decade, mainly because of tourism. But if everyone builds these expensive modern houses, we

will lose what is special about Xishuangbanna and about Dai culture, and tourists will no longer want to visit. Then we will lose a big part of our income.[36]

The chief said he would have to hold a meeting with the villagers and speak
to them about this dangerous architectural trend.

The bureau chief's calculating attitude toward Dai tradition echoes the idea
that culture is an instrument—a resource or tool for political and economic
ends. His concern appeared to be the protection of tourist revenues; architecture was only a superficial problem. Shortly after that conversation, we drove
toward a cultural tourist site, a "Dai cultural village." On the way there, I asked
him how such sites were affecting ordinary Dai people, especially members of
the younger generation who typically staff them. Given his prior tirade, and
given the Party's oft-stated concern with modernization and "spiritual civilization," I expected to hear a laudatory explanation of how working at tourist
sites, and in the tourism industry more generally, brings rural Dai people into
contact with Han, other *minzu*, and visitors from abroad. In other words, I
expected that the bureau chief would provide further commentary on how
participation in an increasingly market-driven society was enhancing Dai
connections to the larger Chinese and globalized world.

The bureau chief's answer surprised me. He explained that because of
tourism, people from the villages, mainly young women, were learning
about their culture, their traditions, and their history as a people, as Dai.
In his view, these sites educated young Dai workers about their own, presumably authentic, customs and practices. He also claimed that when they
returned home, they brought this new knowledge of Dai culture and tradition to their families and neighbors, who might otherwise have known
little about who they, as a people, really are:

> In the past, people did not usually dress up in their traditional nationality cloth-
> ing. But these young women learn about their *minzu* costume when they work
> at the tourist sites, and become used to wearing traditional clothes. When they
> return home, they bring these habits with them, and many more people in their
> villages learn from them and also begin to wear their traditional costume.[37]

His assessment is oddly reminiscent of modernization theory, albeit in
a slightly convoluted way. In his view, Dai participation in the increasingly market-driven tourist economy was helping to "re-traditionalize"
the countryside. He appeared to view this as a positive trend. Certainly
there were financial benefits to be gained by exploiting Dai exoticism. But

Dai people also benefited by becoming reacquainted with (ostensibly) traditional practices, aesthetics, and arts through their labor in the tourism industry. To this official, culture was both a tool for economic gain and an end in its own right, crucial to self-knowledge and a sense of one's history and people.

Both officials and ordinary Dai people have sought creative solutions to the problems created by economic modernization. One such effort includes the planned relocation of one hundred and eighty Dai households to New Manjinglan Tourism Village. The original Manjinglan was once a tranquil village on the outskirts of Jinghong that attracted foreigners to its Dai-style guesthouses and restaurants. As Jinghong grew, Manjinglan was swallowed up in a frenzy of sprawl and construction. By the mid-1990s, Manjinglan was still known for its restaurants and hotels, but, like the newer karaoke bars and beauty parlors, they were mostly constructed in the concrete, cinderblock, and tile style, and the village had become a noisy urban street. Several years ago, officials decided to recreate Manjinglan by relocating villagers. The city government appropriated dozens of Manjinglan paddy fields about one kilometer south of Jinghong along the Lancang River for the construction of the new "traditional" village.[38]

The idea behind the creation of this new Manjinglan is to establish a living, breathing, authentic Dai village that is at the same time a tourist site. Xishuangbanna is dotted with "Dai culture villages," but these are strictly places of commerce, kitsch façades that bear little resemblance to actual communities. Many sites are open just a few hours a day. Manjinglan is intended to be different. It is to be laid out in the fashion of a traditional Dai village, with houses oriented toward the village center and temple. Residents will live in their houses full time. A number of families will be eligible to receive tourists for meals and accommodation. However, planners have not adhered completely to authentic traditions. Planned for the center of the village is a square constructed specifically for song-and-dance performances, and visitors will be able to experience the normally annual water-splashing festival daily. In the eyes of project supporters, these compromises are a sensible response to the need for both cultural preservation and economic modernization.

Similar approaches have been tried elsewhere in Xishuangbanna. The results of these projects are uneven. This is exemplified by the case of Manting Village. Manting, an administrative village in Menghan Township, comprises five natural villages, including Manchunman, the site of the temple rededication festival described at the beginning of this chapter.

Through outside investment and local participation, Manting was transformed into the Manting Dai Minority Village. It has become a mandatory
stop for package tours visiting Xishuangbanna. Whereas before the mid-
1990s anyone could freely travel the dusty roads and alleys of Manting,
today visitors must buy a ticket at an elaborate gatehouse to gain entry. The
former dirt road leading into the village is well paved, and neat hedges line
the side of the main road, limiting views of residents' yards. A typical Dai
village tends to be somewhat dusty (or muddy) and chaotic, with chickens
and pigs roaming freely and farm implements cluttering the underside of
stilted houses. In Manting, the shingled roofs of the large, well-built homes
slope down to neat hedges, making it look more like a Honolulu suburb
than a typical Dai village. In Manchunman, the area in front of the new
temple is crowded with vendors selling faux-ethnic trinkets and religious
paraphernalia to the dozens of tour groups that visit daily.

Revenues from ticket and trinket sales have benefited the village and
freed some residents from the burden of farm work, though most Manting
villagers remain farmers. Thus, while Manting is a tourist site, it is also a
real village. Yet some visitors are dubious. A group of Taiwanese tourists
I talked to at the Manchunman temple said that while they enjoyed their
visit, they wanted to see a real Dai village and temple. I explained that the
village and temple were in fact authentic, but the Taiwanese were not convinced. "No, they're not—they're fake!" one woman retorted.[39]

THE ROCKET FESTIVAL RECONSIDERED

While much of this marketed cultural production is only packaging, with
little existing beneath the surface that visitors see, Dai cultural revival is not
undertaken solely for Chinese or foreign tourist consumption. Many commercial endeavors have been made possible by the resuscitation of grass
roots cultural practices and institutions. Moreover, not all state-promoted
cultural activities are organized for tourist consumption, nor do they all have
such an obviously instrumental function or evince such a superficial character. Rather, many events and institutions in which party and government
officials play a prominent role are organized by and for ordinary Dai people
as well as the Dai elite. Such events can serve as political theater in which
relationships, expectations, and identities among Chinese state, minority
elite, and ordinary Dai people are expressed, affirmed, and contested.

The type of temple rededication ceremony and rocket festivals described
at the beginning of this chapter holds important religious and cultural sig-

nificance for participants and spectators. Such occasions are also opportunities for recreation; in Manchunman, hundreds if not thousands of people came together from all over the township and county to socialize, eat, drink, dance, and otherwise participate in the festivities. Festivals are also venues for officials, especially Dai officials, to demonstrate their commitment to minority autonomy. In doing so they affirm, in symbolic form, Dai political, economic, and social position in a prefecture where historically they dominated, but where Han migrants from the interior are increasing in number. By offering temple donations, requesting sutras for their families, awarding prizes in the rocket competition, and celebrating the renovation of the temple, these officials also affirm Dai distinctiveness and their right to engage in cultural and social endeavors (mostly) unique to them as a people. At the same time, Dai members of the local and provincial party-state apparatus assert their role as mediators between the central state and the Dai people.

Events such as the temple festival are frequent throughout the year in Xishuangbanna, particularly during the Dai New Year. Officials also support a number of long-term, high-profile projects that appear to stimulate the Dai's sense of ethno-cultural identity and unique history. The project for the reconstruction of the imperial palace, for example, is funded by local and provincial government as well as private investors, some of them Thai. The palace will form the focal point of a proposed theme park called "Thailand City."[40] In early 2007, an announcement was posted on the website of the China People's Capital Network regarding investment opportunities in the project, seeking 240 million yuan in capital.[41] In 2005, a real estate development company based in the northeastern province of Liaoning invested 200 million yuan for the construction of the Theravada Buddhism Cultural Center, which opened in October of 2007. The huge complex, located on the outskirts of Jinghong, is formed around the centerpiece of the Mengle Buddhist Temple, now the largest Theravada Buddhist temple in all of China. The complex also serves as the new home of the local branches of the provincial Buddhist Studies Institute and the Buddhist Association, and includes classrooms, offices, and accommodations for several hundred monks. Admission to the center is free for members of the Dai and Bulang minorities, both of which are predominantly Theravada Buddhist; for all other foreign and Chinese visitors the ticket price is one hundred yuan. Ten percent of ticket receipts goes to the Buddhist Studies Institute, while the remaining 90 percent goes to the Liaoning property development firm that constructed and manages the center. Both groundbreaking and opening ceremonies were attended by company officials, religious and government leaders, and members of the former royal family of Sipsongpanna.[42]

Official support for these kinds of projects makes sense, given the benefits cultural revival has had for the economy. However, the contrast between the state's enthusiasm for the restoration of Dai Buddhist temples and its hostility to many (though not all) other forms of religious practice cannot be so readily understood. For instance, in the year prior to the temple rededication ceremony, Beijing officials conducted a crackdown campaign on God of Wealth shrines in restaurants. Unlike many crackdowns on superstition, the anti–God of Wealth campaign was not motivated by fears of nefarious sectarian activity. Rather, the shrines were decried as backward and unseemly. They were examples of superstition not in keeping with the modern image officials believe Beijing businesses should present.[43]

The government is often more flexible regarding the religious practices of minority nationalities. Decentralization is a major factor affecting the variation in the treatment of traditional religious practices. The redistribution of power to localities means that the state as a whole behaves inconsistently. As Kenneth Dean argues, decisions concerning the acceptability and allowable scope of religious activity are often highly localized and variable.[44] Thus, even in Han areas, local officials as well as entrepreneurs promote practices and institutions that might seem like superstition to Beijing counterparts who oppose God of Wealth shrines. For instance, Graeme Lang, Selina Chan, and Lars Ragvald have detailed the role of local Han officials in promoting shrines to the God of Wealth and other deities at Wong Tai Sin temples in Guangdong.[45] As Lily Tsai shows, officials realize that the institutions in which many such "superstitious" practices are embedded can be effective channels for raising revenue.[46] The Beijing crackdown appears to be an unusual case.

One explanation for state support of Dai culture is that officials view the Dai as irrevocably ethnic, exotic, and other, and in continued need of Han assistance both in modernizing and preserving their uniqueness. As such, official support for and even involvement in Dai cultural practices are emblematic of what Louisa Schein calls "internal orientalism."[47] According to Schein, official valorization of minority cultural traditions reflects a larger, Han-centric project of national identity construction. The concept of internal orientalism may help explain the events described above, since, as Schein argues, state-sponsored minority cultural endeavors produce an exotic, traditional, and typically feminized minority "other" against which a modern, masculine Han subject is dialectically constituted.

Schein's concept of internal orientalism can explain much of what is produced for tourist consumption; the scheduled bathing exhibitions by young
Dai women are a prime example. Yet the concept is a poor fit for other institutions and events, including the temple ceremony and rocket festival. One
minor problem is the issue of masculinity. Schein argues that minorities are
primarily constructed as sensual and feminized exotics. Yet the rocket festival was nothing if not a performance, and contest, of hyper-masculinity, as
male villagers competed to see whose rockets would fly highest, straightest,
and farthest. This may simply buttress the idea that minorities are sensualized. Then again, the rocket festival is not an exclusively Dai festival; the
Bun Bang Fay festival, as it is called, is common throughout Tai communities in Laos and northeastern Thailand.[48] By participating in it, these Dai
men were not producing themselves, or being produced, as sensualized
minorities; they were producing themselves as Tai.

Furthermore, the whole idea of internal orientalism rests on a dyad,
a binary opposition between subject and object, Han and minority. In
Schein's formulation it is the construction of the minority as object, as
other, that produces the Han self as subject. The gaze of the subject on the
cultural production of the othered object serves as the mechanism of subject constitution. Yet one of the noteworthy features of the temple rededication and rocket festivals was the multitude of players, subjects, and even
dyads. These dyads included Han and Dai, prefectural and provincial, Chinese and Thai, party and local government, villagers and officials, men and
women. They even included a Dai-Chinese–foreigner dyad, at least briefly
during the banquet when I and the head of the prefecture shared a cup of
baijiu in a toast to demonstrate our mutual regard.

Thus it was not always clear who was performing, or who was in the
audience. For instance, the chanting of sutras during the temple rededication ceremony can be seen as a kind of performance, carried out by a
traditional religious elite whose reconstitution in the last few decades is a
result of favorable Chinese minority policies and foreign (e.g., Thai, Lao,
Burmese) support. Yet the gift offerings and requests for sutras by Thai and
Chinese officials were themselves a performance, one that conceded some
degree of legitimacy to the temple abbot and to the Buddhist infrastructure
of Xishuangbanna. The audience-performer dyad was equally confused in
the rocket festival. The competition was great entertainment for officials
and the hundreds of Dai villagers clustered on the banks of the river. The
demand for and disbursement of prizes, however, turned things around
(and sent them up in the air). Party, state, and consular VIPs became the

performers, captured and held aloft until their displays of cash prizes satisfied their captors, the victors.

While the model of internal orientalism does not quite fit this case, the discrepancies between the government's treatment of Dai religion and its anti-superstition campaigns in other parts of China highlight the centrality of modernization as an ideal and an imperative. That is, the state's seemingly contradictory behavior reflects its overarching goal of modernization. Anti-superstition campaigns are aimed at backward behaviors practiced by Chinese citizens who should be dedicated to the modernization of China's material and spiritual civilization. In this way, clampdowns on superstition echo the anti-religion policies of the Maoist era as well as the campaigns against popular religion of the Republican period.[49] Superstitious practices like God of Wealth veneration do not pose a threat to the state of the sort that Falun Gong and separatist Tibetan activists are believed to pose. Yet they are a feudal and superstitious embarrassment, out of sync with China's modern self-image. In Xishuangbanna, in contrast, religious and other cultural traditions underpin the modernization of the local economy. The markers of economic modernity include such things as a diversified economy, the expansion of manufacturing, and increased revenue extraction; the marketing of Dai culture has served all these ends. Dai minority culture, or some ersatz version of it, is simply one resource among many that further the developmental project.

STATE CULTURAL PROMOTION AND THE DAI RESPONSE

The state uses the mobilization of cultural practice to promote development and enhance its legitimacy among the Dai. Yet it would be simplistic to assume that the effects of valorizing and mobilizing cultural resources are always intended. In fact, by mobilizing cultural resources, the state makes them available to other social and political actors. Regardless of the interests underpinning its actions, in promoting the revival the state sanctions cultural practices and institutions as sites on which identities, goals, and power relations can be asserted and contested. Minority cultural identities do not possess any inherently anti-state, anti-regime tendencies. However, the symbolic and institutional resources that comprise and express these identities can be mobilized for a variety of ends.

Dai people who are recovering and expanding cultural traditions and what they see as an authentic Dai identity want to facilitate genuine Dai cultural expression. These individuals, lay people as well as Buddhist monks, have created several cultural organizations and programs, and in the late 1990s, they established the Dai Culture Association to serve as a formal mass organization to coordinate their endeavors. They also set up a Dai language printing press so they can publish texts focusing on Dai history, folklore, art, and religion. One result of their efforts is the growth of cross-border music festivals involving Tai groups from Myanmar, Laos, and Thailand.

A number of these cultural activists are wary of state-led or business-led cultural endeavors, which they do not see as either benign or as serving the interests of the Dai people. They deride the packaging of supposed traditions for the purpose of economic development, and criticize officials' promotion of what they see as a sham version of Dai culture produced mainly for Han consumption. Yet their understanding of what counts as authentic is paradoxical, and does not necessarily mean traditional. For instance, the Dai literacy courses for both sexes initiated by local promoters are a clear break from the tradition of male-only temple education.[50] The cultural activists also helped put together Dai pop groups and produced DVDs of their music, which is modeled after contemporary Thai pop. One of the key activists, in describing how this very untraditional music expresses a genuine Dai identity, reveals the paradox of cultural expression:

> Our songs are fairly simple: they are about the countryside, village life, and the home. They seem very ordinary, and are not very different from a lot of "Han" popular music, except that the style is like Thai music. But really, we sing about the home because we want to remind people where they are from. We want to make people remember the land, and protect their land, their home. Of course, when we sing about the land and the countryside, we are singing about Sipsongpanna.[51]

As Sara Davis explains, by "creating a hip, contemporary culture" unique to the Dai, pop music promoters "aimed to build the self-esteem of local youth."[52] Their hope is that Dai people in Xishuangbanna will better understand their cultural heritage as Dai, and as members of a cross-national Tai community.

Projects like the ones just described do not spring from simple nostalgia or a longing to recapture the past. These cultural activists explain their endeavors in terms of not just authenticity, but also of "nationality autonomy" and modernization. The Chinese constitution guarantees minority regions certain rights of autonomy, as well as formal protections of minority religion, language and culture. The state rarely if ever balks at suspending these guarantees in the name of expediency or stability, however. In practice, autonomy boils down to the fact that, in counties, townships, prefectures, and other regions designated as minority autonomous areas, certain government positions must be filled by members of the designated groups. The head of the prefecture of Xishuangbanna, for example, must be Dai. There is, however, no restriction on Han officials serving as deputy prefectural or county heads, vice mayors, and so on—there may be four or five of these at a given administrative level. Moreover, the Han-dominated Communist Party retains ultimate say over a wide range of government activities. The ambiguities of nationality autonomy notwithstanding, the fact that members of some minorities are articulating claims based on these guarantees suggests that the discourse of autonomy has taken on a life of its own.

Thus, these cultural activists understand their own projects in progressive and political terms and speak of their activities as efforts to put some real bite into the concept of "autonomy." For them, the idea of Xishuangbanna as an "autonomous prefecture" under the leadership of the Dai people requires that Dai culture and religion flourish. "Without culture," one founding member of the preliminary group explained to me, referring to the Theravada Buddhist-infused Dai traditional culture, "the idea of autonomy is a farce, is meaningless."[53] Even more to the point, he argued that "without culture, there is no power" (*meiyou wenhua, meiyou quanli*)—power understood in a specifically political sense of rights and influence. This individual criticized some members of the Dai party-state elite for their support of, in his view, a bastardized, sham version of Dai culture, and their failure to support programs that might have real efficacy, such as a widespread Dai language literacy campaign.

The recognition of a link tying cultural matters to effective governance has led activists to make changes which seem fairly cosmetic, but which they view as crucial to furthering their agenda. In the mid-1990s they lobbied to change official signs in Xishuangbanna Prefecture that use the Dai written language as well as Chinese. Previously the written Dai on these signs was mostly a phonetic rendering of Chinese phrases in the Dai alphabet. As a result of their lobbying efforts, signs were changed to employ actual Dai words, phrases, and grammar.

This perceived link between culture and power also underpins these activists' educational and even pop music endeavors. Sounding like classical modernization theorists, activists express the fear that increased mobility, opportunity, and the diversity of pop culture lure young Dai away from Xishuangbanna, village life, and Theravada Buddhism to the homogenizing, standardizing cities of China—even if by city they are referring to the commercialized prefectural capital of Jinghong. Granted, these post-Mao changes have given these activists access to the modern pop-cultural milieu of Thailand, from which they derive a great deal of inspiration. They worry that if the practical, everyday features of Dai life are eroded and lose their resonance with the younger generations, then Dai claims of autonomy, even in the limited Chinese sense, is threatened. For this reason, DVDs, concerts, literacy programs, and other projects are pivotal in their struggle to strengthen Dai identity and culture.

Despite the disdain they show for state-led cultural promotion, many of these cultural activists are, ironically enough, party members and state officials. Moreover, close connections with the party-state serve them well. For instance, the deputy mayor of one township described how he used the resources and authority of his office to promote classes in the Dai written language at township schools. This official was responsible for educational affairs in the township, and because of his efforts, several schools were teaching the Dai written language on a regular basis. The Dai pop music festival mentioned above also materialized in great part because of such connections. Organizing something like a music festival in China is complicated, especially when it involves participation by groups from other countries, in this case Myanmar, Laos, and Thailand. Permits must be acquired, forms must be signed and stamped by officials in local and prefectural government, formal invitations must be sent to performers outside the country, lists of participants drawn up and submitted, and visas procured. Without connections to the state, an event such as this one is unlikely to get off the ground. In the case of the Dai music festival, one of its promoters was a township official. Festival organizers decided to hold it in the township where this individual worked. Because of their connections, access to resources, and procedural know-how, the organizers were able to cut through red tape and get the festival approved.

BUDDHIST REVIVAL AND HIV/AIDS PREVENTION

The value of party-state connections is demonstrated by the genesis and development of another fruit of the Dai revival, Home of Buddhist Light (Foguang Zhi Jia). Home of Buddhist Light is an organization of Buddhist monks and laypeople dedicated to preventing the spread of HIV/AIDS. The group operates out of the Central Buddhist Temple (*zongfosi*) in Jinghong (fig. 3.5). It was formally established in 2003, though its founders had been active for a number of years in promoting HIV/AIDS awareness

FIG. 3.5 Offices, classrooms, and living quarters at the Central Buddhist Temple, Jinghong

through the Buddhist infrastructure of Xishuangbanna. AIDS is a growing problem in China, and Yunnan is one of provinces most affected by the crisis. In Yunnan, the Dai minority has been particularly hard-hit. Most Dai infected with the disease, however, reside not in Xishuangbanna but in Dehong, the Dai and Jingpo autonomous prefecture several hundred miles away in western Yunnan. Cases in Dehong are clustered in and around the border town of Ruili, a major transport point for heroin processed in Myanmar. The epidemic was fueled by a spike in prostitution and drug use in the 1980s and 1990s. Xishuangbanna has been far less affected than Dehong: at the end of 2006 there were 557 known cases of HIV and AIDS in Xishuangbanna, less than one-hundredth of a percent of the population.[54] Still, AIDS is a growing problem regionally, and health workers and officials struggle to find effective means of curbing its spread.[55] In recent years the government has mobilized official mass organizations and grassroots civil society groups in the fight against AIDS.[56]

The Home of Buddhist Light organization grew out of a program initiated in the mid-1990s. The group's founders, most of them monks, were inspired by an AIDS awareness program created by Thai monks in the early 1990s, called Sangha Metta. The Dai monks had encountered the program while studying at Buddhist institutions in Thailand. In the late 1990s, representatives of the Thai organization were invited to conduct training sessions in Xishuangbanna. In 2003, Home of Buddhist Light was formally established; it then entered into a partnership with UNICEF.[57] In addition to educating people about AIDS, the group helps people with the disease participate in mainstream society, for instance, by training them to be AIDS educators.

One of the unusual elements of Home of Buddhist Light's approach is that it relies on Buddhist monks to educate people, especially rural villagers, about AIDS prevention. At the Central Buddhist Temple, senior monks give talks every few months on AIDS prevention, which are attended by other monks and lay people alike. Village monks attend training sessions to learn about the disease and how to educate their rural congregations about prevention. During holidays and festivals, monks hand out pamphlets and give sermons on AIDS prevention in addition to their normal duties. Since there are over five hundred temples, six thousand monks, and roughly three hundred thousand Buddhist faithful in the prefecture, the opportunities for AIDS outreach are many.[58]

Buddhist infrastructure and beliefs are central to Home of Buddhist Light's endeavors. In sermons monks discuss the "Five Precepts" of Buddhism, which call on the faithful to abstain from sexual misconduct and intoxicants. Buddhism also encourages compassion and loving-kindness, qualities that may lead to greater acceptance of those living with the disease. One of the founders of the organization is Abbot Long Zhuang, director of the Central Buddhist Temple and the highest-ranking monk in Xishuangbanna.

Government connections were central to the creation of Home of Buddhist Light. Several lay founding members hold positions in local government. Moreover, like other prominent religious leaders in China, Abbot Long is a quasi-political figure. He leads the local Buddhist Association, the Xishuangbanna branch of the Yunnan Buddhist Studies Institute, and has served as a deputy head of the local CPPCC. These are not policy-making bodies, but membership signifies influence and connections to the state. State actions have shaped Home of Buddhist Light in other ways as well. China's trade and diplomatic relationships with Thailand facilitated the transfer of expertise from a religious Thai organization to the monks of Xishuangbanna. Without this favorable political environment, the exchanges that generated the organization might never have occurred. Home of Buddhist Light is not a state-run group, yet its official linkages are clear.

It is difficult to assess whether the organization has helped curtail the AIDS/HIV epidemic. Still, it has improved the lives of many and enhanced awareness throughout the prefecture. Of the over five hundred people in the prefecture known to be infected with the virus, sixty are currently active in Home of Buddhist Light's programs, some as paid volunteers.[59] By using temples and religious festivals as venues for AIDS prevention education, the organization reaches a great many people, perhaps more than state health workers can. The high status of monks accords authority to their anti-AIDS message that other programs may lack.

There is a direct connection between the resurgence of Theravada Buddhism and AIDS outreach. Because of the loss of religious personnel and knowledge during the Mao years, many young Dai monks sought training in the 1980s and 1990s in Thailand, Laos, and Myanmar. There they encountered the ravages of AIDS; those studying in Thailand also encountered Sangha Metta. Buddhist teachings inform the monks' outreach, and religious values encourage ordinary Dai people to accept their message. The revival of Buddhism made Home of Buddhist Light possible, and in turn, the organization benefits Buddhist institutions and practitioners. By being incorporated into the anti-AIDS effort, they are shown to be effective social resources. The Chinese state also benefits. If Home of Buddhist Light is successful, it will help curb the spread of AIDS, prostitution, and drug use. Far from retarding the modernization of the Dai people, Buddhism is central to their economic and social development.

LOCAL IDENTITY AND STATE AGENDA

The story of the Dai experience under both Maoism and the era of reform highlights the ambiguities of minority identity, Chinese national identity, and citizenship. In contemporary China, groups like the Dai are expected to embrace the state's modernizing agenda. At the same time, they are encouraged, if not expected, to resuscitate the traditions and customs that define them as minority. These expectations are interlinked. As Shih Chih-yu argues, minorities "must first recognize their minority status in order to regard citizenship projects with a positive attitude." Doing so has costs, argues Shih, since Chinese civilizing and citizenship projects "reproduce the distinction between the advanced and the primitive who, once enrolled in the projects, will have no perspective to problematize their minority identities."[60]

In Xishuangbanna, one of the more prominent elements of the state's modernizing agenda is the drive to implement a diversified market economy throughout the region. Underscoring Shih's point, Dai practices and institutions—including the traditional village, the Buddhist temple, and habits of personal cleanliness (e.g., bathing)—have been hitched to the developmental project. The presentation of the Dai as backward and exotic has facilitated economic modernization, whether measured by diversification, foreign investment, or tax revenues. Yet does this mean that the Dai lack the critical perspective with which to "problematize their minority [identity]"?

The experiences and projects of Dai cultural activists detailed here suggest otherwise. Many Dai do indeed regard the citizenship project of Chinese modernization with, as Shih puts it, a "positive attitude." They agree, in some respects at least, with the state's goal of modernizing Xishuangbanna and the minorities who live there. Yet they simultaneously challenge the stereotype of the Dai as backward and uncivilized. In doing so, they contest Han-centric understandings of modernity and the processes by which it is achieved, posing instead models of modernity informed by Dai culture and religion. Cultural revival has generated efforts to rethink what it means to be Dai, and Chinese. Contrary to Shih's assertion, Dai appropriations and interpretations of Chinese citizenship projects do indeed problematize both minority and national identities.

This does not mean the state is thwarted in its goals. Cultural revival has been mutually beneficial for the Dai and for the Chinese party-state. Interpretations and understandings may at times diverge, but each makes use of the other in ways that generally, though not always, promote each other's agendas. To some extent, this is because the state and the Dai are not always "others"—the state promoting the revival in Xishuangbanna is partially a Dai state. One benefit for the state is that it can present itself as an effective steward of the customs and livelihood of the Dai people, thereby enhancing its legitimacy among the people of Xishuangbanna. At the same time, Dai cultural revival is viewed by many of its promoters and participants as a means for enhancing their own power, their own rights as minorities and Chinese citizens. For them, cultural revival is a necessary complement to minority autonomy. Their endeavors encapsulate a moral judgment concerning the impact and possibilities of development. If modernization is to truly benefit them it must benefit them as the collectivity of the Dai *minzu*.

—4—

THE BAI AND THE TRADITION OF MODERNITY

One of the hallmarks of nationalist movements and ethnic revivals is nostalgia for pasts real or invented. Longings for a romanticized ideal are obvious in overtly atavistic nationalisms, the Nazi vision of a bucolic Aryan *Lebensraum* being one example of this tendency. Backward-looking romanticism typically celebrates past glories, but great defeats may also galvanize such sentiments. The Serbian obsession with Kosovo, the site of a fourteenth century defeat by the Ottoman Turks, and the recurring motif of humiliation in Chinese nationalism exemplify this phenomenon. Nostalgia and romanticism are responsible in part for the view of nationalist and ethnic movements as inherently irrational, at least when compared to social movements based on ostensibly more instrumental bases such as class. Yet quite "rational," progressive movements may also draw their power from sentimental longing for a bygone era of autonomy, strength, and cultural achievement.

Like the Dai, the Bai have experienced a cultural revival over the course of the reform period. Hundreds of temples have been reopened or newly constructed throughout the Dali Bai Autonomous Prefecture, and local residents have resumed an active religious life; monuments and historical sites have been refurbished; music, dance, and the arts are flourishing; and the long and glorious history of the Bai is widely celebrated in books, magazines, movies, and television programs. This resurgence is spurred on by provincial, prefectural, city, and township officials who hope to promote Dali as a tourist destination and raise its profile among potential investors. Local officials have sought to harness nostalgia for Bai history and culture for the purpose of economic development.

Bai nostalgia, however, is a curious thing. First, the very "Bainess" of the Bai is ambiguous. The establishment of the Bai as an official minority nationality in the 1950s entailed the invention of a great degree of Bai tradition, even to some extent a Bai identity. Second, while government officials have sought to harness Bai exoticism and difference as a means of luring tourist and investor funds, the nostalgia of some cultural activists has a very different focus. Promoters of Bai culture and identity are motivated not simply by the idea of Bai distinctiveness drawn from a distant past, but by an identity rooted in a more recent history of "civilized" achievement and modern economic success. Moreover, much of the cultural revival celebrates not Bai difference but their fundamental "Chineseness," and their contributions to a Chinese past, present, and future.

What makes the Bai unique, or at least unusual, is not their syncretism but their embrace of it. Bai history, like the history of many other ethnocultural entities, is one of fortuitous adoption, adaptation, and integration of diverse peoples and practices. Yet unlike many other groups, the Bai consciously celebrate that syncretism. This syncretism is reflected in the Bai revival. The Bai revival therefore encounters and reveals many of the paradoxes of minority cultural renaissance. One such paradox is that some of the practices and identities being "revived" did not exist prior to the founding of the People's Republic. The party-state, in other words, gave birth to the "imagined community" that is the Bai, as well as some of the cultural artifacts now being revived and developed. For instance, the Bai written language was created in the 1950s by scholars at the Institute of Linguistics at the Chinese Academy of Sciences in Beijing. Yet contemporary promoters of Bai-Han bilingual education see their endeavors as enhancing the status of an ethnic collectivity with ancient roots.

The renaissance of Bai cultural identity reveals that many minority citizens embrace norms and goals that pervade popular and official discourse about what it means to be Chinese in an increasingly market-driven society. These norms and goals include economic modernization, national advancement, and cultural progress. They permeate Bai revival, even those aspects that focus on tradition. To some extent this is because Bai officials and other state-connected elites are often the instigators and promoters of the revival.

This does not mean that revival participants uncritically accept these norms and goals. Instead, they frame them in minority-centric terms. Cultural advancement and economic development are desired goals, but Bai cultural activists regard these through the prism of minority identity.

ORIGINS AND HISTORY OF THE BAI

With a population of just over 1.6 million, the Bai today are the second largest minority nationality in Yunnan.[1] They reside primarily in the Dali Bai Autonomous Prefecture, where they constitute roughly one-third of the prefecture's population of 3.5 million.[2] The Bai are not the largest single group in Dali; nearly half the population is Han. Among the eleven counties and one county-level municipality of which the prefecture is comprised, the Bai population is unevenly distributed. Ninety-two percent of the residents of Jianchuan County are Bai, while in the counties of Weishan, Nanjian, and Midu, the Bai form less than 2 percent of the population.[3] Dali is also home to sizable communities of Yi, Hui, Lisu, Naxi, and other groups.

Dali is located in west central Yunnan, in a geographical region known as the Yunnan-Guizhou plateau. The northern part of the prefecture abuts the foothills of the Himalayas, while the southern end stretches into the lush, subtropical areas of southern Yunnan. The region is blessed with fine, mild weather, and while the climate is somewhat dry, Dali experiences the summer monsoon rains that are a feature of the Yunnan-Guizhou plateau. The prefecture is slightly larger than the state of Maryland, and is the fifth largest prefecture in Yunnan in terms of geography and population. As is the case for Yunnan as a whole, the mountainous character of the prefecture limits cultivation; less than 7 percent of the total area of the prefecture is cultivated for crop production.[4] A substantial irrigation infrastructure draws from the many small streams that flow down off the Cangshan mountain range, an offshoot of the Himalayas, and from Lake Er (Erhai), the second largest freshwater lake in Yunnan. Thousands of tourists from all over China and around the world visit annually, drawn by the region's stunning scenery, its ethnic culture, and the charming cobbled lanes of Dali Old Town (fig 4.1).

Although Chinese law and policy recognize the Bai as a distinct legal and ethno-cultural entity, the issue of Bai identity is complex. As discussed in chapter 2, studies of Dali life and society conducted in the middle of the twentieth century emphasize the essentially Chinese character of the *min-jia*, the group of people later officially classified as Bai.[5] These works also

FIG. 4.1 Tourists and townspeople stroll the main street in Dali Old Town.

demonstrate that many *minjia* rejected the idea of themselves as being ethnic. Bai syncretism and the weakness of their "nationality consciousness" (*minzu yishi*) notwithstanding, their language and traditions were deemed sufficiently unique to justify their classification as minority. Such traditions include *benzhu*, a polytheistic religion involving the worship of local protector gods, many of them figures from myth and history such as Kubilai Khan. At the same time, official studies and popular opinion acknowledged the Bai to be highly acculturated to mainstream Chinese (e.g., Han) social, economic, and cultural practices. This legacy of Bai integration influenced the implementation of Maoist policies in the Dali region. Until the late 1950s, many minorities were subject to policies that minimized the pace of socialist transformation. In contrast, the policies applied in most Bai areas differed little from those implemented among the Han.

THE BAI IN THE ERA OF REFORM

If the Bai experience of Maoist socialism is noteworthy for its "normality," the Bai experience under reform is emblematic of the post-Mao period in

Yunnan Province as a whole. The economy of the Dali Bai Autonomous Prefecture has grown considerably over the last two decades. Much of that growth has occurred in the collective and private sectors through the expansion of township and village enterprises. Industrial and commercial expansion has centered in Dali municipality (Dali *shi*), which includes Dali Old Town and the nearby city of Xiaguan.[6] More than half of the municipality's economy derives from manufacturing, construction, and mining industries, over one-third from services, and just over 10 percent from farming and other primary industries. Tourism is particularly important. By the late 1990s, more than one-fifth of all nonfarm employees in the municipality were employed in tourism and related enterprises.[7] Because of this growth, the municipality is considerably more prosperous than the rest of Yunnan. In 2005, per capita GDP in Dali municipality was ¥16,112, more than twice the provincial average and 15 percent higher than China's per capita GDP for that year.[8]

These figures, however, belie disparities in the prefecture as a whole. Despite the first-blush impression of prosperity and vibrancy that Dali creates, relative isolation and poverty persist throughout the prefecture, as they do throughout Yunnan. The prefecture's economy remains highly agricultural. Major crops include rice, corn, wheat, soy, canola, peanuts, sugar cane, and a variety of fruit and vegetables. Dairy products are also important, particularly in the counties of Binchuan and Eryuan. As in many areas of Yunnan, tobacco is an important cash crop and a key source of local revenue.

Although township and village enterprises have mushroomed over the last two decades, most of that expansion has taken place in Dali municipality. Approximately 18 percent of the prefecture's population resides in Dali municipality, yet in 2005 it accounted for 40 percent of the prefecture's total GDP.[9] That same year, per capita net rural income in the municipality was 54 percent higher than in the prefecture as a whole. Within the municipality, eight individual townships have rural enterprise revenues that exceed those of over half of the prefecture's less well-off, less well-situated counties.[10] Ten of the prefecture's eleven rural counties are designated poor counties and depend on provincial subsidies. Per capita rural net incomes in these counties lag behind the province as a whole, and seven of these are among the seventy-eight counties in Yunnan that suffer annual deficits. Throughout the 1990s, public finance revenues in the counties of Jianchuan, Yongping, and Heqing accounted for less than 40 percent of their expenditures, although in 1998 the counties of Eryuan, Midu, and Weishan were able to "remove their deficit hats."[11]

The disparities between Dali and surrounding counties, along with the relative underdevelopment of the Bai economy, have ramifications for Bai identity and for the Bai post-Mao cultural resurgence. This backwardness is at odds with what, for many people, being Bai means. In popular perception and official policy statements the Bai are, by definition, "relatively advanced." This disjuncture between reality and perception informs the cultural revival. In a sense, the situation is the reverse of that among the Dai of Xishuangbanna. In Xishuangbanna, Dai culture is still seen by many academics and officials as inherently backward, a hindrance to modernization. According to this view, economic development and diversification have occurred in spite of the Dai's traditional worldview with its imputed Buddhist passivity. Yet in Dali, the local economy and society remain relatively backward despite the allegedly advanced culture and character of the Bai.

On paper the economic conditions of Xishuangbanna and Dali are not all that different. Dali municipality is more modern and industrial than Jinghong, if judged by the size of manufacturing and other industries compared to the overall local economy. By other indicators such as public finance revenues, per capita GDP, and income, Dali lags behind Xishuangbanna. The facts of relative development are, however, irrelevant. What is noteworthy is the ongoing effort to understand economic development, or the lack thereof, in terms of minority culture. In the case of the Bai, their allegedly progressive culture has not translated into advancement or modernization of a more practical, material sort. This account of economic development is not a cultural-determinist one, yet Chinese nationality theory, popular thinking about minorities, and concepts of modernization are all marked by just such an understanding of the relationship between "cultural quality" (*wenhua suzhi*) and economic modernization.

BAI CULTURE AND ECONOMIC DEVELOPMENT

Nevertheless, Bai culture, or some version of it, does have some effect on economic development. The cultural revival has aided and abetted economic growth, as evidenced in the rise of the tourist industry in Dali. As in Xishuangbanna, local officials and entrepreneurs have seized on the prefecture's fine climate, scenery, and cultural resources to promote tourism. Officials have also mobilized cultural resources in order to expand trade, outside investment, and manufacturing. A case in point is the Third

Month Market, a market fair that has been in existence since the Tang dynasty. The fair, which takes place over four or five days in the middle of the third lunar month (typically mid-April), is a commercial event that draws thousands of people from all over western and northwest Yunnan for several days of buying, selling, socializing, and horse-racing. As many of the participants and vendors are minorities, the goods they sell are deemed "minority nationality commodities" (*minzu pin*), and the event is advertised as a model of "minority nationality economics" (*minzu jingji*).[12] The fair is well known throughout China, having been memorialized in a popular 1959 movie, "The Five Golden Flowers."[13] Official promotion of the Third Month Market is a way of showcasing state support for Bai history and culture.

Though regularized and policed, the market has historically been a fairly grass-roots affair, with thousands of individuals and families encamped on the hillside above Dali Old Town selling medicinal herbs, skins and furs, jewelry, knives, hats, shoes, and livestock. In recent years local officials have been trying to transform this five-day annual event into a quasi-permanent economic entity. In the late 1990s, officials commenced construction of permanent structures for the market to accommodate the festival annually and possibly turn it into a year-round affair.[14] The prefecture and municipal governments invested nearly 4 million yuan to construct roads within the fairgrounds, build several hundred shops and stalls, and supply these with water and electricity. Within a year of starting the project, officials had garnered over 13 million yuan from outside investors and had sold long-term leases on several hundred market stalls.[15]

State support for local minority culture has also found its way into the township and village enterprise sector. One relative success story is the case of Zhoucheng and its batik industry. Zhoucheng is a large administrative village located at the northern end of Dali municipality, in Xizhou Township. Although agriculture historically is the backbone of the local economy, it was famous for the multicolored batik cloth produced by Zhoucheng residents, which was sold throughout Yunnan, neighboring provinces, and in Burma and Vietnam by the Xizhou-based trading companies. Even the local *benzhu* deity bears witness to the importance of batik production; residents worship a Tang official who, legend has it, brought weaving and dyeing techniques to the villagers centuries ago.

Prior to liberation, roughly a third of the households in Zhoucheng were engaged in batik production. In 1984, Zhoucheng officials established the Butterfly Brand Batik Factory as a village collective enterprise. The factory initially employed just a few dozen workers, but much of the dyeing and design work was contracted out to over four thousand individual household producers throughout the area. The concomitant opening of Dali to tourism helped spur the development of this village enterprise. Five years after its establishment, the total output value of this enterprise was valued at over ¥1.2 million.[16] By 1997, the total output value topped 10 million yuan, and nearly five thousand people in Zhoucheng were engaged in batik production. Touted as a paradigmatic example of "Bai minority style" (*Baizu fengwei*), the tie-dyed, mostly blue fabric is ubiquitous in Dali and is sold in Kunming, Lijiang, Guilin, Beijing, and even for a while in a shop called "Dali" at the top of Victoria Peak in Hong Kong. In recognition of city officials' efforts to modernize the nationality economy of the region, the provincial government in 1997 recognized Dali as a "culturally progressive city" (*wenhua xianjin chengshi*).[17]

BAI MUSICAL REVIVAL AND CHINESE CIVILIZATION

Although Bai cultural identity and institutions are deployed for purposes of economic development, the revival is not reducible to purely material interests. Nor is it the product simply of canny packaging on the part of prefecture officials. Rather, it is shaped by a mix of overlapping goals and interests, including aesthetics, recreation, intellectual curiosity, civic engagement, and ethnic pride, as well as the prospect of financial gain. This mix of objectives is evident in the musical revival taking place in and around Dali.

Music has never been politically neutral in the People's Republic of China. During the more radical periods of the Maoist era, traditional music was disparaged as feudal and reactionary, while more contemporary musical forms were labeled bourgeois.[18] In contemporary China political prohibitions against particular musical styles have mostly evaporated. Central and local governments support professional orchestras, opera troupes, and dance companies; minority dance troupes are featured regularly on television; and a handful of minority groups and performers have won national fame and recognition. However, the vast majority of musicians and dancers are amateurs returning to an art form they enjoyed in the past or are encountering it for the first time. In Dali, hundreds of recreational music groups have sprung up in towns and villages since the early 1980s.

These groups have embraced a variety of musical styles and formats. One style receiving a considerable amount of attention is the music of Nanzhao, a kingdom coterminous with the Tang and Song dynasties that controlled the Erhai region between 738 and 902 C.E. References to Nanzhao and its successor state, the Dali kingdom, are ubiquitous in the region; local officials and tour companies play up the Nanzhao idea as it underscores the uniqueness of the region and its history. In this increasingly capitalistic age, Nanzhao has become a commodity. Yet the fascination with Nanzhao goes beyond its marketable qualities. For many local people, it signifies the political and cultural accomplishments of their forebears.

It is not surprising that the music of Nanzhao is enjoying a revival. Throughout the area, dozens of small, amateur orchestras have sprung up, composed primarily of retired men. In 1997 I encountered one such group in Dali Old Town that at the time performed nightly in the courtyard of a house close to the cafés and gift shops that cater to tourists. The members of this group were all residents of the old city, and thus urban dwellers; they were teachers, party cadres, bureaucrats, doctors, and workers, though most were retired. Most were also Bai, but there were several Han and Hui as well, and for a few months in 1997 a Frenchman joined the group in order to learn how to play the *erhu*, a two-stringed instrument played with a bow. Initially the group was an informal affair, although it had registered with the public security bureau as all organizations, from chess clubs to choral societies, are required to do. The group received no funding, and during the first couple of years of its existence many of its performances were free. When I first made the acquaintance of this orchestra, many of the members were still learning (or relearning) to play the instruments and music, and the conductor, the most experienced musician of the bunch, frequently stopped play to go over difficult sections of the music. The group occasionally performed in more public venues such as competitions and festivals held around the Erhai region.

Several of the group's members explained that the idea for the orchestra was inspired not by other Bai but by a traditional Naxi orchestra in the northern Yunnan city of Lijiang. The Naxi orchestra, established in the 1980s, has garnered national and international recognition; it has performed on television and is written up in many travel guidebooks. Because of the Naxi orchestra's success, some of its members, including its director, have become quite well-off. Not surprisingly, its success inspired the formation of the Dali orchestra.

City officials in Dali Old Town have also taken their cue from other success stories, Lijiang in particular. Lijiang is a popular tourist destination, largely because of the quaint atmosphere of its winding, canal-lined, cobblestone streets. In 1995, Dali officials approved a plan to reconstruct sections of the old town that drew the most tourists, allowing long-established features to be altered. Along the main tourist street, streams that previously ran through underground culverts were opened up and diverted into narrow canals at the side of road. Perfectly good pavement was ripped up and replaced with cobblestone-like paving blocks. Part of one street was restricted to pedestrian traffic and renamed "Foreigner Street" (*Yangren Jie*). Foreigner Street is now one of Dali's main tourist attractions. Chinese tour groups are dropped off daily at the street entrance and given an hour or so to shop, eat, and observe foreign travelers in their natural habitat, the traveler's café, doing foreign things like eating pizza and drinking beer. Participant observation is encouraged.[19]

The artificiality of these promotional efforts notwithstanding, the musical endeavors of the Nanzhao orchestra were hardly false or contrived. While inspired by the Naxi orchestra's success, the Dali men threw themselves into learning "Bai" music for its own sake and derived a great deal of enjoyment from doing so. Their activities were an obvious source of pleasure, an avenue for artistic expression, a mode of civic involvement that put them in touch with visitors and residents of their neighborhood, and an excuse to spend time with old friends.

The benefits these men received from music underscore the fact that the projects that comprise the minority cultural renaissance are not necessarily linked to any ethnic agenda. There is a risk of reducing recreational or aesthetic activities, especially those of minority groups, to political motives, just as there is a risk of interpreting cultural promotion solely in terms of market-based interests. Social scientists in particular may be tempted to impute to such activities some greater significance of which participants may be unaware. In this instance, the members of the Nanzhao orchestra themselves pointed out the greater significance of their endeavors. Their primary motivations for playing music may have been aesthetic or recreational, but these men were self-aware and deliberate regarding their musical aspirations.

This awareness emerged in interviews and conversations with the Nanzhao musicians. On one occasion, while chatting in a pharmacy run by one of them, they showed me their sheet music and described a recent performance on the other side of Erhai Lake. The music they played, explained the pharmacist, was ancient Bai music from the Dali region, but it was not "ordinary" Bai music. Rather, it had influenced the music of the Tang court and been embraced by Tang emperors. The pharmacist elaborated that the music had been given to the Tang emperor, and it became an important part of Tang music. Most people do not know this, but Tang music is Bai music, Nanzhao music. Many of the instruments used in the Tang court were also from Nanzhao. If the Nanzhao king had not given this to the emperor, the music of the Tang would have been very different.[20]

The other musicians nodded their assent, and proceeded to discuss the extent to which Bai music had influenced the music of the Tang.

In making this claim, the musicians echo scholarship on the history and ethnomusicology of the Dali region that stresses the cultural links between Nanzhao and the Tang, scholarship with which these men were familiar. For instance, Dong Mianhan, a scholar in the Department of Music at the Central Nationalities Institute in Beijing, has outlined the exchanges of instruments, songs, and even troupes of musicians, singers, and dancers from Nanzhao to the court of the Xuanzong emperor during the Kaiyuan period of the eighth century C.E. Citing Tang historical records, Dong argues that these transfers were mutual: the Xuanzong emperor gave gifts of musical instruments, musicians and dancers to the Nanzhao king, gifts that "assisted the development of Nanzhao music."[21]

Nanzhao music was itself the product of a variety of influences. The seventh century arrival of Buddhism had brought new musical techniques, instruments, and styles from neighboring Asian kingdoms to the south and west. The subsequent offering of sacred music from Nanzhao to the Tang emperor, Dong argues, was one means by which Buddhist practices and beliefs permeated the Tang dynasty. Subsequent shifts in Tang music show that the "music and dance of border nationalities not only enriched the music of the Tang dynasty, but also became one of the most important components of Tang court music."[22] The "grand occasion" (*shengju*) of the gift of Nanzhao sacred music, Dong claims, demonstrates the extensive contributions of the Bai to Tang musical culture, and the long history of mutual influence among and between the cultures of border nationalities and that of central China.

Noteworthy in Dong's discussion is the transformation of the Nanzhao culture into Bai culture, and the music of Nanzhao into the music of the Bai. Scholars are still divided over the question of whether the Nanzhao rulers were the forerunners of the groups today known as Bai or Yi, or whether Nanzhao was in fact a Shan kingdom, ruled by ancestors of the Xishuangbanna Dai. Despite these historical debates, in popular culture, official and academic accounts, and historiography produced for tourist consumption, Nanzhao has been firmly established as a seminal period in the history of the Bai people. Also noteworthy is the relationship established between the Bai and the Tang. As a *minzu*, as a minority nationality, the Bai did not exist prior to the founding of the PRC. Yet in contemporary Dali, the music of the Bai is the music of the Tang.

The interest in the Bai-Tang connection is of a piece with a broader Bai concern with being "relatively advanced." The fact that this scholar and these musicians seized on Nanzhao links with the Tang is not inconsequential. The Kaiyuan period of the Tang dynasty, when these musical exchanges took place, is widely seen as the zenith of Chinese culture, an era of sublime artistic, religious, literary, and intellectual accomplishment. In asserting their ancestors' role in these achievements and in claiming credit for part of that aesthetic flowering, these Dali musicians and scholars like Dong Mianhan are providing proof of the Bai's relatively advanced character.

Political scientist Crawford Young, who wrote in the 1970s about the global persistence of ethnic and other inter-cultural conflicts in post-colonial states, identified several types of actors who politicize cultural identity and create the groundwork for communal strife. Among these is what Young calls the cultural entrepreneur, who "devotes himself to enlarging the solidarity resources of a community."[23] Cultural entrepreneurs may be historians, folklorists, anthropologists, poets, novelists, curators, or any individual who seeks to identify, classify, and codify the culture of a people. In doing so, such entrepreneurs create for that people an historical narrative the people previously did not possess. The cultural entrepreneur is devoted to expanding a people's symbolic and cultural capital, thereby legitimizing its historical and political existence. Through these endeavors, "founding fathers, the great kings, the triumphant generals, the high priests [are] rescued from obscurity and accorded their place of veneration in the cultural hagiography," and a people, as a self-aware, more-or-less coherent entity, comes into being. For Young, such endeavors are inherently political. They transform unreflective, unselfconscious cultural practices and traditions into "manifest nationalism" of the sort that can bring down empires and divide multiethnic collectivities.[24] The cultural entrepreneur may or may not desire these outcomes, but the creation of institutionalized, ethno-cultural symbolic capital lays the groundwork for that capital to be politically deployed.

The Dali musicians and scholars like Dong Mianhan can be seen as cultural entrepreneurs. What they are promoting is rather unusual, however. By highlighting the links between their current musical endeavors and those of the ancient Nanzhao kingdom and the Tang dynasty and stressing their culture's contributions to China's glorious cultural past, the Dali musicians read themselves into the narrative of Chinese civilization and the Chinese nation. In doing so they position themselves within a Chinese present and a Chinese future, one that celebrates a traditional culture and identity in part because elements of that tradition are progressive and advanced. These musicians have appropriated a Chinese national narrative of historical greatness in such a way that they become central actors in and contributors to their culture's success rather than passive beneficiaries of civilizing projects. To be Bai and to express that identity through the practice of traditional music is to assert the links between Bai and Chinese civilization. It is thus not their separateness as a people that these scholars and musicians are trumpeting, but their undeniable Chineseness and the contributions they and their forebears have made to what is greatest and most advanced about Chinese culture. Their musical and scholarly endeavors weave a collective narrative of the Bai nationality, but this "narrative of national unfolding" places them squarely within the story of the Chinese nation.[25]

MUSICAL REVIVAL AND MAOIST CONTINUITY

Post-Mao shifts in state policy and practice are broadly responsible for the minority cultural revival. However, the renaissance of Bai culture is shaped not only by state retrenchment but by its active role in classifying, cataloguing, and promoting minority culture. Moreover, while official support for minority culture is a feature of the party-state after Mao, the practices and ideological imperatives of Maoist socialism continue to shape the direction and content of that revival. That is, institutional and even ideological elements of Maoism still influence the cultural renaissance of the Dali Bai.

The revival of another style of Bai vocal and instrumental music, called *dabenqu*, illustrates the impact of Maoism on culture. *Dabenqu* has ancient roots in the region, dating back over a thousand years to the period of the Dali and Nanzhao kingdoms. The bulk of the music extant on the eve of Liberation first emerged during the middle of the Ming dynasty. In contemporary Chinese musicology, *dabenqu* is characterized as indigenous, especially in regard to form and meter, yet scholars identify within it a mélange of elements that reflects the social and political transformations of the Dali region over the past millennium.

Dabenqu is performed by a solo singer or by one singer accompanied by another person on the *sanxian*, a three-stringed instrument. Historically, *dabenqu* was performed only by men, unlike other types of Bai folk music. The structure of *dabenqu* is fairly standardized, with a "7-7-7-5" format: four-line stanzas comprised of three lines of seven syllables followed by a closing line of five. Lyrical content varies, and songs can be divided into three main groups or subsets. One includes songs that tell variants of historical tales and myths common in other parts of China, particularly the central and eastern parts of the country. A second subset of songs expresses religious motifs and morality tales based on Buddhism, Daoism, and the local *benzhu* religion of the Dali Bai. The third subset is based on events, myths, and aspects of daily life specific to the Dali region and the people who inhabit it. In this way, *dabenqu* epitomizes how successive waves of conquest, in-migration, and exchange between Dali and the rest of China have shaped the region, its people, and its culture.

The hybrid quality of *dabenqu* is evident also in the languages it employs. Many songs are sung entirely in the Bai spoken language, others in a mix of Bai and standard Chinese or the Yunnan dialect. Many *dabenqu* songs were written down using Chinese characters, and these scores further demonstrate the complexity of Bai music. In some cases, Chinese characters were used to indicate the pronunciation of Bai—or more precisely, *minjia*—terms; that is, the characters are used to approximate sounds, but the meanings of the characters are irrelevant. In other cases, the Chinese meaning of the character explains its usage, but the character possesses a distinctly *minjia* pronunciation. Characters' meaning and pronunciation may also function exactly as they do in standard Chinese. Some scores contain unique characters or symbols created by *dabenqu* composers to convey the meaning and sound of words found only in the *minjia* language. It is not unusual to find these different usages within a single piece of music, even within a single stanza.

Dabenqu is one of many musical styles enjoying a post-Mao resurgence in Dali, thanks to the more liberal and supportive policies toward minority culture. Yet the *dabenqu* resurgence is less a new tack than a continuation of the consolidation and expansion of this art form generated by socialist policies of the 1950s and 1960s. As part of the *minzu* identification project of the 1950s, the Chinese state codified and institutionalized minority arts and music. This project was informed by notions of socialist modernization, by the perceived need to respect the "special characteristics" of minorities, and by the Stalinist conception of nationality that informs policy toward Chinese minority nationalities. Since in the Stalinist view nationality was partly a function of a common "psychological make-up" embodied in distinct cultural identity and practices, the demarcation of minority cultures was a key element in the drive to distinguish and classify minority groups. In a way, culture and its possession justified policy and administrative practice, and culture was one arena in and through which the new socialist state was constructed. As minority autonomy policies were worked out, corresponding state institutions and mass organizations were created to promote minority culture. The designation of the Bai as an official *minzu* required organizations to showcase the ostensibly unique cultural life of the Bai.

In Dali, these developments were a boon for many artists and musicians who found themselves celebrated as representatives of the Bai people and provided with institutional and financial support. According to the *Almanac of Bai Music,*

> After the founding of the People's Republic, in keeping with the Party's arts policies, *dabenqu* arts flourished and developed. First, the Party's policies toward nationality folk arts greatly raised the social standing of *dabenqu* performers, as many older artists became people's representatives and members of the China People's Political Consultative Conference, enabling them to participate in national affairs and receive recognition.... In the period before the founding of the PRC, the number of *dabenqu* artists had dwindled, and only a few remained. Those who remained survived through other occupations such as fortune-telling, and could perform *dabenqu* only during their scarce free time. After the founding of the People's Republic, the Party and government promoted these performers and cultivated a new cadre of *dabenqu* specialists.[26]

Certain noted performers were given positions within orchestras, opera troupes, and the prefectural Bureau of Culture. Government-appointed specialists collected, recorded, archived, and analyzed hundreds of folk songs and operas, presenting research on them in academic publications. Many compositions were scored for the first time, allowing them to be preserved and performed on a scale much broader than before.

Though ostensibly aimed at preserving and promoting minority culture, these actions were also aimed at developing minority traditions in line with the Chinese Communist vision. The aim of all this cultural promotion was not simply the preservation of the past, but socialist modernization. One manifestation of this goal was the creation of a cadre of female singers who were trained in this traditionally male art. Bai musical history was made in 1954 at the Third Month Fair, when Hei Bilang became the first woman to perform *dabenqu* when she sang the lead role in a newly composed opera, "Shi Shance Joins the Collective." This event reportedly created a sensation throughout Dali; shortly afterwards, several hundred young women were selected for cultivation as "backbone" (*gugan*) *dabenqu* performers. These changes "broke through the longstanding male dominance of *dabenqu* music, thereby advancing its progress and development."[27]

Hei Bilang's debut reveals another way in which the state sought to harmonize minority culture with the goals of Chinese socialism. Traditionally, *dabenqu* was performed solo or by a duo, with one singer and one accompanist on the *sanxian*. In 1954, however, Bai musicians and culture workers from the Dali County bureau of culture forged an entirely new form of opera based on the *dabenqu* structure, despite the fact that a type of *minjia* opera, known as *chuichuiqiang*, already existed. New operas incorporated *dabenqu* style and meter, and, in some cases, traditional song content was the springboard for plots. For the most part, however, only the music's formal qualities were borrowed. The new operas told tales not of Bai mythology or traditional morality, but of class struggle, revolution, and life under the new socialist regime. These themes are evident in the titles of the new compositions: "Shi Shance Joins the Collective," followed by "Remembering Fanshen," "The Gate of Socialism," "Two-gun Granny," and "A Flower Grows in the Experimental Field," among others. These operatic adaptations transformed a style from one traditionally practiced by no more than two persons into a collective one that could be performed by dozens of people simultaneously. The operas were staged by troupes organized under the auspices of the Bureau of Culture and the guidance of the *dabenqu* masters whose old-regime expertise had propelled them into positions as representatives of the people. Troupes were dispatched throughout the Erhai region to introduce the new operas and the ideals they conveyed to peasants and townspeople. Singers and culture workers also helped their rural audiences learn the new operas so that they could stage their own amateur productions.

Dabenqu thus served the state-building project. The modified and modernized musical form became a vehicle for the expression and enactment of the ideals and concepts of socialism, collectivization, scientific farming, class struggle, and party leadership. It facilitated the construction of the party-state, insofar as the mass organizations associated with *dabenqu* enabled the party-state to connect with Bai peasants and townspeople and communicate its authority and ideals. It also served as an avenue for the establishment of a cadre of minority officials and people's representatives.

Dabenqu became a cultural interface linking state, minority official, and Bai peasant.

The music itself served a nation-building function as well. In *Imagined Communities*, Benedict Anderson argues that the transmission of the idea of the nation in European states and the non-European colonial world occurred through newspapers and other vernacular print media. Anderson hypothesizes that the regular consumption of vernacular print-media created a sense of experiential and temporal commonality among people living within the boundaries of a territorial state. This sense of shared experience in turn facilitated a collective sense of nationhood. Print-media are not the only means by which that sense of common experience so key to national identity transmission is created; the CCP, for instance, used a unified time zone and nationwide broadcasting system to establish simultaneity and commonality among a far-flung, mostly illiterate population. Art supplemented these devices. Among the Bai, *dabenqu* operas were one means of expressing how their pre-Liberation and revolutionary experiences fit within the broader struggle of the Chinese peasant and proletarian classes. The idea of a revolutionary, socialist Chinese nation, and of Bai membership within it, was communicated through *dabenqu* opera.

This was not a one-way process. Along with other forms of Bai music and dance, *dabenqu* received national attention through television, competitions, and traveling performances. One of the most well-known depictions of the Bai and Dali life is found in the movie "The Five Golden Flowers," which includes *dabenqu* performance. Bai music also garnered international attention. In 1957, singer Zhou Qiongyi, a member of the Naxi minority, performed a traditional Bai folksong at the Sixth World Youth Solidarity Festival in Moscow. Music communicated the fact of Bai membership in the People's Republic of China to a Chinese and socialist international audience.

Promotional and modernizing activities accelerated after the 1956 founding of the Dali Bai Autonomous Prefecture. That year saw the creation of the Bai Song and Dance Troupe. Ironically, the efforts made toward modernizing *dabenqu* also entailed what can perhaps be called Bai-ification. In the traditional *dabenqu*, a substantial number of elements are not unique to Bai culture. A large subset of songs were variants of "Han" songs from central and eastern China, and the language of *dabenqu*, and of the Bai more generally, contained loanwords and characters drawn from Chinese. The instrument that accompanies singers, the *sanxian*, is not unique to the Bai people or to Dali, but is found elsewhere in China. In this way, *dabenqu* serves as a microcosm of Dali and its people; it reflects their longstanding interactions with the greater Chinese cultural and political order.

Beginning in the 1950s, however, a concerted effort was made to compose songs and operas that dealt more specifically with the Bai and their experiences under the old oppressive order and the new regime. Plots and themes of the new *dabenqu* operas in particular incorporated Bai subject matter. Since the vast majority of these operas were composed in the 1950s and 1960s, nearly all of them dealt with politically correct socialist themes. Bai-ification was formalized in 1959 when the prefectural department of culture announced the establishment the Dali Autonomous Prefecture Bai Opera Company, which was to specialize in traditional *chuichuiqiang* opera as well as in the new variant of *dabenqu*.

The ironies of this Bai-ification are many. Because of centuries of cultural and commercial exchange with China's interior, typically Chinese musical forms like Beijing and Yunnan opera—*jingju* and *dianju*, respectively— flourished in Dali. They were popular *and* widely performed; they were in fact integral to the cultural fabric of the Erhai region. But in the view of a bureaucracy operating under Stalinist principles of nationality, they were not unique to and thus not authentically Bai. Consequently they were excluded from the repertoire of the Bai opera company, whose mandate was to perform works specific to the minority nationality they represented. Before 1949, *minjia* language and culture may have been a mélange, but under the cultural apparatus of the PRC, a distinct, bounded, and identifiably Bai culture was called into being, one of and for this minority nationality. The revival of *dabenqu* continues this project.

Not all observers are thrilled with how the revival has proceeded. One Bai scholar of traditional music laments that the great variety of local *dabenqu* music is being ignored and may be lost, as the music garnering local and national attention is generally the nontraditional operatic form created under the new socialist regime. The fact that this ersatz "traditional" *dabenqu* opera is being revived indicates how the Maoist Communist project continues to shape the content and meaning of minority identity. A Bai cultural form rooted in the communist values of the 1950s and early 1960s, and in the state- and nation-building aspirations of the new socialist regime, has assumed a position of primacy in a project that asserts an ostensibly traditional ethno-cultural identity. The resurgence of *dabenqu* opera shows how the specter of Maoism continues to haunt minority identity and practice.

THE BAI-HAN BILINGUAL EDUCATION PROGRAM

Music is an aesthetic phenomenon, and in contemporary Dali, musical endeavors are mostly part-time and amateur, excepting those of professional groups. The development and revival of Bai music, however, reveal the intersection of aesthetics with commerce and of the state's ideological and institutional agenda with amateur pastimes. The words and self-concepts of amateur musicians and the writings of scholars furthermore suggest how Bai identity is embodied in and expressed through cultural endeavors. While traditional Bai music, like other traditions, is no longer the political liability it was during the Mao years, politics and political legacies remain central to the context in which that music is played and performed. The politics of Bai music are not overt, but rather bubble just under the surface.

Politics are more overt, however, in the case of another element of the Bai revival—the effort to promote both bilingual education and the use of the Bai script. This effort culminated in the establishment of the first Bai-Han bilingual primary school, located in the village of Xizhong in Jianchuan County, Dali. The school itself grew out of an experiment in bilingual education initiated in 1986 by county officials and educators. Jianchuan educators are also using Bai-Han bilingual instruction to reduce illiteracy among adults.

The issue of education has a particular resonance for many Bai, given their concern with modernization and cultural development. Moreover, education in China is to some degree synonymous with culture. One's "cultural level" (*wenhua chengdu*) is the level of education one has achieved; when officials speak of raising the cultural quality of minority peoples, they usually mean raising education levels and literacy rates. The educational attainments of a particular nationality are thus both indicators of their progress along the route to modernity and causes of their advancement.

Among the Bai, the focus on education is influenced by the history of *minjia* adaptation of traditional Chinese practices and institutions. Because the Erhai region was politically integrated into the Chinese imperial system during the Yuan, Ming, and Qing dynasties, the imperial system helped disseminate cultural practices of central and eastern China, including classical education, throughout the region. The spread of classical learning was not limited to major population centers. The history of education in Heqing, one of the more remote counties in Dali Prefecture, demonstrates the extent to which *minjia* society was integrated into a broader Chinese cultural sphere. In Heqing, a dozen tuition-free community schools were in operation by the middle of the 1700s, and by the mid-1800s, five classical academies had been established. Chinese cultural tradition was not the only font of learning: French Catholic missionaries established Heqing's first modern primary school in 1890. In the waning years of the Qing, local notables opened a handful of new primary schools that were soon taken over by the local Guomindang government. By the 1920s, Heqing County had 163 elementary schools with nearly five thousand students, both male and female, in attendance. In 1926 the first county middle school opened, and two years later the provincial government established a teacher training college to serve western and northwest Yunnan. Elementary education was thus widespread by the late 1940s: every township had at least one national primary school (*guomin xiaoxue*); the number of public and private primary schools grew to 158; and, according to the *Almanac of Heqing County*, almost two-thirds of the school-age population was in attendance.[28]

The situation of Heqing, which is fairly typical of the Dali region, contrasts sharply with that of the predominantly Dai prefecture of Xishuangbanna. In the late 1940s, there were fewer than eight hundred primary school students in Xishuangbanna, most of them the sons of Han, Bai, and Hui merchants and settlers.[29] However, although education was more extensive in Dali than in most other regions of Yunnan before the founding of the People's Republic, throughout the region high rates of illiteracy were the norm. In Jianchuan, for example, over 90 percent of the population was illiterate.

Today the situation regarding education and literacy among the Bai is mixed. By some measures they are doing well. In the post-Mao era Bai have accounted for approximately 40 percent of all minority university graduates in Yunnan Province, even though they constitute less than 10 percent of the minority population.[30] The Bai are also well represented, as a minority, among the faculties of colleges and universities throughout the province and even nationally. While high illiteracy rates remain a problem in the counties of Yunnan that have been officially designated as at or below the poverty level, rates are relatively low in Dali. By the end of the 1990s, only about 3 percent of Dali youth were estimated to be illiterate, compared to 17 percent of youth in Yunnan. Dali counties were among the first in the province to fully implement nine-year compulsory education.[31] Elementary and middle school enrollment and retention rates in Dali now exceed the provincial average.[32]

In other respects the Bai have fared less well. Despite some important improvements in education and literacy in the first decade of reform, by some measures their situation stagnated. According to the 1982 census, the proportion of people with university degrees was higher among the Bai than among all Yunnan residents and all minorities nationwide. By 1990, however, fewer Bai were receiving university educations, while the proportion of university graduates among all minorities and the population of China as a whole had more than doubled.[33] A similar decline was seen in the proportion of people with a high school education. And while advances in literacy were achieved across the board, improvements were not as dramatic among the Bai. The 1990 census data also showed persistent gender disparities in terms of literacy.

These realities were a source of concern to those involved in the push for bilingual education in the 1980s and 1990s. One supporter of the program explained that while the Bai are known for being relatively advanced, they are so only in comparison to the most backward minorities of Yunnan and other poor provinces:

> According to some people, the Bai *minzu* are comparatively advanced (*bijiao fada*), mainly because they study and use the written and spoken Han language. The use of Hanwen has been of great importance to the development of Bai society, this fact is undeniable. But this line of thinking is one-sided. The so-called progressiveness of the Bai is only in relation to the backwards nationalities of China; in regards to the Han and other advanced minorities, large gaps remain. Moreover, these gaps have reached a point that is beginning to make people worry. . . . In terms of education and the economy, the Bai nationality is not advanced, but still quite backward.[34]

Awareness of these problems and fears of how they might affect the social, economic, and cultural conditions of the Bai people galvanized the educational activists of Jianchuan.

In promoting the Bai language and bilingual education, Jianchuan officials and educators were advancing a minority agenda that in many respects meshes with that of the Chinese government. All minorities in China—in fact, all citizens in general—are exhorted by the state to do their part to raise the cultural quality of the people and advance the national project of modernization. For the Bai, these issues of backwardness and modernization have an added urgency, for they are in fact issues of identity. The conditions of social life and economy in Dali may be backward (*luohou*), but the historical narrative of the Bai is one of relative advancement and cultural sophistication. As in the case of the Nanzhao musicians, the aims of many of the projects of the Bai cultural revival are both to express and to recapture the Bai's advanced status and to bring the realities of Bai life in line with their identity and self-image.

The story of the Xizhong Bai-Han Bilingual Primary School should be seen in this context (fig. 4.2). In the early 1980s, a group of Bai educators engaged the support of UNICEF and its Chinese partner, the China Center for Child Development (Zhongguo Ertong Fazhan Zhongxin), to initiate a six-year experimental bilingual program at a primary school in Jianchuan. Jianchuan lies fifty miles north of the prefectural capital. Mainly agricultural, it has been largely bypassed by the tourism boom that has occurred in and around Dali Old Town. Local officials are trying to develop a local hot springs and lake into a point of interest, and an increasing number of visitors are making their way to the Buddhist grottoes on Stone Bell Mountain. However, most of the tourist traffic is merely passing through on the way to Lijiang and the Tibetan autonomous prefecture of Diqing.

Jianchuan was chosen as the site of the experiment for several reasons. First, over 90 percent of the population is Bai, making the implementation of Bai-Han bilingualism more feasible than it might be in a mixed setting. By some estimates, more than 60 percent of that Bai population cannot speak standard Chinese, let alone write it.[35] The village of Xizhong, located several kilometers from the county seat, is almost entirely Bai, and economically quite typical for the region. There is no industry to speak of, and farmers continue to employ traditional, nonmechanized methods. The county's income, industrial output, and tax revenues consistently lag behind prefectural as well as provincial averages. The gap between Dali municipality and Jianchuan is particularly stark. In 2005, Jianchuan's per capita GDP was ¥4,056, compared to ¥16,112 in Dali municipality and ¥7,835 in the province. That same year the average rural income in Jianchuan was ¥1,296, the lowest among the eleven rural counties in the prefecture. In comparison, the 2005 per capita net rural income in Dali municipality was ¥3,457, roughly two and a half times the level in Jianchuan. The backwardness of Jianchuan's economy relative to Dali's stems in part from the weakness of the rural enterprise sector. The population of Jianchuan is one-third that of Dali municipality, but it possesses just one-fifth as many enterprises, which are considerably less profitable than those in Dali municipality.[36]

The experimental program in bilingual education was launched against this socio-economic background. Program officials chose one out of the

FIG. 4.2 The Xizhong Bai-Han Bilingual Primary School, Jianchuan

FIG. 4.3 Textbooks employing the Bai written language. The Bai alphabet was devised in the 1950s by scholars at the Institute of Linguistics at the Chinese Academy of Sciences in Beijing.

three entering primary school classes to receive education primarily in Bai, both written and spoken. As mentioned earlier, historically the Bai did not possess a written script specific to their spoken tongue. During the period of the Nanzhao and Dali regimes, the ruling elite adapted Chinese characters for use with the Bai tongue, eventually producing works of poetry, calligraphy, history, and religious literature. Most of these Bai works were lost or destroyed during fifteenth-century Ming campaigns to stamp out local written vernaculars; many of those that do remain are unintelligible to contemporary Bai, since the ability to read them has been lost as well. In the late 1950s, however, scholars at the Institute of Linguistics at the Chinese Academy of Sciences in Beijing devised a phonetic writing system based on the Roman alphabet (fig. 4.3). This script has since been revised several times to better harmonize it with the spoken vernacular.

In the experimental program, instructors conducted first-year classes solely in spoken and written Bai. They gradually introduced Chinese characters along with spoken standard Chinese in the second year, and increased education in standard Chinese over the course of the six years, alongside instruction in the Bai language. The thinking behind this program was that students would not only learn to read and write more quickly, since phonetic Bai corresponds with their mother tongue, but they also would be less likely to confuse Bai and Chinese, becoming more aware of Bai and standard Chinese as separate languages and less inclined to apply Bai pronunciation to Chinese characters. The other two classes at the primary school were taught according to the usual methods: standard Chinese was the written language of instruction, although out of necessity the Bai spoken language often predominated in the classroom.

By a number of measures the experiment was a success. Average test scores of students in the experimental class surpassed those of students attending regular classes in Xizhong and at other schools in the township. Students in the experimental class scored higher on Chinese reading comprehension tests taken at the end of their second year, despite the fact that they had spent fewer semesters studying written Chinese. At the end of the six-year program, a greater proportion of students from the experimental class passed the county middle school entrance exams.[37] On the basis of this success, the county decided to turn the entire school into a Bai language elementary school.

In promoting the experimental program, and in trying to implement Bai language education more generally, project supporters were not working blindly, but rather within the context of key national laws and policies regarding minority autonomy and education promulgated in the early and mid-1980s. In 1981, a joint conference of the Ministry of Education and the State Ethnic Affairs Commission established education policies in line with principles of minority autonomy, which led to the establishment of a new Department of Minority Education.[38] Moreover, according to article 37 of the Law on Nationality Autonomy of 1984, schools in predominantly minority areas "should, whenever possible, use textbooks in their own languages and use these languages as the media of instruction."[39] Major education reforms were also announced in 1985 by the CCP Central Committee and in 1986 by the National People's Congress, which called for the nationwide implementation of compulsory nine-year education by the year 2000.[40] Bilingual minority language education in some areas is widespread. By the middle of the 1990s, about ten thousand schools across the country were holding bilingual classes, and an estimated 6 million students from eleven minorities were receiving bilingual instruction.[41]

Despite this favorable legal and political context, and despite the apparent success of the program, bilingual education in Jianchuan ran into roadblocks. After the end of the UN-sponsored experiment in 1992, the government of Dali prefecture refused to provide the funds needed for materials and extra teacher training. Villagers, cadres, and officials in the county government were dismayed by the prefectural government's lack of support. Several characterized the situation as a violation of constitutional provisions for minority bilingual education. They also argued that the refusal to promote Bai language instruction amounted to an obstruction of *minzu* development; one village cadre explained:

> We Bai have always been a comparatively advanced *minzu*. But we never had our own written mother tongue (*muwen*). The Han have *hanwen*, the Dai *daiwen*, and the Hui have Arabic. Now we have a written language, and now we can genuinely say we are an advanced *minzu*. But the government in Dali doesn't support us.[42]

As this man saw it, the possession of a written language was a marker of development, a sign that the Bai were not a backward people. Prefectural officials' disinterest in bilingual education was undermining the "relatively advanced" status of the Bai.

Ironically, one factor that influenced the prefectural government's intransigence is this perception of the Bai as being relatively advanced. Since the Bai have long been well integrated into mainstream Chinese society and culture, Bai language education is viewed by some as a point-less step back. Historically and traditionally, the Bai embraced Chinese culture and learning, so in some respects the Jianchuan program deviates from tradition. Many officials and ordinary Bai people in other parts of Dali also believe that a written Bai script is useless. Since the Bai are only a small, local minority, Bai language has no relevance for students hoping to get ahead in the broader Chinese society. In neighboring Eryuan County, for instance, many Bai families with young children reportedly are eschew-ing the use of spoken Bai in the household in favor of standard Chinese. They are doing so in the hopes that their children will develop a more solid grasp of Chinese than if they spoke Bai as their mother tongue, thereby enhancing their education and employment prospects.[43]

The opposition from officials and ordinary people in the 1990s frus-trated supporters of the program, who had noted its success among pri-mary school students and among adults in literacy classes. Several local officials and educators explained that the government's refusal stems from officials' fear of being labeled "local nationalists." One Dali-based supporter of the program stated that the government's position arises from concerns that the spread of Bai-language education throughout the prefecture's Bai counties would cement nationality consciousness and cohesion.[44]

To be fair to those opposed to the project, many prefectural officials are concerned that bilingual education diverts funds and energy from more pressing and high-profile goals, such as the implementation of universal compulsory nine-year education. Educational officials also face the ongoing task of eradicating illiteracy among youth and adults. The compulsory edu-cation and youth literacy projects—known as the "two basics"—are part of a nation-wide strategy to improve the "cultural quality" of backward regions like Yunnan, and thus improve the prospects for economic devel-opment. While the Jianchuan activists regard their own project as further-ing Bai literacy, many officials believe that furthering literacy in Chinese is a more urgent task. Many Bai people would also prefer that their children learn English; in the nearby town of Jinhua, the Jianchuan county seat, pri-mary school students do not study the Bai script, but they begin learning English in their third year.

The failure of higher authorities in the prefecture to support the pro-gram after its initial success distressed its supporters, including Jianchuan officials and ordinary Xizhong villagers. They perceived this lack of support as denying the Bai the opportunity to advance their culture on their own terms, as the Bai *minzu*. In discussing this dilemma, and in advocating for their cause, local officials used the discourse of modernization and minority development, and even Marxist-Leninist-Maoist thought, to justify their endeavors. As one respected local educator put it:

> To understand the Bai nationality fully, we must see that on the one hand, Bai culture and education are relatively developed; yet on the other hand, among the Bai there is much illiteracy, and the culture is very backward, especially in remote, mountainous areas. Everyone knows that historically the Bai have ... lacked a written language; this is a major obstacle hindering nationality development and progress. After Liberation, Bai writing was invented but not implemented; still Bai culture and education have not developed quickly, and this is the main reason why the quality of the Bai people has not greatly improved.[45]

A Jianchuan official argued that the implementation of the Bai alphabet was both a policy of the party-state and "a right of nationality autonomy" (*ye shi minzu zizhi quanli*). Another supporter, a highly decorated Bai hero of the Chinese Revolution and former head of the Yunnan Nationalities Institute, cited Marx and Lenin in claiming that "socialism cannot be built on a foundation of illiterate masses" and that the use of Bai to "sweep away illiteracy" (*saomang*) is necessary to socialist construction.[46] Along with Marx and Lenin, the twelve-hundred-year-old example of Nanzhao is used to bolster the bilingual position. One supporter has argued that the bilingualism of the Nanzhao rulers was fundamental to their achievements, proof that facility in both the Bai and Chinese languages is conducive to economic and cultural development.[47]

Those in favor of the Jianchuan project view the issue not only as one of cultural development, but also in terms of minority autonomy and rights. Like the Dai activists, these individuals express their support for Bai language education in terms of autonomy. Said one, "we Bai have the Dali Bai Autonomous Prefecture, but we don't have real autonomy. Our officials, especially Bai ones, are afraid of what higher authorities might say."[48]

In early 1998, prefectural officials had a change of heart regarding Xizhong's bilingual program. This switch was due in part to the prodding and lobbying of Zhang Wenbo, a retired teacher and one of the original proponents of Bai-Han instruction. In the mid-1990s, Zhang served as a member of the county CPPCC and as a representative to the prefectural National People's Congress. According to Zhang, he used his position in these bodies to repeatedly raise the issue of Bai-Han bilingual education and request that the prefecture carry through on its promises of support. Zhang also wrote a letter to the Party Secretary of Dali in late 1997 regarding the situation.[49] In January 1998, prefectural head Li Yangde traveled to Jianchuan with other high-ranking officials to investigate the Xizhong School. During his visit Li called for the continuation of the experimental project and promised that funds for the bilingual program would be forthcoming.[50]

Although the program thrived for a number of years after Li Yangde's visit, by 2007 it was moribund. Bai-Han education depends ultimately on the attitudes of local and prefectural leaders, and changes in leadership effectively killed the program. In the last few years the prefectural head, the Jianchuan mayor, and the principal of the Xizhong elementary school have all been replaced at least once and in some cases twice. According to Zhang Wenbo, these newer leaders lack commitment to and understanding of the purpose and nature of the program; they "don't want the trouble" of supporting Bai language instruction, paying for and organizing teacher training classes, and paying for Bai language textbooks in addition to standard course materials. Furthermore, a number of the original proponents of bilingual Bai-Han education, already prominent retired educators and officials in the 1980s when the program was initiated, have passed away. To Zhang, the reluctance of newer officials is misguided, as one of the goals of bilingual education is to improve overall academic achievement as well as literacy in Chinese.[51]

The term "bilingual" is a bit misleading, though, and never quite fit the circumstances of the school. While the program was in force, instruction for the first two grades at Xizhong Primary School was conducted primarily in Bai. Teachers and students spoke Bai, and students learned the Bai alphabet and basic grammar. This enabled them to very quickly develop the ability to write simple sentences and stories in their native tongue. Standard spoken and written Chinese were gradually introduced. By the third year, Chinese became the main language of instruction. From that point on students studied geography, history, math, and other subjects using standard Chinese textbooks. Bai language instruction continued through the upper grades, but was relegated to just several hours per week. Thus from the third year on, Bai was taught much like a second language.

Though he would have preferred more comprehensive Bai language instruction, Zhang Wenbo emphasized the benefits of the program. He is, he states, "the biggest supporter of standard Chinese language literacy in Jianchuan County." The approach, he argues, should be *"xian Bai, hou Han"*—Bai language first, then Chinese. The goal is not to teach Bai at the expense of spoken and written Chinese but to facilitate overall language development, which will assist in the acquisition of Chinese literacy. Teaching young children in a language they do not understand discourages them and retards the development of their reading and writing abilities:

> We must raise the cultural level [*wenhua shuiping*] of the Bai people, but we can't raise them up by pulling on their hair. Instead we must build up the base they stand on. Here in Jianchuan, many children can't understand or speak standard Chinese. How then can we use Chinese to raise their cultural level? We must rely on their actual conditions [*juti qingkuang*].[52]

Those conditions, argues Zhang, include the Bai language.

MODERNIZATION AND BAI IDENTITY

Like the Dai cultural activists discussed in chapter 3, Bai promoters of musical revival and bilingual education are motivated by a variety of goals and interests. Many of them also conceive of modernization and cultural development in a very *minzu*-centric fashion. For these activists, minority autonomy ought to entail the modernization of Bai culture in ways that allow it to flourish and remain distinct. Modernization can benefit them only if it preserves the Bai as a distinct collectivity and preserves that which makes them unique.

These *minzu*-centric understandings of modernization characterize all three of the cases analyzed in this book. However, there is an added level of complexity, even poignancy, in the case of the Bai. For the Bai, literacy, education, and modernization are more than just goals to be achieved—they are normative ideals, constitutive of Bai identity. The renaissance of Bai culture is infused with nostalgia, as many cultural movements are, but it is nostalgia for a past in which their forebears were the cultural and political vanguard of southwest China. Being modern and advanced is what the Bai supposedly are; history proves this notion and the Chinese government has codified it. Many of the cultural projects are intended to restore the Bai to the position of relative advancement that they see as their historical legacy.

Bai musical revival and bilingual activism also highlight the important role played by both elites and those at the so-called "grass roots" level in the resurgence of minority culture. These projects emerge out of complex interactions among ordinary people, local and prefectural cadres, teachers, scholars, and in some cases international organizations and revolutionary heroes. Nevertheless, the state, or parts of it, has resisted projects like bilingual education, often because of practical and resource constraints. Dali officials are under pressure to implement compulsory nine-year schooling and eliminate illiteracy, and many feel that bilingual education diverts scarce resources from these more pressing goals. Yet their reluctance also reflects competing understandings of what it means to be Bai and to be "relatively advanced." In a way, these resistant officials are upholding Bai tradition, although they do not necessarily explain their actions in that way. In fact, throughout history, the forebears of the Bai flourished because of their cultural integration with the Han, and with greater China. Jianchuan activists could even be accused of deviating from that Bai tradition. The supporters of the Jianchuan program, of course, do not see things this way. Like their critics, they are motivated by ideals of modernization and minority cultural development, which they argue are inextricable. In their efforts to promote bilingual education, they advance not just alternative notions of what it means to be Bai, but alternative ways of being modern.

—5—

AUTHENTICITY, IDENTITY, AND
TRADITION AMONG THE HUI

C hinese minorities are frequently portrayed in art, literature, popular culture, and public policy as backward, childlike primitives, in
need of the civilizing assistance of the elder brother Han nationality. Alternatively they are feminized exotics, repositories of authenticity in
an age in which rapid change has all but obliterated the culture and nature
of the Chinese past. These representations are neither entirely negative
nor conditions from which minorities need to be extricated. Instead they
suggest an ideal type, a notion of the "model minority" implicit in much
Chinese discourse. Minorities may be or are alleged to be backwards and
passive, but there is an appropriateness to these qualities and to minorities'
dependence on the modernizing, advanced Han. Passivity, for instance,
translates into "docility" (*wenshun*), always a good thing as far as state
power is concerned. Exoticism has proved to be a lucrative commodity for
minority regions, attracting affluent tourists from abroad and from more
urban, Han-dominated parts of the country.

The Hui are not a model minority. They rarely if ever are portrayed as
exemplars of a passive, eroticized ideal. Though they sometimes seem exotic
to non-Muslim Chinese—"familiar strangers," in the words of Jonathan
Lipman—notions of feminized docility are irrelevant to characterizations
of Hui difference.[1] Moreover, the Hui are not the passive object of Chinese

history—quite the contrary. Where many non-Han peoples have been the target of what Stevan Harrell calls "civilizing projects," historically the Hui often have been the ones doing the civilizing. The history of Chinese civilizing projects in Yunnan is in great part the history of the Yunnan Hui.

Post-Mao reforms have sparked a cultural, primarily religious revival among the Hui Muslims of Yunnan Province. The Hui have rebuilt mosques, established Islamic schools, revived religious networks, and resuscitated practices forced underground during the anti-traditional, anti-religious Maoist years. The cultural ferment involves more than just a straightforward recovery of lost tradition, as participants seek to expand their knowledge of Islam and their opportunities to follow the precepts of their faith.

Hui revival is part of a broader national trend, yet it reflects concerns and goals specific to the Hui as a minority *minzu*. The revival is informed by a historical consciousness of both persecution at the hands of the state and non-Muslim groups and of "rightful resistance" against that persecution.[2] Many Hui view the practice and promotion of their faith in light of a legacy of Muslim rebellion, as a religious requirement to defend their faith and people. Hui cultural activism also challenges official and popular stereotypes of the Hui as violent, clannish, disloyal, and even criminal. Although the Hui locate their political and cultural efforts within a history of resistance against oppression, they also seek to counter negative perceptions of them as unruly troublemakers. To this end many Hui situate their Islamic revival within the broader history of Muslims in Yunnan Province, a history replete with "patriotic" political, social, and cultural achievements.

For the Hui, as for the Dai and Bai, cultural and religious revival is both a return to tradition and an opportunity to modernize their culture and their communities. Religious resurgence has also enhanced the social capital of many Hui communities by revitalizing religious networks and community life. Revival also creates opportunities for Hui to assert the rights and privileges of minority autonomy. Yet the Hui revival is not monolithic. Among the Hui there are differences of opinion regarding the purpose of revival, its meaning, and the traditions and conceptions of Chinese Islam that should be promoted. Some have embraced a Wahhabi-influenced Islam that encourages detachment and insularity from the secular, non-Muslim society that surrounds them. Other Hui support the reconstitution of an existence and identity that is as Chinese as it is Islamic. They justify their vision of an engaged, civil Islam through reference to previous generations of Muslim scholars, writers, officials, and military leaders who were as immersed in the Confucian, Republican, or Communist Chinese cultures of their day as they were in Islam. These competing perceptions of Islamic tradition and identity complicate the Hui people's drive for legitimacy and modernization, and the Chinese state takes notice.

SOCIAL AND ECONOMIC BACKGROUND

The Hui are one of China's ten official Muslim minority nationalities, numbering nearly 10 million nationwide. In Yunnan, the Hui number approximately seven hundred thousand, making them the seventh largest of more than two-dozen minorities in the province. They are dispersed unevenly throughout the province: fourteen counties have Hui populations of fifty or less, while in seventeen counties the population exceeds ten thousand. The greatest concentrations are in the northeast, central, and west-central parts of the province. Even where Hui are numerous, their overall percentage of the population may be quite small; in no county or municipality do Hui account for more than 17 percent of the population. In the four urban districts of the capital Kunming, which is home to over seventy-three thousand Hui, they form less than 3 percent of the population.[3]

The dispersal of the Hui throughout China and within provinces explains their economic and social integration among the Han and other minorities. It also helps explain why, over the centuries, Hui people have absorbed and adopted the language, dress, architectural styles, and even culinary tastes of those other groups among whom they reside, even while attempting to maintain a distinct religious and ethnic identity. Though dispersed, the Hui often reside in tightly knit communities and maintain their identity through worship and dietary practice to some degree. The Hui settlement pattern of concentration-within-dispersal has given rise to the phrase "*da fensan, xiao jizhong*," which translates roughly as "greatly scattered, closely concentrated." In Ludian, a county in the northeastern district of Zhaotong, nearly three-quarters of the Hui population reside in a single township that is 90 percent Hui. In the Weishan Hui and Yi Autonomous County, 90 percent of the Hui population lives in the township of Yongjian.[4]

The Stalinist theory that underpins Chinese ethnography holds that minorities are constituted, in part, by distinct economic practices. However, the geographic variation of Hui communities is matched by a concomitant variation in economic conditions and practices. Historically, many Yunnan Hui were merchants, traders, metallurgists and mule caravan drivers, so many Hui settlements are clustered around commercial and transport centers. The Hui are reputed to possess a propensity for business; they were once a major force in the development of long-distance trade and commerce in Yunnan and throughout China.[5] Popular stereotypes also hold that the Hui tend to be affluent relative to other nationalities, including the Han. Yet today most Yunnan Hui are farmers, and many live in the most impoverished parts of the province. Nearly a quarter of all Yunnan Hui reside in the northeastern district of Zhaotong, whose rural counties are some of the poorest in the province.[6]

Nearly all Yunnan Hui, like most Chinese Muslims, are Sunni. However, within Chinese Sunni Islam there are numerous sects or factions known by a confusing array of names. In Yunnan, most Hui follow Gedimu teachings (from the Arabic *qadim*, or "old"). The Gedimu are colloquially referred to as *laojiao*, or "old teaching." Roughly ten thousand Yunnan Hui are Naqshbandi Sufis, known as Zheherenye or Zhehelinye (from the Arabic word Jahriyya). Sufism first made inroads into Yunnan in the eighteenth century, and is called *xinjiao*, or "new teaching." Another fifteen thousand Hui are members of the Wahhabi sect known as the Yihewani (from Ikhwan, Arabic for "brotherhood"). This group is typically referred to as the *zunjingpai*, or "venerate-the-scriptures faction."[7] Confusingly, this too is called "new teaching," though sometimes the term "new, new teaching" (*xinxinjiao*) is used to differentiate it from the "new teaching" of Sufism. Yihewani Islam was introduced to Yunnan in 1925 by an acolyte of Ma Wanfu, the Gansu *hajji* who initiated the movement in northwest China in the late nineteenth century.[8]

WEISHAN, A YUNNAN HUI COMMUNITY

The religious, geographic, demographic, and economic diversity of the Hui makes it difficult to speak of a "typical" Hui community. However, the township of Yongjian in Weishan County can serve as a general model of a Hui community in Yunnan and shed light on the Hui experience during and after the Maoist period. Weishan is a Hui and Yi autonomous county located in Dali Prefecture, in west-central Yunnan. It is neither the most prosperous nor the poorest of the Hui areas in Yunnan. Still, the county is poor. Like most rural areas far from Kunming, the predominantly agricultural local economy lags behind provincial averages in terms of income, GDP, and industrial development.[9]

Weishan is unusual in that it is one of the two Hui autonomous counties in the province, the other being Xundian in central Yunnan. There are no

purely Hui autonomous counties; Weishan and Xundian are both Hui and
Yi autonomous counties. That Weishan, as an autonomous county, has Hui
designated in its title is somewhat odd, since out of a population of three
hundred thousand, just twenty-one thousand, or 7 percent, are Hui. More
than half the population is Han, and nearly a third are members of the Yi
minority.[10]

Weishan, however, holds a distinctive place in the history of Yunnan
Muslims. It is home to some of the oldest Muslim settlements in Yunnan,
which were founded in the Yuan dynasty by conquering armies under the
leadership of Saidianchi. Many people in Yongjian Township trace their
family genealogies back to Saidianchi and his progeny. Weishan, called
Menghua during the Qing dynasty, is also noteworthy for being the staging ground from which the nineteenth-century Panthay Rebellion was
launched against the Qing.[11] It was from the villages of Yongjian that rebel
leader Du Wenxiu, with a support network of Muslims and Gelaohui secret
society members (many of them one and the same), planned and orches-
trated the attack on Qing authority in Dali.[12] In the wake of that rebellion's
collapse, the Muslim population of Weishan was decimated.

In the late nineteenth and early twentieth centuries, Weishan was an
important religious and educational center for Yunnan Muslims, along
with Shadian in the south of the province and Najiaying in central Yunnan.
Prior to the Panthay Rebellion, there were twenty-eight Muslim villages
in Weishan, each with at least one and sometimes two mosques that provided basic religious courses for the local inhabitants. Mosques in several
of the larger villages established secondary and tertiary schools that drew
students from all over the province and beyond. Most of the mosques were
destroyed in the post-rebellion purges, but by the late 1870s and early 1880s
Islamic religious life had revived. By the end of the nineteenth century,
Weishan mosques were again functioning, as was Islamic and Arabic education. Education in Weishan was not focused solely on Islam, however.
During the Ming and Qing dynasties, the Hui community of Weishan produced one successful imperial exam candidate (*jinshi*), twelve successful
provincial-level exam candidates (*juren*), and several others who passed
local exams (*gongshen*). Several of these individuals attained high positions
in the imperial bureaucracy.[13]

Though the economy of Weishan is today primarily agricultural, in the
late nineteenth and early twentieth centuries the local Hui economy was
more reliant on commerce, cottage industries, and other nonfarming pursuits than it is today. For a variety of reasons related to settlement patterns

and persecution during the late Qing, Hui in Weishan were engaged in a wide range of trades. Long-distance transport and trade were mainstays of the local economy. In 1950, the area supported one hundred caravan teams, called *mabang*, comprised of 5000 mules and horses; households in the village of Huihuideng owned almost half of these teams. An investigation in 1951 found that in Huihuideng, half the 380 households derived their livelihoods entirely from transportation and trade. Another ninety households made their livelihoods half from farming and half from transport and cottage industry, while only one hundred households relied solely on farming for their income.[14]

The widespread reliance on nonfarming pursuits is often attributed to an innate Hui propensity to engage in commerce, a propensity often explained in ethno-racial terms. The Hui affinity for commerce, the explanation goes, is inherited from their forebears, the Arabic and Central Asian Muslim traders who settled in northwest China. Also contributing to the Hui's alleged propensity to trade was the need for people to adapt in the face of anti-Muslim persecution. Following the collapse of the Panthay Rebellion, Muslim-owned properties were confiscated, which severely reduced the landholdings of Hui families. Yet despite the steep decline in the Muslim population from deaths and out-migration after the Panthays were defeated, per capita land holdings were still much lower among the Hui than among the Han, Yi, and others in the region. As Muslim villages began to recover in the late 1870s, the experience of persecution led Hui people to live in tighter, more closely knit and guarded communities, which increased the density of settlements and exacerbated land shortages.

HUI LIFE DURING THE SOCIALIST ERA

The centrality of Islam to Hui culture and society and the reliance on commerce and trade as centerpieces of the economy meant that post-1949 socialist construction and collectivization were particularly transformative of Hui life. Because of linguistic, cultural, and economic reasons the Hui were classified as being at the same high stage of development as the Han. Like the Bai, they were thus subject to the same sorts of land reform and collectivization policies as the Han, which were implemented soon after Yunnan was declared liberated in 1950. Land reform entailed the confiscation of most of the farmland occupied and controlled by mosques, land that had provided resources to support the mosques. Official accounts suggest that cadres showed some restraint in carrying out land reform in Hui areas, at least initially. In Weishan, mosque landholdings were reallocated only to poor and lower-middle Hui peasants, as were lands belonging to rich Hui peasants and Hui landlords, according to the *Annals of Weishan County*. The *Annals* record that cadres also restricted non-Hui people from participating in struggle and denunciation sessions against Hui landlords, due to lingering fears and enmity stemming from previous inter-ethnic strife.[15]

Since collectivization applied to draught animals as well as land, the horse and mule teams of the long-distance caravans were removed from private ownership and put under the control of the communes.[16] State ownership of transportation firms, the growing use of motor trucks, and the construction and improvement of the Yunnan road system increasingly rendered this pre-modern mode of transport mostly obsolete, although in isolated Yunnan horse and mule teams remained necessary to the local economy.

The Great Leap Forward appears to have been as thorough and destructive in Weishan as it was elsewhere in China. Strides were made in land reclamation and irrigation system construction, but much of the investment and labor of this period was wasted. One Weishan commune invested ¥50,000 in steel production and produced nothing; another put ¥24,000 into a distillery and produced only a few liters. In Yongjian, farm labor and funds were diverted into the production of steel and even motorized vehicles. Over-reporting of grain yields decimated the food supply, and much farmland went unplanted. Neglect and misallocation of funds and labor resulted in severe food shortages, famine, and disease.[17] During the Cultural Revolution, the emphasis on class struggle, the resulting attacks on capitalist elements, and the drive to make grain the centerpiece of the economy (*yi liang wei zhu*) spelled the complete demise of commercial activities. The resulting simplification of the economy and emphasis on agriculture was particularly problematic in the Hui communities of Weishan, given the dearth of farmland.

The transformations wrought during the Maoist era greatly affected Islamic faith and practice in Weishan. For the first few years after the founding of the PRC, mosques remained open. Religious leaders, called *ahong*—graduates of Arabic and Islamic study programs who lead religious instruction and ceremonies—were allowed to continue their duties. Mosques continued to offer Arabic and Islamic instruction, though Weishan's first Chinese-Arabic middle school, the Xingjian School, was reorganized as a secular state school and Arabic and Islamic instruction eliminated.[18] As collectivization intensified in the mid-1950s, all remaining mosque lands were confiscated and subsumed into the collectives. The Anti-Rightist Campaign, which began in 1957, led to the near-complete curtailment of religious worship and instruction. Religious leaders and scholars were labeled "counterrevolutionaries in religious garb" and sent away for re-education, as were party cadres who had followed earlier directives to respect the special characteristics and religious practices of the Hui.[19] Public worship ceased entirely with the beginning of the Great Leap Forward in 1958. During the Cultural Revolution all mosques in Yongjian were closed, wrecked, or turned into granaries or performance halls.

Details concerning the course of the Cultural Revolution in Weishan's Hui villages are somewhat murky, as is information regarding Hui participation in the factional conflicts of this period. The county as a whole was split by dozens of factions, most of which eventually coalesced into two main groups, although whether the splits were marked by ethnic strife or not is unclear. According to *The Annals of Weishan County*, "during the Cultural Revolution, the Hui people of Weishan never participated in factional fighting, nor were they influenced by outside provocation; from start to finish they upheld peace and unity and maintained production."[20] People today who remember those times insist that the Hui in Weishan did not fight amongst each other. However, another source hints that conflicts between villages were quite serious, with some villages transformed into "fortresses."[21]

Throughout the province, Hui most certainly did participate in and suffer from the factional fighting of this era. The Cultural Revolution was perhaps more devastating for Hui in Yunnan than for any other minority group. Mosques were stripped of religious references, turned into meeting halls, movie theaters, granaries, and pigsties, or simply destroyed. *Ahong*, the religious teachers, were singled out for rectification. Wells in some Hui communities were contaminated with pork, and Hui were required to eat in communal canteens that were not *qingzhen* (*halal*), that is, did not adhere to Muslim dietary guidelines and restrictions. Irreplaceable religious and historical records, sites, graves, and buildings were destroyed, including the family record of the explorer Zheng He, the nineteenth-century engravings used to print the first Chinese Koran, and scores of Yuan and Ming dynasty mosques.[22] Violence and persecution were by no means specific to Muslim communities in Yunnan or elsewhere. Yet Islamic laws and dietary taboos left Hui vulnerable to insults and degradation in ways other minorities were not.

These atrocities were not always perpetrated by other groups. When asked, Hui officials and educators typically attributed factional strife to "outsiders" (*waidiren*). This claim was also made by Dai officials regarding the course of the Cultural Revolution in Xishuangbanna, though ordinary villagers told a different story.[23] One official in the Dali branch of the Islamic Association, for instance, insisted that factional strife did not occur in the rural area where he lived, owing to the cohesiveness of Hui people. Yet there are reports of conflict among Hui, sometimes between followers of different religious sects, although these reports employed the language and symbols of revolutionary struggle.[24]

Intra-Hui conflict played a role in the most notorious and bloody incident of the Cultural Revolution in Yunnan, the Shadian Incident. Dru Gladney recounts the circumstances and trajectory of this event in his book *Muslim Chinese*, though details surrounding the bloody incident remain opaque. Shadian, a large Hui village in southern Yunnan not far from the border with Vietnam, had been a prosperous commercial and religious community prior to the Communist era, and an important stop for Hui traders and caravans heading toward Southeast Asia. In the late 1960s, as the Cultural Revolution was well under way throughout the rest of the country, "leftist" and "revisionist" factional splits emerged among Hui, with the leftists advocating the abandonment of Islam and its laws and taboos, including abandoning the taboo on the consumption of pork. Some versions of the conflict hold that these "leftists" threw pork into Shadian wells to contaminate them and perhaps force the issue.[25] Such contamination is not unusual in rural Han-Hui conflicts, but in this case Hui were apparently among the perpetrators. Like many Cultural Revolution conflicts, this one turned violent. After simmering for a number of years, factional strife reemerged in 1975. This time the army stepped in to quell the discord by force. In the end, the village was virtually destroyed, and roughly a thousand Hui were killed.[26]

Today, Hui and non-Hui still speak of the horror and bloodshed of that crackdown that arose from a local disagreement. For Hui, the Shadian Incident serves as a grim reminder of the necessity of unity, the need to oppose repression, and the precariousness of Hui existence. It is part of the long and tortuous history of anti-Hui persecution that for many Hui is a defining feature of their identity. For the state, Shadian remains an embarrassment, although it has gone to great lengths to make reparations to the people of Shadian. Officially, the responsibility for the Shadian Incident was placed on Lin Biao and the Gang of Four. To make amends, the party-state has pumped money into Shadian, rebuilding the village, creating new industries, replacing destroyed mosques and schools and constructing new ones, and organizing pilgrimage trips of village elites to Mecca for the hajj. Because of these efforts, Shadian has prospered. In 1993 Shadian was named "southern Yunnan's first 100-million-yuan rural town."[27] Today Shadian is held up as a model of what economic reform and "nationalities' unity" (*minzu tuanjie*) can achieve in rural areas.

The legitimacy and authority of the Communist Party were sorely damaged by three decades of leftist excess. Deng Xiaoping's reforms that jump-started economic growth and allowed greater social and cultural freedoms were designed to restore the Party's reputation. Among the Hui the task facing the CCP was particularly fraught with difficulties, given the debacle at Shadian and nearly three decades of anti-religious policies and persecution. The Party's standing among the Hui was consequently very weak, and the need for reforms pressing.

Hui settlements were among the first in Weishan to respond to new economic policies by dismantling the communes and making the shift to household contracting. The reform process was not exactly smooth; despite the central government's call to implement the household responsibility system, the Weishan Party Committee issued thinly veiled criticisms of the new arrangements several years after reforms were initiated. In one document from 1982, the committee described those implementing household contracting as "backward economic elements." Just two years later, however, the committee had apparently progressed in its thinking and was promoting the household responsibility system. The subsequent economic transformation of Hui life has been considerable, despite the fits and starts of reform. In Yongjian, grain production and the per capita grain ration nearly doubled between 1978 and 1998, despite constraints on arable land. In the 1990s alone, overall rural earnings increased six times over.[28]

The economy of Weishan continues to be dominated by farming, fishing, animal husbandry, and other agricultural pursuits. As both an officially designated poor county and a minority autonomous county, Weishan receives subsidies from the provincial government for specific projects and to make up shortfalls in revenues. Many counties that receive subsidies continue to run deep deficits year after year. Weishan, however, has actually managed to bring its spending in line with its revenues, and in 1998 it was able to "remove its deficit hat."[29]

To address the continuing problems of rural underemployment, local officials in Weishan, as elsewhere, have pushed the development of private and collective enterprises. Officials and entrepreneurs have sought to capitalize on cultural preferences, skills, and requirements in this develop-ment process. In the early 1990s, township officials in Yongjian set up a *qing-zhen* beef curing and packaging plant in Huihuideng Village. Dried cured beef, or *niurou ganba*, is a Hui specialty; since the enterprise produces *qing-zhen* beef, it can take advantage of Muslim as well as non-Muslim markets in China and abroad. The "Huihuideng" brand has become well known throughout the region.[30] The Weishan Hui are also well known regionally for their tea, and county officials have been promoting tea production and processing in the more mountainous parts of Yongjian.

Problems still remain, however. Land remains scarce, with disparities in access to land persisting between Hui and non-Hui. The dearth of land has created religious as well as economic problems; Hui Muslims eschew cremation, but constraints on land limit the space available for burial plots. New economic opportunities have created problems of their own. One development that troubles officials concerns the Hui practice of hiring Han laborers to farm their lands. This practice is not unique to the Hui. In Xish-uangbanna, Dai households engaged in rubber cultivation are hiring Han workers from the nearby state-run farms, who are lured by wages higher than those paid by the Farm Bureau. In Weishan, some officials worry that a "master-servant" (*zhupu*) relationship is developing between Hui entre-preneurs and their Han workers, and that this may aggravate resentment and mistrust between groups.[31]

Local officials blame persistent economic backwardness and under-employment for the most troubling development in Yongjian—drug traf-ficking. The trafficking of heroin and opium from the Golden Triangle reemerged in the 1980s, and Hui from several villages in Yongjian have been major players in its reemergence. In 1999 Yongjian was identified as one of seventeen national "drug problem areas." A five-year "Strike Hard" campaign against trafficking resulted in the conviction of 381 drug criminals and the confiscation of 66 properties. In September 2004, the central government allowed Yongjian to remove its "drug problem area hat." However, since then there have been several major drug arrests in or linked to Yongjian. In April 2005, police in Weishan broke up a joint Burmese-Yongjian trafficking oper-ation, nabbing eight suspects, over eight kilograms of heroin, and ¥11,600.[32]

RELIGION AND CULTURE IN THE ERA OF REFORM

The transformation of religious and cultural life has been at least as impres-sive as the transformation in economic affairs. Within months after the conclusion of the Third Plenum in 1978, physical and institutional rebuilding was well underway. The government set up branches of the Nationality Affairs Committee in minority counties throughout Yunnan, including Weishan, in early 1979. In early 1980, the Islamic Association, a nationwide mass organization that oversees Muslim religious affairs, opened a Weishan branch in the Hui village of Daweigeng.[33] Similar institutional reorganization occurred in Hui communities around the province.

Mosque reconstruction commenced immediately as well. During the Cultural Revolution, mosques had been closed, neglected, or used as theaters, granaries, and performance halls. At worst, they were razed, burned down, or used as pigsties and thus contaminated. Renovation and rebuilding was necessary, and the 1980s saw a spate of mosque construction and reconstruction all over Yunnan. In Shadian, reconstruction was spearheaded by a penitent state in partial compensation for the 1975 massacre. Typically, however, renovation and construction have relied on private funds from the faithful collected through tithing and donations. In some cases, overseas Chinese Muslims have donated large sums for the construction and reconstruction of mosques in their ancestral villages.[34]

Many new mosques in Yunnan, as in Hui communities throughout China, incorporate physical elements drawn from Arabic and other Middle Eastern architecture. Pre-communist era Yunnan mosques resemble Chinese temples in style and construction, with wooden columns, curving tiled roofs, and elaborately carved doors. Some newer structures echo the traditional style, but others include domes and spires similar to those featured in photographs of Middle Eastern mosques that hang on the walls of many Hui homes (figs. 5.1, 5.2). In the Weishan villages of Daweigeng and Xiaoweigeng, the mosques, completed in 1990, were the first to incorporate these Middle Eastern elements. The new mosque in Huihuideng melds Middle Eastern with traditional Chinese Islamic architectural elements.

These stylistic shifts are symptoms of greater wealth and access to a broader variety of building materials. They are also the fruits of increased contact between rural Muslim communities like the villages of Weishan and the greater Islamic world that reforms and prosperity made possible. These contacts have allowed more and more Chinese Muslims to make the hajj. Increasing numbers of young people are also going abroad to Muslim countries for higher education. Although variations in mosque style are related to the divergent views of different Islamic sects, these architectural trends are not clear indicators of one or another sect.[35] They do, however, suggest that Hui Muslims increasingly see themselves as defined

FIG. 5.1 Entrance to old mosque, Three Family Village, Weishan. The sign reads "Three Family Village Mosque" (*Sanjiacun qingzhensi*). The original date of the mosque is unclear; however, it was renovated several times during the twentieth century, most recently in 1977.

FIG. 5.2 New mosque constructed in 1997, Three Family Village, Weishan.

by a religious identity that links them to a global Islamic community. These trends point to a growing Islamic consciousness facilitated by cultural opportunity and economic growth.

Whether built in the traditional way or in the newer, quasi-Arabic style, Yunnan Hui mosques share a number of characteristics. They are generally constructed around a four-walled courtyard (*siheyuan*), at the end of which sits the main building, typically a one-level prayer hall (*libaisi*). Adjoining the main yard is a small room or courtyard where pre-prayer ablutions can be performed. The other main building in a typical mosque complex, the *jiaobailou*, is a three- or four-storey tower from which the call to prayer is broadcast. Mosques may also feature classrooms and living quarters for religious teachers or a resident caretaker. Larger mosques that offer secondary and tertiary education in Arabic and Islamic studies, such as those in the villages of Daweigeng, Xiaoweigeng, and Huihuideng, include dormitory quarters and dining halls.

The interiors of prayer halls are usually bare, in comparison to Daoist and Buddhist temples with their plethora of gods and goddesses. Mosques contain neither statues or figures nor anything resembling an altar, since Islam forbids the worship of idols and graven images of animate beings. The carved wood panels in the doors of traditional Chinese-style mosques adhere to this injunction and lack such representations, but sometimes include abstract images of flowers and plants. They also may show objects relevant to the practice of Islam, such as a Koran, a crescent moon, or, as seen on one Weishan mosque door, a carving of a toothbrush and tube of toothpaste indicating the importance of cleanliness.

Along with serving as sites of worship, Hui mosques function as civic and economic institutions. Mosque communities raise funds to support a variety of public needs, such as mosque operating expenses, teachers' salaries, instructional materials, and special events. Funds may also support public goods and services that benefit non-Hui as well. Since the middle of the 1990s, mosques in Yongjian together have raised several million yuan for the construction of village roads and public schools.[36]

In contemporary Yunnan Hui villages, Islam increasingly shapes the rhythms of daily life. The call to prayer is broadcast over loudspeakers ten times a day, twice before each of the five daily prayers. First broadcast is a preliminary call, which alerts the faithful to put aside whatever tasks they are engaged in and prepare for prayer by washing face, hands, and feet. This is followed five or ten minutes later with another call indicating that prayers are about to commence—a signal for men to make their way to the mosque and for women to don a veil and lay out a prayer mat at home.[37] The walls of homes are laden with Islamic paraphernalia, such as photographs of Mecca, Arabic calligraphy, and calendars featuring pictures of famous mosques in China and the countries of the Middle East.

Religious festivals and holidays have been resurrected, including Ramadan and the Feast of the Prophet (also called Muhammad's Birthday). Not all Yunnan Hui observe holidays like Ramadan; adherence appears to be inversely correlated with urbanization. Many Hui I spoke to in Kunming and Dali stated that they do not fast during Ramadan because the demands of their urban jobs and lives make fasting too difficult, or because fasting draws unwanted attention from curious non-Muslims. Yet in Weishan, as in many other rural areas, Ramadan is strictly observed. Distinctly local festivals and holy days have also been revived. One of these is Wangren Jie, which commemorates those who died following the collapse of the Panthay Rebellion and the concomitant destruction of Weishan Muslim settlements. This holiday has no fixed date; in a given village it is typically held on the lunar date when that village was attacked and destroyed by Qing forces. Hui communities in other parts of Dali also observe the holiday. Each year, close to the anniversary of Du Wenxiu's suicide and posthumous decapitation, Dali Hui head to a site at the base of the Cang Mountains famous for its pink-hued rock slabs for prayer and remembrance.[38] Though such rock formations result from mineral deposits, they are seen as a symbolic manifestation of the spilled blood of Muslims massacred more than a century ago. Hui people offer prayers and recount the bitter history of Yunnan Muslims under the Qing, re-etching the event into Hui memory and myth.[39]

These holidays and festivals are more than just religious events. They are opportunities for the expression of Hui and Muslim identity and solidarity. Wangren Jie, for instance, is a local affair that reinscribes, through prayer and ritual, the historic tenuousness of Hui existence and the need to combat repression. In contrast, Ramadan temporally and ritually links Hui to a global Muslim community through fasting and prayer. Like the rocket festivals and temple rededication ceremonies in Dai communities, and like *benzhu* worship and pilgrimage circuits resurrected by the Bai, these events are also opportunities for socializing beyond the boundaries of village, township, county, and even prefecture.

These events can also serve as occasions of moral or political instruction, forums in which local elites remind the faithful of their religious and civic duties. The Feast of the Prophet is a case in point. In the parts of the

Muslim world where this holiday is celebrated, it is typically held on the twelfth day of the third month of the Muslim calendar. In Yunnan, however, the date on which it is celebrated varies from mosque to mosque, making it possible for Hui from neighboring communities to join in the festivities.[40] It is often combined with other events such as the dedication of a new mosque.

At one holiday event I attended in Dali in 1997, held in conjunction with the graduation of *ahong* from the Dali Muslim Culture College, an Islamic college attached to the mosque, visitors came from surrounding villages, Dali Old Town, the nearby commercial city of Xiaguan, and neighboring counties. Many visitors were friends and family of the graduates and other students; there were also a number of Hui elites from the municipal government and the Dali Islamic Association. The centerpiece of the event was the commencement ceremony for eight young men and women. Festivities included Arabic songs, recitations from the Koran, and a demonstration of Arabic conversation by children from the mosque school. After the ceremonies concluded, those in attendance were served an inexpensive lunch in the school cafeteria. Along with the performances, the feast, and the conferring of degrees, the event also included a sermon by a representative of the Islamic Association, in which he exhorted the faithful to fulfill the precepts and observe the prohibitions of Islam, especially prohibitions against alcohol and drugs. He stressed that because the use and sale of drugs are activities that transgress the laws of the country, they violate Islamic belief. Patriotism, he reminded his listeners, "is one aspect of religion" (*aiguo shi zongjiao de yibufen*); drug trafficking was unlawful and unpatriotic, and therefore un-Islamic.[41]

Holiday festivals such as this one highlight the extent to which Muslim networks and community linkages have been reestablished and expanded. A number of the secondary religious schools in Yunnan draw students from all over the province and even other provinces. Most students at the Dali Muslim Culture College are from Yunnan, but some come from as far away as Henan, Fujian, Gansu, and Xinjiang. Most are Hui, but several students and teachers are members of other Muslim *minzu*. Many of the larger schools occasionally host delegations from Saudi Arabia and other Muslim countries, whose members give lectures and evaluate curricula.

The reestablishment of inter-community networks is both a result of Islamic revival and a cause of its expansion. The mobility and openness of the reform years has allowed increased contact with the global Islamic world. International and domestic linkages also allow more orthodox

Yunnan Muslims to monitor the condition of the faith in scattered settlements. In several cases this has produced re-conversions of Muslim communities that had strayed from the precepts of Islam, such as the Hui-Dai of Menghai County in Xishuangbanna Prefecture. The Hui-Dai are descendents of a handful of Muslims who fled south from Dali after the defeat of the Panthay Rebellion. They settled in two villages among the Dai people of Xishuangbanna, and over time adopted local customs and the Dai language. They also adopted local dietary and religious customs, including pork consumption and the practice of animist and Buddhist rituals. In the late 1980s, religious and community leaders in the central Yunnan Hui community of Najiaying got wind of this situation, and dispatched a group of religious teachers to Menghai to reacquaint the Hui-Dai with Islamic beliefs and practices. From all appearances, and from conversations with students and the local imam, the re-conversion appears to have worked (fig 5.3).[42]

Re-conversion has also occurred in one remote village in Shangri-la County, a Tibetan autonomous county in northwest Yunnan (formerly called Zhongdian).[43] The village, called Haba, is in a Naxi autonomous township eighty miles from the county seat. Hui reside in two of the several natural villages that form Haba, which also includes Tibetan, Yi, Naxi and Han settlements. Haba lies in a remote valley at the base of snow-capped mountains. Public transport to the area is infrequent and irregular; buses go only as far as the township, and getting to the village requires several hours on foot or hiring a car.

Because of Haba's geography, for most of the twentieth century its residents were cut off from Muslim commercial and religious networks and other Hui communities. Like the Hui-Dai, the Haba Hui adopted many local habits and customs. This was often a matter of survival: the village is situated roughly 8,800 feet above sea level, the terrain is mountainous, and the region bitterly cold in winter. Consequently Muslims in Haba adopted local—that is, Tibetan—agricultural practices; they grow wheat, barley, corn, peppers, and raise yaks as well as lowland cattle and goats. Tibetan-style cheese and butter tea are staples of the local diet. In language and dress, too, the Hui adopted local practice. Their speech contains grammatical elements from the local Tibetan dialect, and some men and women continue to wear the thick, brightly embroidered, multicolor Tibetan-style wool robes and aprons of the region, at least in winter. For these reasons the Hui of this area are called "Zang Hui," or Tibetan Hui.[44]

Like the Hui-Dai, the Haba Hui also adopted the religious beliefs and practices of the groups around them. Post-Mao religious revival before

FIG. 5.3 Mosque melding traditional Chinese and Arabic elements, Menghai County

2000 had sparked a resurgence of Tibetan Buddhist, Naxi Dongba, and other folk rituals and practices—though not Islam. In 2000, Haba's situation was brought to the attention of Islamic leaders in Shadian, which is over five hundred miles southeast of Haba, not far from the border with Vietnam. These leaders, including the principal of an Arabic school, the directors of the Shadian Great Mosque, and the executive committee of the Shadian Foundation, raised funds to send copies of the Koran, teaching materials, and religious instructors to Haba. Hui from Kunming, Tonghai, Dali, and other regions also contributed to the effort. A wealthy entrepreneur from Shadian donated money to build a new mosque.[45] Today Islam appears to be flourishing in Haba. The village has a new mosque, a substantial grey brick structure built in the traditional Chinese style situated at one of the highest points in the village (fig. 5.4). Most villagers, men and women alike, pray at the mosque five times daily. Before praying, villagers wash in the hot and cold running water of the newly constructed bath facilities, also built with funds donated by affluent Yunnan Muslims from Shadian and other communities. Muslim head coverings are now ubiquitous, and some residents even pepper their speech with Arabic phrases.

This thoroughgoing and swift transformation underscores the strength of Hui religious and commercial networks. It also demonstrates the extent

FIG. 5.4 New mosque, constructed in 2000, in the traditional style, Haba, in Shangri-la Tibetan Autonomous County

to which the practice of Islam is central to the contemporary Hui self-understanding. Religiously observant Muslims from all over Yunnan are proud of Haba's re-conversion, seeing it as evidence of the power of their faith and the will of Allah. The Haba Hui have been brought back onto the straight and narrow, pure and true path. No longer are they "confused and perplexed in their spiritual yearnings," as the head of the Shadian Arabic School put it, the condition that presumably drove them to un-Islamic superstition in the first place.[46]

While Haba's Islamic revival is celebrated by the Hui, it has generated some problems regarding intra-village, inter-ethnic relations. Non-Muslim residents of Haba are perplexed by the rapid transformation among their Hui neighbors and their refusal to participate in non-Islamic rituals they had previously embraced. Others are bothered by the placement of the new mosque, which stands near a grove of trees, a mountain stream, and several springs considered sacred by Naxi, Yi, and other non-Hui from the surrounding villages. One Tibetan man who summarized the complaint argued, "A *minzu* must pay attention to and respect another *minzu's* religion and culture. Where the Hui built their new mosque is not good, it doesn't show respect. They could have built it a little lower down the mountain, away from the other [ritual] sites." While this man supported the Hui's right to practice their religion, he felt that some of their actions disrespected the religious beliefs of other groups.

Overall, however, the Islamic revival has benefited the Haba Hui, often in very tangible ways. It has ameliorated their isolation, ignorance, and to some extent their poverty. For some of Haba's young people, the revival has given them the opportunity for an education that otherwise would be beyond their reach. Many have received scholarships to study at Islamic schools in Shadian. Their studies focus almost exclusively on religion and Arabic. However, they are also learning to use computers and navigate the Internet. Some hope to continue their studies at colleges in Pakistan, Malaysia, or, ideally, Saudi Arabia. The revival of Islamic tradition, ironically, is thus a catalyst for the modernization of Haba, though the village is hardly modern even by rural Chinese standards. When I visited in 2002, most of the village lacked electricity owing to the breakdown half a year earlier of a nearby hydroelectric generating station. Pointing to an unusable washing machine, one villager expressed his frustration that while the rest of China was leaping ahead, Haba was going backwards ("Zhongguo fazhan, women tuibule!"). Still, the reintegration of the Haba Hui into Islamic networks in Yunnan and beyond has brought better sanitation, new well-constructed houses, and opportunities for Haba's young people to get an education. Islam serves as a vehicle through which the Haba Hui, especially the younger generation, encounter China's modernization and capitalist transformation.

Religious Education

Islamic education has been resuscitated along with other religious institutions; in parts of Yunnan, the post-Mao recovery of religious education, called *jingtang jiaoyu* in Chinese, was swift. In Weishan, religious courses were established in several mosques by the end of 1978, shortly after the completion of the Third Plenum. By the end of 1979, over two thousand students were enrolled in twenty mosque schools, each school offering at least basic instruction in Islamic belief and practice, the Koran, and elementary Arabic. Several of the largest mosques quickly established intermediate and advanced programs for youth in their late teens and twenties.[47] There are now more than a dozen secondary and tertiary Arabic and Islamic schools and colleges throughout Yunnan, many of them outgrowths of advanced programs based in the larger mosques. Funding for religious education comes from a variety of sources. Students at the middle and high-school level typically pay tuition, but operating expenses are also supported by community donations and tithes offered on holy days throughout the year.

Religious education is an important component of Hui Islamic identity and practice in China, central to the propagation and maintenance of the faith. It has a long pedigree in Yunnan; during the eighteenth and nineteenth centuries and up until the 1950s, Islamic schools in Shadian, Weishan, Tonghai, and other communities with sizeable Hui populations were renowned throughout the region. These schools drew students from around the province and across China. Weishan even earned the moniker "Little Mecca," since so many Muslim students and scholars traveled there to teach and study. Historically, religious education in Yunnan was not limited in focus to Islam and Arabic (or Persian). Instead, the education offered was *zhong'a bingshou*, "Chinese-Arabic dual education." The curriculum at these religious schools was nearly identical to that offered at non-Muslim private academies, except that the former included courses on Islam, Arabic, and sometimes Persian in addition to classically Chinese fare.

The dual educational approach continued into the twentieth century. The curriculum of many private Hui schools established after the May Fourth Movement reflected that movement's concern with modern science and culture. The most well known of these was the Mingde School, established in Kunming in 1926 by prominent local Muslim intellectuals, many of them May Fourth activists.[48] In rural Weishan, the local branch of the China Islamic Association established the Xingjian Middle School in 1943, which offered courses in Chinese language and literature, history, math, natural science, music, physical education, Arabic, and Islam. Although most Xingjian students were drawn from the local Hui population, non-Hui students also attended, primarily because of the quality of the Chinese education these schools provided.

Today, many Islamic schools focus almost exclusively on religious subjects and the Arabic language skills necessary to study Islam. They do so partly because students are expected to acquire a standard, Chinese education in state schools. Islamic education is supposed to be supplemental, not unlike the Confraternity of Christian Doctrine (CCD), an after-school religious instruction program for Catholic children who attend public school in the United States and elsewhere. Courses on Islam for younger children and working adults are typically offered in the evenings, outside of normal

FIG. 5.5 Hui children in a village mosque school, Menghai

school hours (fig. 5.5). Full-day intermediate and advanced programs enroll students who in theory have already graduated middle or high school. Yet in practice that is not always the case: at a girls' school I visited in Weishan, most of the two dozen or so students had finished middle school, but a handful possessed only primary school diplomas.

Despite the narrow focus of contemporary Islamic instruction, students are enthusiastic about its practicality. According to one student enrolled in a school that focuses almost exclusively on Islam and Arabic, learning about Islam was helping him to become a better Muslim. Arabic, he stated in all earnestness, "is the mother tongue of the Hui, because we are Muslim. It is important that I learn to read and speak the language of my *minzu*." It should be noted that the mother tongue (*muyu*) of the Hui is typically the Chinese dialect of the regions where they live, a fact which did not trouble this young man's analysis. Like many students, he expressed the hope that after graduating he might go abroad to continue his studies, in which case knowledge of Arabic would serve him well. Naïvely or not, this student saw his future as linked to an Islamic world, not necessarily a Chinese one.

Officials and some educators, including many who are Hui, are concerned about the neglect of nonreligious subjects at Islamic schools. As mentioned, this narrow focus should not be a problem, since religious education is intended to supplement a regular, state education. However, some Hui regard religious education as a replacement for mainstream schooling, and a superior one at that. They see Islamic education as necessary for the protection and advancement of their people and their faith. The decision to pull students out of public school and enroll them in religious courses is a repudiation of state education and even of mainstream Chinese culture, a repudiation driven by the history of persecution from the Qing era until the leftist excesses of the Mao years. According to the authors of a study on minority education, this history still resonates among contemporary Hui:

> Many worry that Islam may die out in China, and that Hui cultural traditions and customs may be lost. In recent years, due to the Party's new policies, the Hui masses have acquired the right to religious freedom. . . . Still, many people fear that . . . the religion of Allah is disappearing in front of their eyes, so they let their children quit school and enroll in mosque education instead. This problem is very serious and has even disturbed the normal system of education, causing enrollment, continuation, and graduation rates in Hui areas to drop.[49]

Far from assuaging Hui fears, policies of religious freedom have exacerbated a sense of urgency regarding the preservation of Islam and Hui culture. Sending children to mosque rather than state schools is an effort to counter anti-Hui threats, real or perceived, and the tide of secular assimilation. Because of the historical experience of persecution, argue the study authors, some Hui "despise" and "underestimate" all elements of Han culture—that is, Chinese culture, including Chinese education—and reject it in favor of Islam.[50]

This situation is compounded by broader problems concerning education and literacy in rural Hui communities. As with Buddhist temple schools in Xishuangbanna, the revitalization of Islamic education in the 1980s and 1990s coincided with a drop in public school enrollment rates. This drop was partly the result of economic reforms. Schooling became more expensive as new economic opportunities created incentives for parents to put their children to work, on the farm or in the marketplace. The shift to the household responsibility system and a market economy, along with increases in school fees, led rural families throughout China to pull their children out of school. However, in Hui regions, the economy is not the only culprit; the availability of Islamic education exacerbates this trend. Over the last three decades, enrollment rates in many Hui communities have lagged behind those of neighboring Han and other minority communities, even where Hui communities are economically better off than their neighbors.[51]

The complexity of such matters shows that they are not simply manifestations of cultural identity. Rather, they result from interactions among a variety of cultural, economic, and historical phenomena, such as poverty, new entrepreneurial opportunities, inter-ethnic mistrust, and the collective remembrance of repression. They highlight the dilemmas posed by Islamic revival, especially for officials. Certain customs at times undermine party-state objectives. Yet if it improves relations between the Hui and the party-state, tolerance for Muslim identity and practice can buttress state authority and help maintain the social order.

Tradition and Identity in Islamic Education

Many Hui educators, officials, and religious leaders are conscious of the negative consequences of Islamic revival and have sought ways to reconcile religious goals with official objectives. For instance, in the field of religious education there are alternatives to the Arabic- and Islamic-only approach. A few of the Islamic schools established in Yunnan in recent years offer expanded curricula, which updates the tradition of *zhong'a bingshou* for the twenty-first century. Two examples are the Kaiyuan Arabic Vocational School and the Dali Muslim Culture College (fig. 5.6). Both are patterned after state-run technical or vocational schools (*zhuanke xuexiao*). At the Kaiyuan Arabic School, students study Islamic theology, philosophy, history, and the classical Arabic needed to read religious texts, but they also take courses in modern Arabic conversation, comprehension and composition, business Arabic, newspaper reading, Chinese literature, and Chinese history. English and computer science are offered as electives. The college in Dali offers a similar curriculum, along with geography, math, and science. It also offers a program in Chinese language education; graduates of the program who pass state exams are qualified to teach Chinese in elementary or middle schools. For many students, the degrees they receive there are likely to be their highest. However, some go on to study Arabic in foreign language departments of Chinese universities, or to universities elsewhere in the Muslim world. In this way, for Hui and other Chinese Muslim students, Arabic and Islamic education can be a means of enhancing their skills and improving their employment prospects.

Teachers at the college in Dali claim that their goal is to train students to be both devout Muslims and productive members of China's rapidly

FIG. 5.6 Mosque flanking basketball courts at the Dali Muslim Culture College, Dali. The mosque was completed in 2001.

modernizing society. Several express concerns about the trend toward an Arabic and Islam-only curriculum at other Islamic institutions. According to the retired principal of the college, this trend is "based on narrow thinking":

> Some Muslims wish to separate themselves from all non-Muslims and believe that the only suitable course of study is an Arabic and Islamic one. At the same time, many people believe that non-Muslims should not study Arabic or anything having to do with Islamic religion, philosophy, or history.[52]

The problem with Islamic education in Yunnan, the retired principal explains, is twofold. First, although Islamic school organizers are supposed to secure government approval prior to establishing Islamic schools, there are few if any curricular requirements such schools must meet, with the exception of a few self-study courses like the Chinese language education program offered in Dali. Second, Muslim religious educators themselves had not yet established a set of standards, and consequently curricula varied from school to school, depending on the personal views of religious leaders and teachers.

From the principal's perspective, the phenomenon of Arabic- and Islamic-only education, while seen by some as a return to the past—to "fundamentals"—ignores the history of Yunnan Hui Muslims. That past, he argues, was one of engagement with and achievement in Chinese society, which traditional Hui education reflected. The most accomplished Hui scholars in history, he points out, knew the classics of Chinese culture as well as the sacred texts of Islam. The retired principal also compares the practices of his school to traditional Islamic education in Yunnan, which except for its religious component was indistinguishable from the education offered in non-Muslim schools of the period. In his view, the Dali Muslim Culture College epitomizes authentic Hui tradition, while the Islamic and Arabic-only trend spurns it.

In making his case, this retired principal echoes the claims of scholarship on the Hui, much of it produced by Hui researchers, educators, and officials. This scholarship, which includes provincial, county, and national histories, social scientific analyses of contemporary Hui life, and studies of Islam in China, typically advances several key points. First, scholars emphasize that the Hui possess a historical and cultural "Chineseness." The Hui are who they are because of the melding of Islamic and Han cultural elements; the combination of these two streams of culture gave rise to this nationality. As one Yunnan Hui scholar writes, "without Islamic culture there would be no Hui, just as without Han culture there would be no Hui minority."[53] In the words of another, the culture of the Hui is "Islam with Chinese characteristics."[54]

Much of this scholarship further stresses that acculturation to Han culture has long been a central component of Hui culture and tradition. The Hui are a "relatively advanced" *minzu* in great part because of their adoption and adaptation of Han *wenhua*, or Han culture. Yunnan Muslim adaptability enabled the Hui to attain great economic, political, and social influence, from the Yuan Dynasty to the present. As writers on the subject are apt to point out, the adaptation of Chinese culture is no threat to a "pure and true," *qingzhen* Islamic existence. This latter claim is buttressed by references to the efforts of Islamic scholars during the Ming and Qing who used Confucian, Daoist, and Buddhist principles to explain the truths of Islam to a Chinese audience.[55] Finally, this scholarship argues that the Islamic revival must embrace this tradition of integration and acculturation, since it is central to Hui advancement. It is central also to the development of China: "the revival of the greatness of the Chinese nation requires that Islam advance with the times, and the development and progress of the Islamic faith of the Hui is inseparable from the greatness of the Chinese nation."[56]

Critics of mosque education fear that in its current incarnation, it is an obstacle to the continued vitality and development of the Hui. Consequently, they advocate a curriculum that can respond to the spiritual needs of Muslims and the demands of contemporary life. Some reformers have even proposed that mosque schools offer, along with a conventional curriculum, technical training in subjects such as agricultural technology, enterprise management, and computers. Educators, these critics and reformers argue, ought to model themselves on earlier generations of Muslim teachers and religious leaders; *jingtang jiaoyu* should "meet the needs of Hui masses in the twenty-first century."[57]

Although calls for the modernization of education are informed by concerns regarding practicality and relevance, they are simultaneously an assertion of identity—of a particular understanding of what it means to be Hui and of the traditions that constitute and express that identity. What worries many of the writers on this topic is that the widespread embrace of an Arabic- and Islamic-only education entails not just a rejection of a modernizing Chinese society but a repudiation of genuine Hui identity and tradition. Furthermore, one writer explains in an article on a mosque's website, the neglect of Chinese culture and language hinders the development of the faith by preventing Hui Muslims from comprehending great Chinese texts on Islam:

> When we look back at the great [Chinese] Muslim scholars . . . we see that their many contributions to their country and their nationality are inseparable from their deep comprehension of the Han language. If they had lacked this fundamental knowledge of the Han language, would we be able to read the great variety of works they produced?[58]

The genius of the Hui in bygone eras, those who promote a Chinese-Islamic identity argue, was their ability to meld Islamic and Chinese cultural elements. This melding was more than useful—it is who the Hui were in the past and who they are now.

These arguments dovetail with the views and interests of the Chinese state. In expressing their concerns and plans for reform, Hui teachers, scholars, and officials are articulating an officially sanctioned position. Most of these individuals are directly or indirectly linked to the state: party and state cadres, scholars at universities and research institutions, and promi nent members of the Islamic and Hui studies associations. Moreover, the books and articles that contain their views are published by state-approved and state-managed presses and journals. Their concerns reveal that the Chinese state is interested not only in what minorities do, but also in how they think about themselves and their place in Chinese society. Behavior and practices are chief among the government's preoccupations, and it seeks to contain or quash those that appear to contravene its political and economic agenda. Yet identity and tradition and how they are defined are also matters of state concern, as the discourse on Islamic education reveals.

The reformist writings of Hui scholars, educators, and officials, however, are not mere expressions of the party line. While scholars and educators are limited in what they can publicly advocate, by challenging the isolationist tendencies of contemporary religious education, these scholars counter what they see as a false tradition with one they view as authentically Hui. A Hui identity that is as Chinese as it is Islamic, as modern as it is traditional, resonates in interviews with teachers, students, and ordinary people, including the retired principal of the Muslim college in Dali.

Yet the strictly Arabic and Islamic focus of much contemporary religious instruction and existence also has roots in Chinese Muslim tradition, specifically the Yihewani movement of the late nineteenth and early twentieth centuries. The leaders of the Yihewani, who were influenced by Wahhabi fundamentalist teachings, advocated an Islam stripped of the Chinese aesthetic and ritual elements that characterized much Chinese Muslim practice. Its founder, Ma Wanfu, promoted a purified, Arabic aesthetic in dress, speech, architecture, and education. Ma Wanfu even called for the separation of Muslim and non-Muslim communities, and according to Jonathan Lipman, "refused to learn to read and write Chinese, forbade his children to learn Chinese, and insisted on Arabic and Persian education as the foundation of Muslim orthopraxy."[59] Although members of subsequent generation of Yihewani were ardent Chinese nationalists and modernizers, the Salafiyya, a movement that grew out of the Yihewani in the 1930s, called for what Gladney describes as "a return to nonpoliticized fundamentalist Wahhabi

ideals."[60] In some Yunnan Hui communities, the influence of the Yihewani
in the early twentieth century was profound, despite the numerical strength
of the Gedimu.[61] Yihewani teachings continue to shape religious practice
and education because of this history and the growing global prominence
of Wahhabi Islam. Though hard to quantify, Wahhabi and Salafi influence
in China itself is increasing. The Yihewani are estimated by some to be the
"predominant force" within the national Islamic Association.[62]

The efforts of some Hui to create an existence apart from mainstream
Chinese social and cultural life must be seen within a broader context than
immediate concerns for preserving religious identity. Isolationism and
withdrawal are inherent neither in Islam nor in Hui Muslim identity and
beliefs. Rather, the Hui's motivation to withdraw from surrounding society
is borne of centuries of conflict between Chinese state and Muslims and
between Muslims and other social groups—conflicts in which Muslims
have often been singled out for discrimination, repression, and violent persecution. Tensions between the state and Chinese Muslims are aggravated
by the global War on Terror, which has provided the government an excuse
to crack down on Islamic activities that it alone deems troublesome, with
little if any condemnation from abroad. The desire to constitute a life separate from non-Muslim society may stem from a self-protective impulse
more than anything.

MODERNITY, TRADITION, AND HUI IDENTITY

Religious revival among the Hui is not aimed simply at resurrecting the
past but also at developing and modernizing cultural identity and practice. Even Yihewani fundamentalism is in some ways a neo-traditionalist
attempt to grapple with modernity and its implications for the faith. For
some Yunnan Muslims, celebration and exploration of their Hui identity
also involves probing what it means to be Chinese. As is the case throughout China more generally, where rapid social and economic change has
altered the relationship of Chinese people to their past and their traditions,
debates about tradition and identity are embedded within a broader discourse of modernization and development.

While religious concerns underpin Hui desires to study and practice
Islam, including efforts to go abroad for these purposes, the issue is more
complex. Many Hui discuss Arabic and religious education in terms of
minzu improvement and development. One teenage girl studying at a village mosque in Weishan and preparing to become a teacher put the matter

this way: "I feel that my *minzu* will develop quickly. I want to improve my Arabic and knowledge of Islam so that I will be at the forefront of that development, so that I can participate in the development of my *minzu*."[63] For this girl and for others, the study and promotion of Islam is a matter of minority development. Among the Hui, as among the Dai and Bai, the concern with modernization and development is minority-centric.

The modernity of Islam and its compatibility with modernizing Chinese ideals is asserted in a number of ways. Islam is argued to be particularly suitable for a reforming socialist market economy. In contemporary Chinese writing on minorities, the market is increasingly seen as the answer to minority backwardness, and the solution to the task of national integration. Numerous official and academic publications from the early 1990s onward describe, in laudatory terms that would make Karl Marx blush, how the market is breaking down local barriers, eroding regional differences, linking disparate minority groups in a web of commodities exchange, and enhancing the mutual interdependence among all the *minzu* who comprise the Chinese nation. In response to this valorization of the market, Muslim scholars are quick to highlight Islam's affinity with trade and commerce. Books and articles on the relation between Islam and economics note that many of the original Muslims in China were Arabic and Persian traders and that the Hui dominated commerce and long-distance trade in Yunnan during the nineteenth and early twentieth centuries. That Muhammad himself engaged in commerce before dedicating himself to the spread of the faith further enhances the close connection between the two; "trade and commerce are enterprises loved by Allah."[64]

Basic religious principles underlie arguments that Islam is particularly conducive to a market economy. Monopolies, including state ones, and restricted markets are inconsistent with Islamic belief. If all things under Heaven are created by Allah, then, according to one Chinese Islamic scholar, "closed markets are antithetical to this [belief], since they . . . restrict the free flow and exchange of all that Allah has created." Islam's this-worldly emphasis on striving and engagement rather than renunciation, continues the writer, also coheres with reformist, market-oriented goals:

> Among the world's great religions, Islam not only emphasizes this world more than others, it is a religion that enters the world, and simultaneously advocates trade, commercial activity, markets and market standards. In Islamic classic texts . . . there are many references to commerce and markets, much more than in the texts or thought of other religions.[65]

Because it emphasizes worldly striving and self-improvement, and because of the respect it commands for all that Allah has made, "for Islam, trade, commerce and the expansion of markets are noble enterprises."[66]

To assert the modernity of Islam, Hui also draw distinctions between their religion and the "superstitious" practices of other minorities. The teenage girls at the women's mosque school in Weishan repeated this distinction frequently. They elaborated, for instance, on the sensible and scientific thinking behind requirements to wash one's hands, feet, and face five times a day before prayer, and on the logic behind other basic precepts. In their view, the syncretic mix of Buddhism, Daoism, and other folk beliefs of the Han, Yi, Bai, and others was useless superstition and idol-worship that lacked a rational basis.

Science and the alleged scientific basis of Islam are preoccupations among many Chinese Muslims. Islamic websites and written publications are brimming with articles discussing the rationality of religious practices and how Islamic beliefs prefigure modern scientific discoveries such as the Big Bang, interstellar matter, plate tectonics, embryonic development, and others.[67] At the Dali Muslim Culture College, a retired science teacher who now teaches courses on science and Islam expounded on the need to demonstrate their compatibility. Understanding the scientific basis of Islam is essential if one is to appreciate the truth and logic of Islam, he explained. In addition, in a world of skepticism, appealing to science is a way of drawing people in, of piquing their interest. Using science allowed him to demonstrate the truths of Islam and the Koran and to prove that the latter is "the only Bible."[68]

There are a number of reasons for this concern with Islam's scientific and anti-superstitious tendencies, some of which are practical and strategic. For one thing, it distinguishes Islam from "mere" superstition. For many Hui, Islam's scientific basis is both indisputable and a mark of its superiority. Although Yunnan Muslims are convinced of Islam's truth on religious grounds, comparisons to the "superstitious" beliefs and practices of other groups bolster that sense of its superiority. The Hui's insistence that Islam is scientific and therefore nonsuperstitious also seems pragmatic because the Chinese state, while officially supporting both religion and science, is hostile to what it deems superstition, although the definition of that term is ambiguous. The focus on science is, however, more than a strategy, for defense or otherwise. In *The Battle for God*, Karen Armstrong argues that the effort to reconcile faith with scientific truth and method is a feature of contemporary fundamentalist movements, regardless of creed.[69] Islamic movements in the Middle East increasingly stress the religion's connection to science and modernization.[70] The Hui preoccupation with the compatibility of faith and science reveals the extent to which Chinese Islam is tied to trends in global Islam. As seemingly remote as many Hui villages are, Islamic schools like the colleges in Dali and Kaiyuan are linked to currents in international Islamic thought, practice, and culture.

The emphasis on science and modernity also reflects the influence of the Yihewani. As discussed above, although the movement called for a return to scriptural and ritual purity, proponents also sought to modernize religious study. Key leaders studied in Egypt and Arabia, as well as Japan and the United States, in the late nineteenth and early twentieth centuries. There they were influenced by trends in Islam and by overseas Chinese student associations promoting modern Chinese nationalism; the Yihewani movement became a kind of May Fourth Islam.[71] The influence of the Yihewani on religious belief and education in Yunnan resonates in contemporary ideals of national development and scientific progress.

ISLAMIC RESURGENCE AND ITS DISCONTENTS

While the Islamic revival at times conflicts with state policy, as the example of mosque education shows, for the Hui in Yunnan their religious resurgence is a source of pride and satisfaction. They view this resurgence through the lens of their "tortuous and winding" history and a heightened awareness of their forebears' accomplishments in the spheres of religion, politics, culture, and economics. They are also cognizant of the role of oppression in shaping their past and present. The Hui revival is informed by the rich history not only of political and military success and economic prowess, but also of persecution at the hands of non-Muslims and the Chinese state.

Several Hui students and teachers I interviewed in 1997 linked the revival of their faith to a sense of obligation to "oppose oppression" (*fandui yapo*), which one student at the Dali college described as an integral element of Islam. They are quick to defend their religious practices and educational endeavors and their right to engage in them. Like the Dai and Bai cultural activists, many Hui are concerned with rights and autonomy, particularly with the right to practice their religion. The students and teachers witnessed what they believe were violations of these protected rights; their fear that what they have seen constitutes repression is not without foundation. Officials have in fact tried to restrict the expansion of mosque schools as part of the drive to implement compulsory education. Since 1994, the government has also required all religious institutions to register with the authorities and submit to inspections.

Yunnan Hui perceive some spillover from the crackdown on Muslim separatism and religious practice in Xinjiang that began in the mid-1990s. In 1996 and 1997, following a series of bombings in Urumqi and Beijing, the government stepped up its efforts to quell Uyghur separatist activity in Xinjiang Province. The crackdown expanded to include limitations on ordinary worship activities, Islamic education, the publishing of religious texts, and the construction of new mosques. A report on Xinjiang Television in May 1996 "stressed the need to 'consolidate and cleanse the book and magazine market'" specifically of books "privately printed and circulated without the state's prior examination and approval."[72] The Communist Party in Xinjiang also moved against religious party members and called "for efforts to sternly deal with party members and cadres, especially leading cadres, who continue to be devout religious believers, despite re-education."[73] That same year Xinjiang police shut down a number of "illegal" mosques and religious schools, confiscated religious material for being "reactionary," and clamped down on illegal religious activities on college campuses.[74]

While the crackdown focused on Xinjiang, several thousand miles to the northwest, teachers and students interviewed in 1997 in Weishan and Dali knew of it and were angered by the obstacles their co-religionists faced in promoting religious education. "It is getting very difficult to open new schools in villages," one teacher explained, "and when schools are established, they are only allowed to have three or four students." They attributed these difficulties to the state's hostility toward Islam. When asked whether the situation for Muslims had not in fact improved greatly during the reform period, they were skeptical of the rights and autonomy ostensibly promised by the state. In the view of one female student, "that is just a show for foreigners. In reality, the government wants to control religion, especially Islam."[75] Many Yunnan Hui went out of their way to explain that Islam in no way contravened their loyalty to China. More than one person reiterated the slogan painted on walls and buildings throughout rural Hui villages: "*Aiguo shi zongjiao de yi bufen*" (Patriotism is one part of religion). Hui view official and unofficial restrictions on religious practice as not just a hindrance but an insult.

Despite the limitations to religious practice, many indicators suggest that materially and spiritually, life is better now for the Hui—in Yunnan at least—compared to the pre-reform period. Prejudice and persecution exist, but the contemporary situation bears little resemblance to the anti-religious environment of the Maoist era. Rising economic and religious expectations may account for some of the frustration, though the Hui's resentment of the increased suspicion of all Muslims due to Xinjiang unrest is genuine. Ongoing surveillance and regulation do not appear to have quelled Islamic life in Yunnan, which is thriving.

HUI VERSUS ISLAMIC REVIVAL

The concerns about the treatment of Islam in Xinjiang reveal that not only ethnic but also religious identity is a central feature in the Hui revival. Officially, being Hui means being a member of a minority *minzu*. The state perceives Hui identity as having an ethnic or ethno-national character rather than a religious one; being a member of the Hui *minzu* does not mean that one follows a certain religion, just that one shares certain ethno-cultural characteristics with other members of that group. However, a distinct criteria of Hui identity is belief in Islam, even for those whose beliefs and practices have lapsed.

Prior to the twentieth century and the minority classification project initiated by the Communist regime, Muslims in China were typically called "Hui-Hui" or "Hui-min," terms which refer to a religious rather than an ethnic identity. "Hui-Hui" was, in theory, an inclusive concept that could be applied to many Chinese Muslims. The term Huizu (or Hui *minzu*) is exclusive and applies only to a single officially recognized group of Chinese Muslims. Some members of that group might not even practice Islam.

Dru Gladney has argued that the Hui in contemporary China generally accept the ethnic implications of the official classificatory system. Though Hui identity is elaborated and expressed in a variety of ways, he argues that many Hui understand their identity in ethno-cultural rather than religious terms. Maoist and post-Mao policies have caused ethnonyms like Huizu to harden; that is, Hui and other minorities are increasingly identifying themselves as members of their respective *minzu* and engaging in collective action on the basis of those identities:

> A process of ethnogenesis has . . . brought [Hui communities] closer together in dialectical interaction with state policy and local traditions. Through acceptance of the ethnic label assigned by the state, increased communication, education in special state minority schools, and the desire for more political power through larger numbers, ethnic groups are beginning to argue for the national

unity of their people—a process of pan-ethnic nationalization noted by Benedict Anderson.[76]

Gladney finds evidence for this ethnogenesis in shifting interpretations of the saying *"Tianxia de Hui-Hui shi yi jia"* (All Hui-Hui under Heaven are one family). In this phrase, "Hui-Hui" historically referred to all Muslims. However, as Gladney finds, it "is now taken by the Hui as referring only to the unity of their own people," e.g., the Hui *minzu*. Thus, where the term Hui-Hui once referred to people who followed the Islamic religion, contemporary Hui see themselves as members of an ethnic collectivity distinct from other Muslim groups.

Gladney's findings may reflect the fact that much of his research has focused on Hui communities in China's northwest and in Beijing, where a variety of Muslim minorities co-exist and where intra-Muslim differences and boundaries are more significant.[77] In Yunnan, however, nearly all Muslims are Hui, with the exception of some recent immigrants and itinerant traders from other provinces. Consequently, the term Hui more often than not means "Muslim." It is not an exclusive, ethnic designation, but rather the name for all those who practice Islam. In Yunnan, the terms Hui and Han are used interchangeably with the words for Muslim and non-Muslim (Musilin and *fei* Musilin, respectively); several people I spoke to even referred to Saudi Arabia and Iran as "Hui" countries. In rural Hui areas, the first question most people asked me was, "Are you Hui or Han?" This was usually followed by, "What is your religion?"—a question only Chinese Muslims asked. On occasion people simply assumed that I was Hui, that is, Muslim. At a wedding I attended in the company of a group of teenage girls studying to be *ahong*, a middle-aged woman, seeing me with a group of head-scarf wearing young women, ran to me, grabbed my arm, and exclaimed, "Tai hao ni shi Huizu!" (It's so great that you're Hui!). I would have been happy to let her persist in her error, as she seemed overjoyed to meet a foreign Muslim. However, it seemed imperative that I explain that I was not Muslim, though Hui history in China was of great interest to me.

At the women's mosque in Weishan and at the college in Dali, students and teachers gently tried to convert me. Several of them expressed the hope that as I continued to spend time with them and learn more about Islam, I would inevitably recognize the scientific and religious truths of Islam. As one teacher put it, "We hope that you will convert to Islam and become a famous Muslim scholar." If I did convert, she continued, my experiences studying the Hui would be vastly different. Doors would open to me, people would consider me as "one of their own family," and I would be shown great hospitality. This puzzled me, as their hospitality had been more than generous.[78]

For these Hui, religion appears to be the relevant marker of identity. As one man explained, "the special characteristic of the Hui is this: other nationalities are first a *minzu*, then develop a religion. However, the Hui had religion first, and then became a *minzu*. The Hui were made by, created by religion."[79] This man further insisted that to understand the Hui, one must read the Koran; without doing so one could not comprehend what it means to be Hui. Being Hui means being Muslim, non-Hui is a synonym for non-Muslim, and Han can be a synonym for non-Muslim as well. This broad interpretation of the term Han is not unique to the Hui; in rural villages in Xishuangbanna, children on occasion called me "haw hoa leung," Dai for "yellow-haired Han."[80] Officially designated ethnonyms such as "Hui" are widely accepted, yet their meanings are fluid and contested.

These shifting interpretations are not limited to rural Yunnan. Urban Hui often use the terms Hui and Muslim, or Han and non-Muslim, interchangeably. Some Hui in Kunming expressed cynicism regarding government-imposed categories. One Kunming noodle shop proprietor dismissed the official minority classification scheme: "Hui, Uyghur, Dongxiang—we're all the Islamic *minzu*!"[81] The term he used, "Yisilan *minzu*," is not an officially recognized category. The use of separate terms to draw distinctions among Muslim groups, he argued, is "the government's attempt to keep us apart." In his view the state fears that Chinese Muslims might indeed behave as "one family under Heaven," so it splits Muslims into ten distinct *minzu*. Yet the state often treats Muslims *as* Muslims, as members of a single entity rather than as separate *minzu*, in its efforts to monitor Muslims and Islam.

LIMITS TO HUI INCLUSION

In their efforts to promote Islamic revival, many of those involved assert the legitimacy of their goals by situating them within contemporary Chinese discourses concerning national modernization, science, patriotism, and the market economy. They draw on official PRC policy in their efforts to promote religious education and transnational Islamic connections. Doing so reduces their "opportunity costs" by rendering their activities and ideals palatable to the state. Yet their actions are also aimed at expanding the meaning and practice of minority autonomy and at holding the state to its legal and political promises.

Hui cultural activism is informed also by the history of Muslim rebellion against persecution. The party-state has tried to appropriate this into a broader history of class struggle and revolution, which presents the Hui with opportunities and constraints. If Hui history is viewed as part of the history of class struggle, then Hui struggles for religious autonomy are justified through historic and ostensibly patriotic models of resistance. At the same time, showing Hui history as part of the history of revolution contributes to an image of the Hui as an aggrieved people who are on guard against attacks on their communities, their livelihoods, and their religion. This need for communal vigilance has not been alleviated by twentieth-century attacks on Muslims and on Islam.

Hui people see the defense of their religion as a righteous struggle against oppression, existing within the context of Chinese national narratives of modernization and development. Unfortunately, their ability to use this context to full advantage is hindered by non-Muslim, popular views of the Hui as simply being contentious—the Hui propensity to cause trouble. Some non-Muslim Chinese take a dim view of Hui religious and cultural practice, ironically due, in part, to Chinese assumptions regarding modernization and its presumed incompatibility with religious identity and belief. As one Han man I talked to exclaimed, "Why don't the Hui just admit that they're modern and give up their religion?"[82]

Part of the problem for the Hui is that they are regarded as "relatively advanced." They do not fit the stereotype of the docile, passive, backward minority. Instead they are noted for their cohesion, commercial savvy, and cultural accomplishments, and for their adherence to practices that other Chinese find strange, such as abstention from the consumption of pork. They are both assimilated and separate—nonexotic others who maintain a distinct identity even though they lack characteristics typically associated with minorities. In the face of their obviously advanced character, Hui adherence to faith and practice is viewed by some non-Muslims as a willful attempt to assert their separateness and claim minority privileges on the basis of an outmoded identity. Non-Hui suspicion of the Hui stems from the widespread notion that Hui behavior and belief ought to reflect their "modern" existence. If the Hui can define the modern and themselves in a way that is simultaneously Hui, Muslim, and Chinese, they may find a way out of this dilemma.

—6—

CONCLUSION

Cultural revival among the Dai, Bai, and Hui has taken a variety of forms. Members of these groups have plumbed the past for inspiration and have explored new modes of identity articulation. They have both resuscitated tradition and established new organizations and practices. The revival is an outgrowth of the post-Mao state's more tolerant and even supportive stance toward minority cultural expression and institutions. This accommodating attitude is a dramatic change from how the state treated minorities during the radical phases of Chinese socialism, from the high tide of collectivization through the Cultural Revolution. Colin Mackerras argues that the state's altered attitude entails a return to some of the policies and practices of the years immediately following the founding of the People's Republic of China.[1] At that time, the CCP wanted to enhance its authority among a diverse population, much like Deng Xiaoping's regime did at the start of the reform era. Among groups like the Dai that had been only minimally integrated into the economy, polity, and culture of pre-Communist China, the CCP's state- and nation-building efforts relied on established cultural institutions and a traditional elite, many of whom were integrated into the new party-state apparatus.

Today, however, tolerant cultural policies have been extended toward ostensibly assimilated or integrated groups like the Hui and Bai, whereas in the 1950s, they were subject, for the most part, to assimilative policies applied in Han areas. Their identities are now generally celebrated and promoted. The reasons for the shift are many. For one thing, officials have had to acknowledge and respond to disasters perpetrated during the Cultural Revolution against minorities, especially the Hui. This response at times appears superficial, since Lin Biao and the Gang of Four, rather than the CCP itself, are still blamed for the destruction and persecution of that era. Nevertheless, the government has demonstrated remorse and a commitment to minority cultural autonomy, as in the example of the Muslim community of Shadian.

The post-Mao treatment of minorities is distinctive also for the manner in which minority and economic policy intersect. Minority culture, and even minorities themselves, are regarded as resources to be developed and deployed for the purpose of economic growth. The packaging and consumption of exotic cultural artifacts and practices fuel development, and in so doing they help diversify the economies of minority areas. County and township officials have tried to meld ostensibly traditional handicrafts with modern manufacturing methods and market incentives to spur the growth of the rural enterprise sector. Such efforts are more successful in areas like Dali and Xishuangbanna, where minority exotica combined with climate and scenery entice tourists and investors. Officials in less geographically favored areas, including remote parts of these same prefectures, are also trying to capitalize on the cultural resources at hand, though their efforts face serious challenges. Among the Hui, who are regarded warily by the state and by non-Muslims, ethno-cultural identity is somewhat less available as a resource for commercial exploitation. This is partly because, after centuries of integration into Chinese society, the Hui are not considered exotic.

The state regards cultural revival among the Dai, Bai, and Hui groups differently. The Dai and Bai have the advantage of long being seen as both cooperative and exotic, though the Bai are considered less exotic than the Dai. In a way, the phenomenon of "internal orientalism" identified by Louisa Schein—that is, the idealization by a majority group of minorities as alien, feminized others—benefits them. The Bai and Dai and the leaders of their respective autonomous prefectures have successfully packaged their identities to exploit market opportunities.[2] Because they are perceived as cooperative, even docile, the risk that cultural revival will foment any group solidarity that might be at odds with national cohesion is seen as small. Furthermore, these two groups are politically powerful in their respective prefectures. The participation of CCP officials in religious ritual and cultural practice is acknowledgment of the groups' local power and position. The relative influence of minorities in the prefectures, counties, and regions where they live may be a key variable in determining the treatment they receive from the state, in particular the extent to which the state supports their religious and cultural endeavors.

The party-state in Yunnan also tolerates a range of religious expression among less easily marketable groups like the Hui. It even supports activities like the hajj which enhance transnational Islamic ties. By allowing minority cultures to flourish, the contemporary party-state tries to distinguish itself from its repressive predecessor and thereby enhance its standing with minority peoples. Officials recognize the indispensability, to use Duara's term, of a minority "cultural nexus": local, heterogeneous, symbolic, and meaning-laden cultural institutions that facilitate state power and legitimacy. At times the state behaves like a "cultural entrepreneur," hard at work expanding the "solidarity resources of the community" and the identities these resources express.[3] However, while the state's actions suggest that it sees the cultural revival as instrumental in improving the economic status and political stability of local regions, many officials, especially minority ones, promote the cultural revival for reasons that go beyond utility.

The desire of the Dai, Bai, and Hui to recover long-suppressed traditions and practices drives their cultural revival. For many members of these groups, cultural revival is also an expression of their desire for modernization, albeit in minority-centric terms. Modernization is a goal and an ideal; it is an object of attachment, an emotionally resonant symbol of progress valorized in many of their cultural endeavors. At the same time, cultural activists wield ideals of modernity as justification for their projects.

For groups like the Dai and Hui, revival has enhanced connections to transnational collectivities and identities. These groups have benefited from foreign assistance in rebuilding sites of worship, religious schools, etc. Dai connections to Thailand, Laos, and Myanmar, and Hui ties to Muslim countries and global Islam, have thus contributed to the vibrancy of religious and cultural life. Despite official pronouncements and laws against foreign intrusion in the sphere of religion, the state frequently supports minority identification with a pan-Tai or pan-Islamic cultural entity—as long as this identification does not appear to split the motherland.

These transnational linkages inform Dai and Hui interpretations of the national and the modern. Many Dai point to the rapid growth of the Thai economy as proof that economic development is compatible with "their" culture, despite frequent official and scholarly assertions to the contrary.

Many Hui see the prosperity and modernity of Malaysia, Turkey, Saudi Arabia, and other Muslim states in a similar light. The scientific legacy of Islam and the history of commercial activities among Muslims—including Mohammad himself—are held up as proof of the compatibility of Hui identity and practice with Chinese national goals of economic modernization.[4]

The type of legitimacy that these two groups gain through identification with non-Chinese groups may not seem available to the Bai, given that Bai people reside only in China. However, for the Bai, an historical Bai subject, fictionalized or invented though it may be, serves an analogous function; the commercial, cultural, and educational successes of their *minjia* forebears inform contemporary Bai critiques of their present condition of "relative backwardness." Identification with the past also influences efforts to overcome that backwardness and to retrieve an identity bound up with ideals of cultural and economic achievement.

What implications do these developments have for the cohesion of the Chinese nation? Might they lead to the unraveling of the unity of the Chinese nation-state? As explained in chapter one, conceptions of the nation based upon theoretical paradigms as diverse as modernization theory, rational choice theory, and post-modernism may lead to the logical conclusion that minority cultural revival threatens national unity.[5] Moreover, from some angles, the revivals among the Dai, Bai, and Hui bear many of the hallmarks of ethnic nationalism. The main task of the nationalist, writes Anthony Smith, is "to discover and discern that which is truly 'oneself,' and to purge the collective self of any trace of 'the other.'"[6] This task is accomplished, he argues, through "the rediscovery, authentication, and correct interpretation of a unique ethnic past [that is] the focus of national labours."[7] What Smith describes is in many respects what Dai, Bai, and Hui cultural activists and revival participants have tried to do. The success of their endeavors indicates that a movement akin to cultural nationalism has been germinating for some time.

Real-world nation-states are and always have been heterogeneous entities, an obvious point that has been emphasized by much scholarship on nations, culture, and identity.[8] Cultures are not bounded and coherent, nor is there a simple and straightforward positive correlation between culture and group identities.[9] Yet the idea that cultural, ethnic, and religious minorities undermine national cohesion persists in much popular, journalistic, and academic discourse about many countries.[10] One journalist has characterized the minority revival in China as "splintering the image of a homogenous Han majority and heightening the distance between the provinces and Beijing."[11]

Yet the cases analyzed in this book show that expressions of diversity within the nation can also reflect national goals, such as the desire for economic development and modernization. The Dai, Bai, and Hui revivals entail ethnically and religiously informed interpretations and appropriations of broad Chinese national values and ideals. Expressions of minority identity can be ways of participating, or attempting to participate, in the imagined community of the nation. These interpretations and appropriations are critical ones that allow aspects of the revival to function both as expressions of minority identity and as citizenship practice.

Both the idea of citizenship as practice as well as actual citizenship practices among the Chinese people, especially the Han, are worth revisiting to understand minority identity as more than neutral characterization or simple rhetoric. Citizenship is a formal legal category, a state-imposed identity that individuals typically possess in passive fashion. With the exception of naturalized citizens, most people's behavior and choices have little bearing on their citizenship status. Practice, in other words, does not enter into it. Yet citizenship is practice, in that the actions of states and citizens expand, contract, or otherwise alter its boundaries and applications. In China, as in the United States, citizenship rights to education, freedom of speech and religion, and so on are more or less fixed in law, and they apply, in theory, to those who enjoy citizenship status (and sometimes to those who do not). Yet the actual content and meaning of these citizenship rights depend on actions, expectations, and political context. The interplay of government attempts to limit these rights, citizen efforts to expand them, and broader societal understandings renders citizenship rights mutable and dynamic.

Recent studies have explored the meaning of citizenship and how it is expressed in China. Much of this work examines popular responses to post-Mao legal reforms and the growing emphasis on the rule of law. Kevin O'Brien and Lianjiang Li, for example, have studied the explosion of administrative litigation among rural Chinese, who are suing the state over corruption, property confiscation, illegal fines, pollution, physical mistreatment, and a host of other concerns. While O'Brien and Li caution that many Chinese still view the law as an instrument of state domination, they demonstrate that legal awareness is growing; administrative litigation "may play a part in enlarging the still small bundle of rights that villagers possess."[12] As Margaret Y. K. Woo argues, "Adjudication is not only a source of private dispute resolution, but also a process by which public rights are determined and articulated."[13] In the legal cases analyzed by O'Brien, Li, Woo, and others, citizenship practice does not mean blind acceptance of state authority, or of the categories and norms the state tries to impose. Rather, these examples of citizenship practice are thoroughly contentious, as ordinary people challenge officials in the name of the law and its alleged guarantees.

Along with litigating more, Chinese people are also experimenting with new modes of participation in public affairs. Since the mid-1990s, civic associations, nongovernmental organizations, charitable foundations, and other types of citizen-led social groups have mushroomed. According to the Ministry of Civil Affairs, in 2005 there were approximately three hundred and fifteen thousand registered "people's organizations" (*minjian zuzhi*) throughout the country.[14] Some scholars estimate there may be as many as 2 million such organizations, when unregistered groups are taken into account.[15] Many of these are resuscitated traditional organizations, though others are wholly new, and focus on contemporary concerns such as women's rights, disability, autism, and the environment.[16]

Identity also informs contemporary Chinese citizenship practices, including those within the sphere of law. For instance, Woo's work analyzes the role of gender-based concerns in women's litigation in China. Woo suggests that public actions like collective litigation can have a feedback effect on identities like gender. Women's collective litigation that promotes the idea of the "collective gendered citizen" may strengthen Chinese women's consciousness of their rights as both women and citizens.[17]

What about other forms of identity-based action? The focus of this book is not the legal system or civil society per se, but minority cultural revival. Can participation in and promotion of cultural and ethnic institutions really function as citizenship practice? Here a comparison with the Han is instructive. Han communities, like minority ones, have experienced a remarkable cultural and religious revival since the start of the post-Mao period. This revival is also driven by a variety of interests and motives. Elites and ordinary people alike have sought to recreate meaning and authenticity in their lives and to rebuild organizations that traditionally served to anchor their communities. Identity-based organizations such as ancestral halls and temple societies also serve important social and economic functions, and are promoted, or manipulated, by local officials seeking to increase revenues, fund public services, generate tourism, and attract investment from overseas Chinese and others.[18] An increasing number of the civil society groups discussed above are faith-based, that is, civic associations with some connection to Buddhism, Daoism, Christianity, and other faiths.[19]

As among minority cultural institutions, the relationship of Han cultural institutions to the norms and values of Chinese national membership and identity is complex. By participating in religious and lineage rituals, donating money to religious charities, making temple offerings, supporting the arts, etc., Han people demonstrate community solidarity, civic duty, filial and religious piety, social status, and economic prowess. They present and perform themselves as moral, upstanding citizens, good sons and daughters, loyal members of the clan, village, town, or city, and exemplars of contemporary Chinese socio-economic values.[20] Yet Han, or predominantly Han, religious and cultural practice can also subvert such norms, or be seen to subvert them. The Chinese government's antipathy toward Falun Gong and similar groups reflects its wariness, influenced by centuries of history, of the power of religion to generate counter-hegemonic challenges to the state.[21] Han cultural practice can violate mainstream norms in more subtle ways as well. Mayfair Yang has shown how ritual practice in Wenzhou—a showcase of China's market economy—subverts capitalist and state socialist norms, even as it fuels and is fueled by Wenzhou's capitalist economic growth.[22] Moreover, for Han associations of a religious nature, the simple fact of operating within the bounds of an atheist state makes them inherently problematic, regardless of their goals and actions. Their religious worldviews, argues Richard Madsen, "are always at least partially at variance with the government's legitimating ideology."[23] Nevertheless, local, particularistic Han cultural practices can serve as vehicles for the expression of national and civic identities, as well as religious, ethnic, or kinship ones, though they do not always do so. The cultural practices of the Dai, Bai, and Hui are likewise both potentially subversive and expressive of national and civic identities.

Much of this analysis reveals similarities among the Dai, Bai, and Hui, showing how the state tolerates and supports their cultural endeavors. Yet there are important differences among them. First, the strategies of identity revival available to each group are constrained or facilitated depending on the social and cultural resources they possess. The scope of the Bai revival is limited because the Bai lack any institutional, ideational, or historical ties to transnational entities. In contrast, cross-national linkages and identification are integral aspects of the Dai and Hui revivals. This situation renders their revivals politically more complex, and for the state, potentially more troubling, because of the state's longstanding suspicion of cultural heterogeneity and foreign influence. Yet the state's reaction to the Dai and Hui varies considerably. In the Dai case, the state is almost wholly supportive of expanded cross-border linkages. In the Hui case, transnational linkages are more problematic, and the state is more ambivalent.

How revival affects identification within China's borders in turn affects the way these groups are regarded. The resurgence of Theravada Buddhism, the transformation of Xishuangbanna into a packaged homeland-cum-theme park, and the reconstruction of the pre-Liberation royal palace in Jinghong all encourage Dai identification with the defined, geographically contained territorial space that is Xishuangbanna. Even cross-national linkages encourage this; the thousands of Thai tourists who visit annually enhance the salience of Xishuangbanna as a homeland, a point of origin, as much as they enhance pan-Tai cultural community. The location of Xishuangbanna thus to some extent constrains Dai cultural revival. In contrast, the Hui have no defined place—and how can they be expected to stay in their place if they do not have one? Muslim cultural revival is problematic to the state in part because it encourages Hui to identify not as a territorially delimited minority but as members of a religious collectivity that stretches across the country and around the globe.

The ambivalence and mistrust between the Yunnan Hui and the Chinese state are not merely a result of cultural factors. Despite the transformations wrought by both Chinese socialism and market reforms, and despite state attempts to make amends for past injustice, a kind of habitus of Hui-state interaction that emerged during the Qing persists today.[24] This habitus—institutionally embedded "traditions" of persecution, mistrust, protest, and rebellion—continues to color Hui revival and the reactions to it of others, including the state.

Yunnan has not seen the kind of ethnic separatist unrest that simmers and sporadically explodes in Xinjiang and Tibet. However, Yunnan is not free of inter-ethnic tension and conflict. Many of the most worrisome examples of such conflict have occurred between Han and Hui groups, usually between residents of villages and settlements in close proximity to one another, or between Hui communities and local state organizations. The Shadian Incident of 1975 is a particularly horrific example of this phenomenon. These incidents are not new in Yunnan; they are part of a pattern going back at least as far as the early nineteenth century. Many Hui view the treatment of Muslims in the "incident" at Shadian as typical of the way Muslims have been treated from the Qing to the present, although the incident is unusual given its origins in intra-Hui, Cultural Revolution factionalism. Yet the Shadian incident resembles other cases of inter-ethnic violence in that it emerged not out of separatist sentiments, but rather local, interpersonal conflict.

The following episode illustrates the trajectory that many such conflicts follow. In late December 1996, violence erupted between adjacent Han and Hui settlements in Nagu Township, which is in the central Yunnan county of Tonghai. The origins of the conflict were rather petty. Apparent road rage during a traffic jam led to a fight between drivers and passengers in two trucks near Nagu Township. In the course of the fight, one of the drivers tried to drive his vehicle away; accidentally or not, he hit and killed at least one of those involved in the dispute. The participants were from neighboring Han and Hui villages in Nagu Township, and the fight escalated into a conflict between the two settlements. Exacerbating the conflict was the fact that historically Nagu was a center of metallurgy, in particular gun and knife manufacturing that was allegedly halted in the early 1950s. In actuality, the manufacture of guns and knives persisted, so not surprisingly, when the fight in Nagu Township escalated into a pitched battle, it became violent and dangerous.[25]

The battle lasted for several days, until it eventually was quelled by the People's Armed Police. For months the police were stationed everywhere in and around the town, particularly around the Hui settlement of Najiaying (Na Family Homestead). Though meant to dissuade further violence, their stance appeared protective of the Hui settlement, perhaps out of sensitivity regarding the Shadian Incident and other Han-Hui riots that have occurred in the region. Checkpoints were set up along the main road into the county. On the hillside above the township, someone had arranged dozens of painted white rocks to form a phrase in huge Chinese characters clearly visible from the windows of passing vehicles: "One family is not complete, ten thousand families are complete" (*Yi jia bu yuan, wan jia yuan*). The reference was to the "family" (*jia*) of the Hui settlement, Na Family Homestead (Najiaying); the message was in support of ethnic harmony.

Though indicative of longstanding inter-ethnic mistrust, incidents like the one in Nagu Township do not amount to separatism. Local conflicts can and do lead to anti-state violence, though; state mishandling of similar conflicts sparked the nineteenth-century Panthay Rebellion. Whether or not local disputes provoke anti-state action depends greatly on how officials respond to them. To understand minority conflicts in China, rather than scrutinizing "cultural nationalism" for secessionist tendencies, we should examine how the state deals with such matters, such as its efforts to create parity among minorities and the Han and its overall support for minority cultural expression.

While cultural identities and inter-ethnic relations in Yunnan are at times a source of concern for the state, the state also poses problems for minorities. Although this book provides many instances of state support for minority cultural practices, the long-term prospects for this support are ambiguous. The government remains hostile toward "heterodox" institutions that are not amenable to official monitoring or co-optation. The state also retains the power to determine what does and does not threaten national unity, and officials have few qualms about using excessive measures to squelch activities and organizations perceived as threats. Efforts to eliminate secessionist Islamist elements in Xinjiang, which include restrictions on religious practice, publishing, and education, demonstrate that seemingly inoffensive cultural practice can be suppressed in the name of stability.

There are other, less obvious ways in which minority cultural practice may be constrained and marginalized over the long run. For example, official and unofficial beliefs about modernization, what it entails, and the duties of Chinese citizens in light of the modern ideal affect official rhetoric. The state's vision of Chinese modernization is mostly one of a rationalized, homogenized, superstition-free society. Minorities may have appropriated the language of modernity to justify their endeavors and themselves, but such efforts are limited by the neo-culturalist expectations regarding minority and Chinese citizen behavior analyzed in chapter one. Contemporary neo-culturalism valorizes certain behaviors and attitudes as civilized and modern, while disparaging others as superstitious and unseemly. It pervades both popular and official thinking about what it means to be Chinese, and is not entirely compatible with minority cultural practice and identity.

One problem for minorities is that despite official distinctions between "real" religion and superstition, religious worship is still characterized in the media as unbecoming of an increasingly modern, cosmopolitan society, and is seen as such by many Chinese people. This situation may be changing; in recent years top officials have announced that religion has a role to play in constructing a "harmonious society."[26] Nevertheless, official and popular conceptions of modernization have been slow to make room for religious identity and practice. To a certain degree, minorities are protected from these kinds of criticisms, in that religion is one of their special characteristics and thus was more or less legitimized by the Constitution in 1982 and the Law of Minority Autonomy in 1984. Yet these protections underscore the dilemma that minorities face. Modern, cosmopolitan, sophisticated people—good Chinese citizens, in other words—do not engage in un-modern behaviors. Minorities, however, are expected to engage in them.

The dilemmas created by this way of thinking are evident in the ambiva-lence many Han express toward the Hui practice of Islam. Hui religiosity is seen by some Han as something of a sham, incompatible with the eco-nomically "advanced" and integrated lives that many Hui lead, especially those who live in urban areas. While this hostility reflects inter-ethnic mis-trust, it also results from the somewhat transgressive quality of Huiness. The Hui are perceived as a not-quite-minority, not-quite-Han people who obstinately refuse to acknowledge their modernity. The Dai, in contrast, are held to a different standard of behavior. Religiosity among the Dai is still a quaint and marketable expression of their exotic character; among the Hui, it constitutes willful resistance to modernity.

In *Rescuing History from the Nation*, Prasenjit Duara argues that the study of nationalism ought to be broadened to include a variety of "nation-views and other narratives" of the nation. Nationalism, he points out,

> is often considered to override other identities within a society—such as reli-gious, racial, linguistic, class, gender, or even historical ones—to encompass these differences in a larger identity. However, even when or where such an encompassment has been temporarily achieved, the way in which the nation is represented and voiced by different self-conscious groups is often very differ-ent. Indeed, we may speak of different "nation-views," as we do "world-views," which are not overridden by the nation but actually define or constitute it. In place of the harmonized, monologic voice of the Nation, we find a polyphony of voices, contradictory and ambiguous, opposing, affirming, and negotiating their views of the nation.[27]

The cultural revivals of the Dai, Bai, and Hui are multilayered endeavors, polyphonies within themselves. They spring from a diversity of motives and interests: grass-roots religious faith, the desire for an authentic life, academic interest, fun, orientalist fascination, the push for market share, etc. A great deal of the ferment in minority areas entails a straightforward and fairly unreflective resurrection of everyday practices and institutions, but at other times it is deliberate and self-conscious. The Dai, Bai, and Hui are redefining national goals and ideals in ways that allow them to be minority, modern, and Chinese. Their contradictory "nation-views" nego-tiate a Han-centric vision of the Chinese nation, providing voices of both opposition and affirmation, rife with ambiguity and paradox.

CHINESE GLOSSARY

ahong 阿訇

Bai 白

benzhu 本主

Bulang 布朗

Dai 傣

daimeng 傣勐

Daizu *fengwei* 傣族风味

Dali 大理

fei musilin 非穆斯林

Foguang Zhi Jia 佛光之家

fojiao 佛教

Fojiao Xiehui 佛教协会

Haba 哈巴

Han 汉

Hani 哈尼

Heizhao 黑召

Hui 回

huoxi 火西

Jinghong 景洪

Kunming 昆明

Menghai 勐海

minying 民营

minzu 民族

minzu jingji 民族经济

musilin 穆斯林

Naxi 纳西

neidiren 内地人

qingzhen 清真

qingzhensi 清真寺

renmin 人民

Shangri-la   香格里垃

shaoshu minzu   少数民族

shuangyu   双语

waidiren   外地人

Weishan   魏山

Xishuangbanna   西双版纳

Yao   瑶

Yi   彝

yisilanjiao   伊斯兰教

Yisilanjiao Xiehui   伊斯兰教协会

Yunnan   云南

Zang   藏

zhaomeng   召勐

zhaopianling   召片领

Zhongguo   中国

NOTES

BSLD	*Baizu shehui lishi diaocha*
DSLD	*Daizu shehui lishi diaocha*
WYHZMZZ	*Weishan Yizu Huizu zizhi xian minzu zongjiao zhi*
XDSZD	*Xishuangbanna Daizu shehui zonghe diaocha*
YHSLD	*Yunnan Huizu shehui lishi diaocha*
YHXD	*Yunnan Huizu xiangqing diaocha*
YMGS	*Yunnan minzu gongzuo sishi nian*
YTN	*Yunnan tongji nianjian*
ZSMJS	*Zhongguo shaoshu minzu jiaoyu shi*

INTRODUCTION

Chapter epigraph: Pye, "How China's Nationalism was Shanghaied," 129.

1. National Bureau of Statistics, "2005 nian quanguo 1% renkou chouyang."

2. Townsend, "Chinese Nationalism," 130.

3. Hirschman, *Exit, Voice, and Loyalty*.

4. Chen, "Healing Sects and Anti-Cult Campaigns."

5. See Gordon White et al., *In Search of Civil Society*; also Wank, "Civil Society." For a critical dissenting view, see Wakeman, "The Civil Society and Public Sphere Debate."

6. Gladney, *Muslim Chinese*, 62.

7. Litzinger, *Other Chinas*, 191–92. "Governmentality" is Foucault's term. See Burchell et al., *The Foucault Effect*.

8. Kaup, *Creating the Zhuang.*

9. Gladney, "Representing Nationality"; Schein, *Minority Rules.*

10. Harrell, "Introduction: Civilizing Projects."

11. Litzinger, *Other Chinas,* 187–92.

12. See Notar's discussion in *Displacing Desire,* chapter 4, on how the reconfiguration of the tourist infrastructure in the Dali Bai Autonomous Prefecture has been shaped in great part by a fictional and fantastical martial arts movie. "Preposterous" is her assessment.

13. Harrell, "L'état, c'est nous, or We Have Met the Oppressor and He Is Us." Harrell argues the need to "question the assumption that minority cadres are nothing but stooges for the majority" (226), and presents examples of cadres mobilizing state resources in service of local ethnic interests.

14. Pearson, "The Janus Face of Business Associations"; Unger, "Bridges"; Foster, "Associations"; Wank, "Private Business."

15. Gillette, *Between Mecca and Beijing,* 227.

16. Cited in McKhann, "The Naxi and the Nationalities Question," 47.

17. Ibid.

18. On civilized and uncivilized land use, see Sturgeon, *Border Landscapes,* 27–36, 62–63. As Sturgeon points out, the characterization of shifting cultivation as "primitive" has long been challenged.

19. Kaup, *Creating the Zhuang,* 88–89.

20. Diamond, "Defining the Miao," 92–116.

21. Gladney, "Representing Nationality"; McKhann, "The Naxi and the Nationalities Question"; Schein, *Minority Rules.*

22. Blum, *Portraits of "Primitives",* 50–54. Blum delineates multidimensional categories by which Han classify minorities, such as the "fetishized, ethnic other," the "resistant, disliked ethnic other," "colorful, harmless ethnic others," and the "almost us."

23. Hsieh, "On the Dynamics of Tai/Dai-Lüe Ethnicity."

24. Mackerras, "Aspects of Bai Culture," *Modern China,* 14, no. 1 (1988): 51–84.

25. Fitzgerald, *The Tower of Five Glories;* Hsu, *Under the Ancestor's Shadow.*

26. Lipman, *Familiar Strangers.*

27. For a history of state-sanctioned anti-Hui persecution during the nineteenth century, see Atwill, *The Chinese Sultanate,* especially chapters 5 and 6.

28. In 2005, Yunnan's population was estimated at 44.5 million; about 15 million are minority.

29. Giersch, *Asian Borderlands,* 11–12.

30. *Dangdai Zhongguo de Yunnan,* 269.

31. "2006 nian Yunnan nongcun jumin shouru cengzhang sudu mingxian jiada" (Incomes of Yunnan rural residents grow rapidly in 2006), February 12, 2007, http://finance.sina.com.cn/g/20070212/11193333822.shtml (accessed May 25, 2007).

32. World Bank, *China: Overcoming Rural Poverty,* report prepared by Alan Piazza et al., 38.

33. Some comparative studies include Hansen, *Lessons in Being Chinese;* Blum, *Portraits of "Primitives";* and Sturgeon, *Border Landscapes,* which compares Chinese Akha

with Akha in neighboring states. Some of Harrell's work on the Yi compares subgroups of the Yi, and examines their relations to each other and to the very idea of the Yi *minzu*.

34. See Blum, *Portraits*, 7–8; Harrell, "L'état, c'est nous," 234–36; and Litzinger, *Other Chinas*, 33–35, 238–42, for discussion of minorities and the Chinese nation.

1 CULTURE, THE NATION, AND CHINESE MINORITY IDENTITY

1. Bhabha, *Nation and Narration*, 1.

2. The classic account of identity formation and the crises it entails is found in Erikson, *Young Man Luther*.

3. Anderson, *Imagined Communities*.

4. Fichte, *Addresses*.

5. Classic examples of this paradigm are Deutsch, *Nationalism and Social Communication*; Lerner, *The Passing of Traditional Society*; Inkeles, *Becoming Modern*.

6. Gellner, *Nations and Nationalism*, 55.

7. Weber, "On The Nature of Charismatic Authority," 53–54.

8. Hechter, *Containing Nationalism*, 23–24.

9. Duara, *Rescuing History*, 66.

10. Deutsch, *Nationalism and Social Communication*, 14.

11. Bauman, *Postmodern Ethics*, 141.

12. Gergen, *The Saturated Self*.

13. Foucault, *The History of Sexuality*; Deleuze and Guattari, *Anti-Oedipus*.

14. For American attitudes on multiculturalism, see Citrin et al., "Multiculturalism in American Public Opinion."

15. Rosaldo, "Cultural Citizenship"; Ong, "Cultural Citizenship as Subject-Making," 737–51.

16. Taylor, *Multiculturalism and "The Politics of Recognition."*

17. Kymlicka, *Multicultural Citizenship*, 83.

18. Taylor, cited in Bhabha, "Culture's In-Between," 57.

19. Kymlicka, *Multicultural Citizenship*, 76.

20. Bhabha, "Culture's In-Between," 57.

21. Kymlicka, *Multicultural Citizenship*, 76.

22. Gupta and Ferguson, "Culture, Power, Place," 1.

23. Gilroy, *The Black Atlantic*.

24. Eagleton, *The Idea of Culture*, 15.

25. For applications of the concept see the essays in Werbner and Modood, eds., *Debating Cultural Hybridity*. For a critique of how hybridity masks power dynamics see Dirlik, "Bringing History Back In."

26. Ortner, "Thick Resistance," 140.

27. Dirks, "Ritual and Resistance."

28. The quote is from Terry Eagleton, *Walter Benjamin: Towards a Revolutionary Criticism* (London: Verso Press, 1981), 48, cited in Dirks, "Ritual and Resistance," 486.

29. Dirks, "Ritual and Resistance," 487–88.

30. Duara, *Culture, Power and the State*, 35.

31. Perry, *Shanghai on Strike.*

32. Goodman, *Native Place, City, and Nation*, cited in Wong, "Two Kinds of Nation," 119.

33. Wong, "Two Kinds of Nation," 120.

34. Snow and Benford, "Master Frames and Cycles of Protest."

35. Somers, "Citizenship and the Place of the Public Sphere," 587–9.

36. Limits to the concept's applicability to China are explored in Wong, "Citizenship in Chinese History."

37. On symbolic practice, participation, and membership in revolutionary France see Hunt, *Politics, Culture, and Class in the French Revolution.*

38. Among the most influential of these is Dreyer, *China's Forty Millions.*

39. Schein, "Gender and Internal Orientalism," and *Minority Rules.*

40. Gladney, "Representing Nationality."

41. Harrell, "Introduction," 49.

42. Scott, *Domination and the Arts of Resistance*, chapter 1. Scott distinguishes between what he calls a "public transcript," aimed at authorities, and a "hidden transcript," expressed by marginal actors among others who share their social status. In addition, Scott theorizes the existence of an intermediate realm in which officially sanctioned discourse and behavior is manipulated toward subversive ends.

43. Thornton, "The New Cybersects"; Xu Jian, "Body, Discourse, and the Cultural Politics of Contemporary Chinese *Qigong*"; Chen, "Urban Spaces."

44. Rothschild, *Ethnopolitics.* This is what Harrell notes in his analysis of Confucian, communist, and market-socialist "civilizing projects"; he argues that contemporary attempts to modernize the economies and societies of minority *minzu* should be seen in terms of this history of paternalistic, chauvinistic improvement of peripheral, barbarian peoples.

45. MacKerras, *China's Minorities.*

46. Litzinger, *Other Chinas*, 20.

47. Gillette, *Between Mecca and Beijing.* Sidney White discusses the cultural importance of being modern for the Naxi nationality in "State Discourses, Minority Policies."

48. Chow, "Introduction: On Chineseness," 6.

49. For an analysis of applications and critiques of Levenson's culturalism-to-nationalism thesis, see Townsend, "Chinese Nationalism."

50. Cohen, "Being Chinese," 88.

51. The term is Hegel's, who uses it to describe how citizens in civil society are "educated up" to freedom via the state's penetration of that realm. The term has a distinct moral connotation, and is apropos for the Chinese case, since education in Confucian cultural traditions are what made one a civilized human being. See Herman, "Empire in the Southwest."

52. This is Townsend's summary of James Harrison's thesis, in Townsend, "Chinese Nationalism," 98.

53. Ibid., 99.

54. Ibid.

55. Leo Ou-fan Lee, "The Cultural Construction of Modernity," 33.

56. Strand, "'A High Place Is No Better,'" 126.

57. Duara, *Rescuing History*, 95–110.

58. Ibid., 94.

59. Barmé, "To Screw Foreigners Is Patriotic."

60. One example is the controversial 1988 television series "He Shang" (The River Dies Young). This series criticized the inhibiting effect of Chinese culture on China's modernization, and employed the mythology of the Yellow River and other quintessential Chinese symbols as metaphors for the Chinese nation. In defining Chinese nationhood in terms of a mythologized racial lineage, the series reveals the problems of applying the term "Chinese" to non-Han peoples. See "Culture in Debate: The River Dies Young," in *Beijing Review*, January 23–29, 1989, 20.

61. See Friedman, *National Identity and Democratic Prospects*, especially chapter 10.

62. Ben Xu, "'From Modernity to Chineseness'"; Wang Hui, "Contemporary Chinese Thought"; Dirlik, "Modernity as History."

63. Leo Ou-fan Lee, "On the Margins of the Chinese Discourse."

64. Ibid., 212.

65. Crossley, *A Transluscent Mirror*.

66. Interview with prominent Dai official and member of the former royal family, Jinghong, March 12, 1997; interview with Dai man, Menghan, April 26, 1997.

2   THE DAI, BAI, AND HUI IN HISTORICAL PERSPECTIVE

1. McKhann, "The Naxi and the Nationalities Question," 46.

2. Duara, *Rescuing History*, 4–6.

3. Moerman, "Ethnic Identification in a Complex Civilization."

4. Hsieh, "On the Dynamics of Tai/Dai-Lue Ethnicity," 303–10.

5. The terms *zhaopianling*, *zhaojingha*, *daimeng*, and *zhaomeng* are pinyin versions of Chinese terms that are themselves transliterations from the Dai. *DSLD*, vol. 2, 35–39; *zhaopianling* is a Chinese transliteration of the Dai term *chao phaendin*. See Hsieh, "On the Dynamics of Tai/Dai-Lüe Ethnicity," 303.

6. *Jinghong shi wenshi ziliao*, 6–11.

7. Herman, "Empire in the Southwest."

8. *XDSZD*, vol. 1, 48–61; *DSLD*, vol. 10, 8–13.

9. Moseley, *The Consolidation of the South China Frontier*, 22.

10. McKhann, 41–43.

11. In waging war and revolution, the CCP also demonstrated ideological flexibility in Han areas of central and northeastern China by forging alliances with a variety of local factions and power-brokers. See Chen Yung-fa, *Making Revolution*.

12. Ma Zhuo, *YMGS*, 152.

13. Interview with retired prefecture head Zhao Cunxin, March 19, 1997.

14. Ibid.

15. Zhao Cunxin, quoted in "Zai Cheli xian gongzuo de huiyi" (Remembering work in Cheli County), *Jinghong shi wenshi ziliao*, 125–33.

16. *DSLD*, vol. 2, 20–28.

17. See *DSLD*, vol. 10, 91–102, for a list of *huoxi* obligations by village. Interview with Dai teacher Ganlanba, April 26, 1997.

18. *DSLD*, vol. 2, 26–27.

19. Ibid., 27.

20. Ibid.

21. Ibid., 49.

22. Ma Zhuo, *YMGS*, 153.

23. Xishuangbanna underwent five land reforms; however, two of these (the third and fifth) were rehabilitative measures to correct the excesses of previous redistributive campaigns. Interview with Zheng Peng, Jinghong, March 14, 1997.

24. Interview with female Dai villager, Jinghong, April 5, 1997.

25. Interview with former village head, Jingha, April 25, 1997.

26. In Tang and Song accounts of the Nanzhao and Dali kingdoms, for example, the rulers of these states were called the *bai man*; those whom they vanquished were referred to as the *wu man* (*man* connoting savage or barbarian). The *wu man* are considered by some scholars as the forerunners of the minority today known as the Yi. *Baizu jianshi*, 24–31.

27. "Common people" is Mackerras' translation of the term *minjia*. See Mackerras, "Aspects of Bai Culture," 51. Fei Xiaotong translates the term as "civilian households," as cited in Wu, "Chinese Minority Policy," 2.

28. Hsu, cited in MacKerras, "Aspects," 53.

29. According to Fitzgerald, "More than half the vocabulary and the grammar" of Bai are "wholly unlike the Chinese language." Cited in Mackerras, "Aspects," 53. Mackerras points out that although Fitzgerald saw "the Bai as a people distinct from the Han, he cites numerous examples showing their culture as very similar and subject over the centuries to very great Han influence."

30. Li Donghong, "Baizu benzhu chongbai," 82–86. My translation; unless otherwise noted, all translations are my own.

31. Mackerras ("Aspects," 54) states, "The Bai people place no emphasis on categorizing religions by name. They are quite happy to accept deities from the local pantheon, or from a Buddhist or Daoist. Shamanistic rites coexist with Buddhist. However, although religious beliefs are vague, their traditional strength is considerable."

32. Congruence between irrigation networks (or gate societies) and temple hierarchies was a feature of peasant society throughout China. See Duara, *Culture, Power and the State*, 31–32.

33. *BSLD*, vol. 3, 297.

34. The syncretism of the *benzhu* religion has on occasion led to some sticky situations. One village near the town of Xizhou worships Saidianchi, the Bukharan Muslim who served as Yunnan's first governor during the Yuan. Some years ago the villagers decided that, since Saidianchi was a Muslim, their prayers might be more effective if they went to

the nearby mosque to pray and make offerings. They gathered up the idol, incense, offerings, and other paraphernalia from the *benzhu* temple and walked over to the mosque to continue their activities. This horrified the Hui, since Islam stipulates that there is no god but Allah and forbids the use of incense and graven images. The *benzhu* worshippers were quickly thrown out and fortunately a more serious confrontation was averted. Conversation with two Hui men, Dali, August 27, 1997.

35. Wu, "Chinese Minority Policy," 2–4.

36. Ibid., 11.

37. *Baizu jianshi*, 99.

38. Ibid., 92.

39. The Yong Chang Xiang firm, established by investors from Xizhou Town and Jiangxi, had branches in Hongkong, Shanghai, Chengdu, Haiphong, and a number of other Chinese cities. Chen Runpu, "Yan Xiecheng," in *Yunnan laozihao*, 187–205.

40. See Su Songlin, "Dali Baizu shanghao," in *Yunnan laozihao*, 288–93.

41. Yang Taojun, ed., *Yunnan Huizu shi*, 2; also *Yunnan shengzhi: zongjiao zhi*, 165.

42. One folk account claims that during the Tang dynasty, in 748, a group of sixteen or so itinerant Arabian merchants combined resources to construct Yunnan's first Muslim prayer hall. By the end of the Tang and beginning of the Song, the Arabic community had grown to roughly forty households, and a proper mosque was constructed. Other accounts, however, indicate that the mosque in question, located in the southern part of Kunming, was built in the mid-thirteenth century after the Yuan conquest. *Yunnan shengzhi: zongjiao zhi*, 165–66; Wang Yunfang, "Kunming diqu qingzhensi," 97–99.

43. Ma Gongsheng, "Saidianchi Shansiding shiliao sanjian," in *YHSLD*, vol. 1, 138–40.

44. Ma Zhuo, *YMGS*, 39–41, 86–88.

45. *Yunnan shengzhi: zongjiao zhi*, 66–67.

46. Rossabi, *Kubilai Khan: His Life and Times*, 202–03.

47. Ma Zhuo, *YMGS*, 40.

48. Rossabi, *Kubilai Khan*, 202.

49. Ma Zhuo, *YMGS*, 40; Rossabi, 203.

50. Nasr al-Din was later implicated in an assassination attempt and executed. Rossabi, 203.

51. *Yunnan Huizu shi*, 49–50.

52. *Weishan xianzhi*, 43–44; also *Yunnan shengzhi: zongjiao zhi*, 167.

53. *Yunnan Huizu shi*, 56–57.

54. Mote and Twitchett, eds., *The Cambridge History of China: Volume 7*, 144.

55. Ma Zhuo, *YMGS*, 41–43.

56. *Yunnan Huizu shi*, 74–75.

57. Lipman, *Familiar Strangers*, 72–85.

58. *Yunnan Huizu shi*, 68–73, 91–93; *Yunnan shengzhi: zongjiao zhi*, 201.

59. On the role of economic competition in Han-Hui strife, see Atwill, *The Chinese Sultanate*, especially chapter 5.

60. Ma Weiliang, ed., *Yunnan Huizu lishi yu wenhua*, 26–33.

61. *YHSLD*, vol. 2, 73.

62. Du was a prominent member of the Menghua (Weishan) branch of the *Gelaohui* secret society, called *guanggun* ("glorious scoundrels" or "glorious rods") by local adherents. *Gelaohui* headquarters in the Hui village of Xiaoweigeng served as a base of operations for the uprising. *Weishan xianzhi*, 900–02.

63. Other rebellions of the period include the Nien in Eastern China (1853–1868), Yakub Beg's Muslim uprising in Northwest China (1862–1873), a Miao revolt in Guizhou, and a series of interlocking uprisings in Yunnan involving the Yi, Hani, Dai, and other groups. Ma Zhuo, *YMGS*, 57–59.

64. Atwill, *The Chinese Sultanate*, 178–84.

65. *Yunnan Huizu shi*, 309–18.

3   DHARMA AND DEVELOPMENT AMONG THE XISHUANGBANNA DAI

1. The amount and event of the donation are recorded on a plaque on the temple grounds. The donation is also noted in *1997 Xishuangbanna nianjian*, 213.

2. Anderson, *Imagined Communities*.

3. *2006 YTN*, 712–13.

4. In the mid-1990s the Jinghong State Farm, the largest rubber-producing farm in the country, invested over one hundred million *yuan* to build the Xishuangbanna Nationalities Song-and-Dance Hotel in a city in Jiangsu Province. *1997 Xishuangbanna nianjian*, 320.

5. Interview with temple abbot, Ganlanba, April 26, 1997.

6. Xi Yunhua, "Xishuangbanna zhou zongjiao wenhua chanye fazhan: diaoyan baogao" (Research report: The development of religious culture in Xishuangbanna Prefecture), April 22, 2006, http://www.sdci.sdu.edu.cn/detail.php?id=8469 (accessed Feb. 24, 2006); Mi Yunguang, "Shilun zhengque," 119–211.

7. Cohen, "A Buddha Kingdom in the Golden Triangle." See also Davis, *Song and Silence*, 157–59, 172.

8. Mi Yunguang, "Shilun zhengque," 121.

9. Ibid., 120; See also *ZSMJS*, 1034, and Hansen, *Lessons*, especially chapter 5.

10. Fewer than half of all primary students who started school in 1970 graduated in 1975. *ZSMJS*, 1024, 1033.

11. Ibid., 1030.

12. Ibid., 1033.

13. Mi, "Shilun zhengque," 122–26; *ZSMJS*, 1031–36.

14. Interview with temple abbot, Damenglong, April 3, 1997.

15. Hansen, *Lessons*, xv. Hansen uses the terms "Tai" and "Sipsong Panna" where I employ "Dai" and "Xishuangbanna."

16. *Menghai xianzhi*, 720.

17. *ZSMJS*, 1024–36.

18. In 1983, the land-to-person ratio in Xishuangbanna was 2.4 mu of cultivated land per person, of which 1.84 mu was paddy; in Yunnan as a whole there was 1.49 mu of cultivated land per person, with just 0.57 mu of that being paddy. Tan Leshan, "Xishuangbanna Daizu shehui de bianqian," 278–81.

19. Ibid., 280.

20. Interview with official from the Minority Work Department, Jinghong, March, 28, 1997.

21. Interview with Zheng Peng, Jinghong, March 10, 1997.

22. In 2005, trade between China and the GMS countries was valued at closed to US $32 billion. That same year, trade between China and all other ASEAN countries was estimated to be $130.4 billion. Between Yunnan and the ASEAN countries, the value of trade was $1.05 billion in 2004, double the amount in 2001. "Six-nation Mekong River basin trade grows tenfold," *Japan Economic Newswire*, July 3, 2005; "China ASEAN trade tops 130 billion US dollars."

23. Baruah, "Taking a New Route to Change in the Mekong Delta," *The Hindu*, November 21, 2005.

24. Ibid.

25. "China-Laos Mekong passenger route to open on June 26," *Deutsche Presse-Agentur*, June 13, 2001; "$5.9 Million Invested in Construction of Jinghong-Mekong Port in Yunnan," *Chinese News Digest*, July 15, 2004 (Lexis-Nexis) (accessed February 19, 2006).

26. Zhong Gong Xishuangbanna Zhouwei, *Xishuangbanna wushi nian*, 2.

27. Since the late 1990s TVE earnings have dropped, in great part due to falling prices for natural latex. Earnings plummeted from a 1999 high of 3.5 billion yuan to 1.02 billion in 2001. *2004 Yunnan jingji nianjian, 2002 Yunnan jingji nianjian*, various pages.

28. "Fazhan shitou lianghao, minying qiye dingqi Yunnan xiangjiao chanye banbian tian (With good developmental momentum, civilian-managed firms push forward Yunnan's rubber industry, holding up half the sky)" Dec. 19, 2005, http://info.chem.hc360 .com/HTML/001/020/113391.htm (accessed February 17, 2006).

29. Interview with Dai villager, Jingha, Xishuangbanna, April 25, 1997.

30. *2006 YTN*, 754–55; *1999 YTN*, 437–40, 457–60.

31. *1999 YTN*, 437–40, 457–60; *2004 YTN*, 772–79.

32. In 2005, Xishuangbanna had slipped back to tenth of sixteen among prefectures in terms of per capita revenues. *2006 YTN*, 740–41.

33. Many other scholars note the linkages between commoditized *minzu* culture and the tourist industry. See Harrell, *Ethnic Encounters*, 183–88; Schein, "Internal Orientalism"; Swain, "Commoditizing Ethnicity."

34. See note 13.

35. Ibid.

36. Interview with county bureau chief, March 25, 1997.

37. Ibid.

38. Huang Huikun, "Xishuangbanna Manjinglan lüyou xincun," 53–62.

39. Conversation with Taiwanese tourists, July 15, 2002.

40. Interview with retired prefectural head Zhao Cunxin, March 16, 1997. See also Huang Huikun, *Cong Yueren dao Tairen*, 284–93.

41. "Xishuangbanna Mengle gugong jingqu huifu jianshe xiangmu" (Project to restore the Xishuangbanna Mengle palace), *Zhongguo Minjian Ziben Wang* (China People's Capital Network), February 9, 2007, http://project.ourzb.com/6641.html (accessed May 29,

2007). Information on door receipts provided in interview with official of the prefectural Minority and Religious Affairs Bureau, February 17, 2008.

42. Su Yunhua, "'Nanchuan Fojiao Wenhuayuan' potu donggong" (Groundbreaking and construction begin on the 'Theravada Buddhism Culture Center'), May 11, 2005, *Xishuang-banna Daily*, http://www.xsbn.gov.cn/govinfo/bnnews/200505/510.html (accessed January 15, 2006).

43. McCarthy, "Gods of Wealth," 28–29.

44. Dean, "Ritual and Space," 172–75.

45. Lang, Chan, and Ragvald, "Folk Temples and the Chinese Religious Economy."

46. Tsai, "Cadres, Temple and Lineage Institutions, and Governance"; Ashiwa and Wank, "Politics of a Reviving Buddhist Temple."

47. Schein, "Internal Orientalism."

48. Lefferts, "Time out of Time in Time."

49. Duara, *Rescuing History*, 95–110, 160–68.

50. Interviews with Dai pop music group founders, Jinghong, April 7, 1997; interview with Dai literacy promoter, Jinghong, July 18, 2002.

51. Interview with pop music producer, Jinghong, April 7, 1997.

52. Davis, *Song and Silence*, 72.

53. Interview, music producer, Jinghong, April 7, 1997.

54. "2007 Foguang Zhi Jia gongzuo jihua" (2007 Foguang Zhi Jia work plan), *China Sangha Metta*, April 4, 2007, http://www.chinasanghametta.org/article/news_view.asp?newsid=573 (accessed May 15, 2007).

55. On the socio-cultural and gendered dimensions of AIDS in Yunnan, especially Xishuangbanna, see Hyde, *Eating Spring Rice*. See also Hyde, "Selling Sex and Side-stepping the State."

56. Another organization involved in AIDS prevention and education is the Jinghong Women and Children's Psychological and Legal Counseling Service Center. The center was established in 1997 by activists in the Xishuangbanna Judicial Department and the Women's Federation, with assistance from Save the Children, UK. Though the center advocates in a variety of issue areas, HIV/AIDS prevention and awareness are a major component of its work. In 2006 the center won a US $250,000 Peace and Social Justice Grant from the Ford Foundation. "Law and Rights Project Digest," *China Development Brief*, January 1, 2002 http://www.chinadevelopmentbrief.com/node/170 (accessed February 12, 2007).

57. "Monks teach, practice tolerance for HIV-AIDS victims," *People's Daily Online*, October 26, 2005, http://english.peopledaily.com.cn/200510/26/eng20051026_216985 .html (accessed January 10, 2006); "Rang renmen yuanli aisibing de qinrao" (Helping people escape the AIDS invasion), *Legal Daily Online*, November 20, 2000, http://www.legal daily.com.cn/gb/content/2000-11/30/content_9424.htm (accessed January 10, 2006).

58. "Xishuangbanna senglü jiji canyu aisibing xuanchuan fangzhi gongzuo (Xishuang-banna monks participate enthusiastically in AIDS prevention education work)," *China Buddhist Information Net*, September 5, 2005, http://news.fjnet.com/jjdt/jjdtnr/t20050811_12727.htm (accessed January 10, 2006).

59. China Sangha Metta, "2007 Foguang Zhi Jia gongzuo jihua."

60. Chih-yu Shih, "Ethnic Economy of Citizenship," 237.

4 THE BAI AND THE TRADITION OF MODERNITY

1. *2006 YTN*, 700.

2. Ibid., 712–13.

3. In Midu, less than one-half of one percent of the population is Bai. Ibid., 713.

4. *1996 YTN*, 637–38.

5. Fitzgerald, *The Tower of Five Glories*; Hsu, *Under the Ancestors' Shadow*.

6. Dali is the name of a prefecture (Dali *zhou*), a county-level municipality (Dali *shi*), and an old walled city, Dali Old Town (Dali *gucheng)*. Dali *shi* is comprised of Dali Old Town, the small city of Xiaguan, and ten rural townships. Dali prefecture is comprised of Dali *shi* and eleven rural counties.

7. *1998 Dali zhou nianjian*, 249; *1999 Dali zhou nianjian*, 163. In 2002, municipal revenues from tourism amounted to ¥18.8 billion. *2003 Dali zhou nianjian*, 304.

8. In 2005 Dali *shi* ranked ninth among Yunnan's 131 counties and county-level municipalities in terms of per capita GDP. *2006 YTN*, 687–88. Per capita GDP in China in 2005 was ¥14,040.

9. Ibid., 685–66.

10. *2003 YTN*, 731.

11. *1998 Dali zhou nianjian*, 170.

12. Ibid., 166–67.

13. As Notar shows, "Five Golden Flowers" continues to shape popular perceptions of the Bai throughout China, thereby influencing tourism (especially domestic tourism) within Dali prefecture. In so far as sightseeing itineraries and other activities are organized around sites and representations from the movie, much Chinese tourism in Dali, she argues, is aimed at "avoiding authenticity" rather than experiencing it. See *Displacing Desire*, chapter 3, especially 60–61.

14. *1999 Dali zhou nianjian*, 271.

15. Ibid.

16. *Dali shizhi*, 351–52.

17. *1998 Dali zhou nianjian*, 251–53.

18. See Kraus, *Pianos and Politics*.

19. On the evolution of "Foreigner Street" in light of increasing domestic Chinese tourism, see Notar, *Displacing Desire*, 37–46.

20. Interview with orchestra members, Dali, July 15, 1997.

21. Dong Mianhan, "Baizu yinyue dui Zhongguo gudai," 81–83.

22. Ibid. Dong argues that certain instruments and pieces of music that had been included in the tributary gift became some of the most frequently played.

23. Young, *The Politics of Cultural Pluralism*, 47.

24. Ibid., 46–47.

25. Bhabha, *Nation and Narration*, 1.

26. Wu Guodong, *Baizu yinyue zhi*, 69.

27. Ibid., 24.

28. Ibid., 579–89.

29. By 1956 the number of primary school students in Xishuangbanna had ballooned to over 10,041. Xie Jingqiu, *Yunnan jingnei de shaoshu minzu*, 193.

30. *2003 YTN*, 676.

31. *1996 Zhongguo jiaoyu nianjian*, 137.

32. *1999 Dali zhou nianjian*, 221–24.

33. Ibid.

34. Ibid., 159.

35. Zhang Wenbo, "Jianchuan Xizhong," 35.

36. Total TVE revenue in Jianchuan in 1998 amounted to 5.7 percent of the revenue of Dali prefecture as a whole. Jianchuan firms earned an average of 15,460 yuan, compared to 41,414 per firm in Dali. *1999 Dali zhou nianjian*, 137.

37. Zhang Wenbo, "Bai Han shuangyu jiaoxue yanjiu," 240–41; Yang Mei, "Analysis of the Bai Nationality Bai-Han bilingual education sixteen-point experimental program" *China Education and Research Network*, December 12, 2001, http://www.edu.cn/20011205/3012879.shtml (accessed September 8, 2005).

38. Mackerras, *China's Minority Cultures*, 134–35.

39. Ibid., 142.

40. Ibid., 135.

41. *1996 Zhongguo jiaoyu nianjian*, 260–61.

42. Interview with retired Xizhong village official, August 5, 1997.

43. Interviews with Bai villagers and official from the Eryuan County Education Department, Eryuan, August 6, 1997.

44. Interview with Bai retired educator, Jianchuan, Yunnan, August 5, 1997.

45. Zhang Wenbo, "Jianchuan Xizhong," 34.

46. Ibid.

47. Dong Jianzhong, "Renzhen zongjie Baizu de lishi," 160–61.

48. Interview with Bai educator, Jianchuan, Yunnan, August 5, 1997.

49. Interview with Zhang Wenbo, Jianchuan, August 4, 2002.

50. *1999 Dali zhou nianjian*, 213.

51. Interview with Zhang Wenbo, August 11, 2007, Jianchuan. Zhang himself is in his late 80s.

52. Interview with Zhang, August 4, 2002.

5 AUTHENTICITY, IDENTITY, AND TRADITION AMONG THE HUI

1. Lipman, *Familiar Strangers*, 1997.

2. Kevin O'Brien uses the term "rightful resistance" to describe grassroots actions against official policies that participants defend in terms of legal guarantees or theoretical principle. Such resistance may include vandalism and sabotage, behaviors considered criminal by the state, but which perpetrators see as morally appropriate. O'Brien, "Rightful Resistance," 31–55.

3. In 2005, the Hui population in Yunnan was estimated at 689,928. *2006 YTN*, 700–05.

4. *2003 YTN*; *1997 Zhaotong nianjian*, 277, 283; *1999 Weishan nianjian*, 81.

5. This stereotype can sometimes work to their advantage. Maris Gillette argues that because of this alleged propensity Hui have received "official support and encouragement to take advantage of the state's economic reforms." Gillette, *Between Mecca and Beijing*, 45.

6. In 2005, the per capita net rural income in the Hui town of Nagu in Tonghai was ¥6,447 (roughly $806). In Ludian it was ¥1,286 ($161). *2006 YTN*, 754–55.

7. The translation is from Gladney, *Muslim Chinese*, 55.

8. On the diversity of teachings in China, see Gladney, *Muslim Chinese*, appendix A, 385–92; see also "Yisilanjiao xinyang (The Islamic faith)," *Cultural Yunnan*, July 25, 2005, http://www.wenhuayunnan.com/2005-07/07251057401.htm (accessed May 22, 2007).

9. In 2005, the per capita rural income in Weishan was ¥1,538, three-quarters the rural income for Yunnan as a whole, and less than half the national average of ¥3,255. *2006 YTN*, 754–55.

10. In 2005, the county population was 309,600; 21,774 of those were Hui. *2006 YTN*, 712–13.

11. For a comprehensive account of the Panthay Rebellion, see Atwill, *The Chinese Sultanate*.

12. Du was a member of the Hong Bang (the Red Gang), a local offshoot of the Gelaohui secret society. His position in the Hong Bang was that of "Fifth Brother" (*wuge*), a kind of public relations officer or emissary to the outside world. *Weishan xianzhi*, 900–901. Casualty figures are hard to come by, though census data before and long after the rebellion give some idea of the devastation. Five years before the rebellion in 1851 the Muslim population of Weishan was approximately 50,000. In 1923, more than fifty years after the rebellion, a census conducted by the Nationalist government put the Muslim population of Weishan at around 6,000. WYHZMZZ, 3; Gao Fayuan, ed., *YHXD*, 183.

13. Ma Chaoxiong, *Weishan Huizu jianshi*, 68–75; also *YHXD*, 183.

14. *YHXD*, 164–65; also *YHSLD*, vol. 1, 22–23.

15. *Weishan xianzhi*, 158.

16. Ibid; also *YHXD*, 165.

17. The population of the county, which grew at an annual rate of 2 to 3 percent from 1950 through 1957, fell 8.8 percent between 1958 and 1961. *Weishan xianzhi*, 611–12.

18. *Weishan xianzhi*, 689–90.

19. *YHXD*, 183–84.

20. *Weishan xianzhi*, 615–19.

21 *YHXD*, 174.

22. *Yunnan Huizu shi*, 317; *Yunnan shengzhi: zongjiao zhi*, 208.

23. The personal experiences of the elite may have something to do with this; members of the upper strata were often singled out for struggle and persecution by Red Guards comprised of sent-down youth, students, etc., who were in fact predominantly Han from other parts of Yunnan and China.

24. Interview with Hui official from the Islamic Association, Dali, August 22, 1997.

25. Interview with sociologist from Mengzi, near Shadian, Kunming, May 17, 1997.

26. Gladney, *Muslim Chinese*, 137–40.

27. Provincial and local governments rebuilt Shadian and turned it into a showcase of *minzu* unity and economic reform. The government established factories to make roof tiles, shoes, electrical appliances, textiles, and other manufactured goods. In 1994, the average income in Shadian was just under ¥1,400, compared to ¥803 for the province. Shadian District Party Committee and Government, eds., *Shadian de zuotian, jintian*, 45–56.

28. *Weishan xianzhi*, 621; *YHXD*, 165–66.

29. *1998 Dali zhou nianjian*, 170.

30. *1999 Dali zhou nianjian*, 304–05.

31. *YHXD*, 142, 166.

32. "Yunnan Weishan Yongjian diqu zhaidiao 'dupin zhongmiequ' maozi" (Yongjian district in Weishan, Yunnan takes off its "drug destruction area" cap), *Yunnan Daily*, October 27, 2004; "Zhongguo gong'an jiguan gongbu jinqu pohuo dupin da'an qingkuang" (China public security agencies report on recent major drug arrests), http://www.cnr.cn/home/column/zgjd/jdxd/200506100310.html (accessed June 15, 2005).

33. *WYHZMZZ*, 328.

34. *YHXD*, 184.

35. On Islamic factions and mosque architecture, see Gladney, *Muslim Chinese*, 55–56.

36. Hu Xuefeng, "Jianlun qingzhensi," 47–49.

37. Hui women in Weishan pray in the home (or in school buildings if they are students), not in the mosque. A prayer mat is unrolled and placed so that one will be facing west, toward Mecca.

38. On Du's posthumous decapitation, see Atwill, *The Chinese Sultanate*, 181–83.

39. *WYHZMZZ*, 325; also *Weishan xianzhi*, 162. This day of remembrance resembles collective Hui rituals in Northwest China that commemorate the victims of other nineteenth century massacres and failed rebellions. Gillette describes one such commemorative feast day in the Hui quarter of Xi'an, in *Between Mecca and Beijing*, 160.

40. Personal observation; also *WYHZMZZ*; 143, *Shadian*, 95.

41. Speech by a representative of the Dali Islamic Association at the graduation ceremony of the Dali Muslim Culture College, Wuliqiao Village, Dali, 1997.

42. Interview with *ahong*, Menghai County, July 21, 2002.

43. On the name change, see Hillman, "Paradise under Construction."

44. Ma Weiliang, *Yunnan Huizu lishi yu wenhua*, 133–51. See also Ma Weiliang and Wang Yunfang, "Diqing Zangzu zizhizhou Huizu diaocha," in *YHSLD*, vol. 3, 43–50.

45. Nu Lunding, "Mingji lishi; zhongshi jiaoyu," 49–50.

46. Ibid., 49.

47. *WYHZMZZ*, 328–29.

48. *YHSLD*, vol. 3, 120–24.

49. *ZSMJS*, 105.

50. Ibid.

51. In some Hui communities with the worst enrollment rates, rural incomes far outpace those in Hui areas with better records. In the two largely Hui townships of Shouwang and Taoyuan in Zhaotong District, primary school enrollment rates in 1990 were 58 per-

cent and 76 percent, respectively, compared to 82 and 84 percent in the counties in which these towns are situated. Yet per capita net rural incomes in Shouwang typically exceed those in Taoyuan several times over, and exceed those in more Han parts of Zhaotong. I do not have figures for 1990, but in 1995 the per capita net income in Shouwang was nearly four times greater than that in Taoyuan (¥1,703 compared to ¥446). The 1995 per capita net rural income in Yunnan was ¥1,011. *YHXD*, 221, 247; *1996 Zhaotong nianjian*, 212, 220; *2000 YTN*, 497.

52. Interview with retired principal of the Dali Muslim Culture College, August 2002.

53. Gui Limei, "Cong duo xueke jiaodu," 167.

54. Kong Lingwen, "Huizu minjian jiaoyu de zouxiang," 242.

55. Lipman, *Familiar Strangers*, 72–85.

56. Kong Lingwen, "Huizu minjian jiaoyu de zouxiang," 243.

57. Ma Bin, "Guanyu Xi'an huifang jiaoyu," 202.

58. Ma Zaixian, "Emphasize Han Language Education," Web site of the Najiaying Mosque, Feb. 28, 2004, http://www.njy.cn/ (accessed July 16, 2005).

59. Lipman, *Familiar Strangers*, 205.

60. Gladney, *Muslim Chinese*, 55–56. On Wahhabism and modernization in China see also Lipman, *Familiar Strangers*, 204–11, and Gillette, *Between Mecca and Beijing*, 76–79.

61. *Shadian*, 91–92.

62. Israeli and Gardner-Rush, "Sectarian Islam and Sino-Muslim Identity," 452–57.

63. Interview with young woman studying to become an *ahong*, Weishan, Yunnan, July 21, 1997.

64. Zhang Yongqing et al., eds., "Yisilanjiao kending jingying shangye," 387.

65. Zhang Yongqing, Ma Ping, and Liu Tianming, *Yisilan yu jingji*, 387.

66. The full quote from this section is as follows: "The condition of man is such that no individual can acquire, by him- or herself, all that he needs or wants; human beings must rely on each other—mutual reliance. The exchange of commodities in markets—trade, buying, and selling—helps satisfy the needs of people. Because of this, for Islam, trade, commerce, and the expansion of markets is a noble enterprise." Ibid., 23–24.

67. "Islam and Science," http://www.kyaz.com/English/IslamAndScience.html (accessed August 25, 2006).

68. Interview with retired science teacher, August 15, 1997. As the teacher explained, "I use science to make them see and understand the scientific rationality of the Koran."

69. Karen Armstrong, author of *The Battle for God*, on National Public Radio, "Fresh Air," March 29, 2000.

70. Ravetz, "Prospects for an Islamic Science."

71. Lipman, *Familiar Strangers*, 208–11.

72. Xinjiang Television report of May 14, 1996, as quoted in "Religious Repression in China," Amnesty International Report ASA 17/69/96, July 1, 1996, 17.

73. *Xinjiang Daily*, May 22, 1996, reported in *BBC Summary of World Broadcasts*, June 8, 1996.

74. *Xinjiang Television*, June 7, 1996, reported in *BBC Summary of World Broadcasts*, June 3 and 11, 1996.

75. Interview with Hui students and religious studies teacher, Dali Prefecture, August 14, 1997.

76. Gladney, *Muslim Chinese*, 312.

77. As Fredrik Barth has argued, the boundaries between groups, rather than any ethnic traits or content, are often the focus of efforts to promote and maintain group identity. Barth, *Ethnic Groups and Boundaries*, 14–15.

78. Conversation with religious studies teacher in Dali, August 10, 1997.

79. Interview with vice-principal of an Islamic school, Dali, August 15, 1997.

80. Similarly, people in Taiwan would often tell me that my hair was golden (*jinhuangse*) and that I was tall (*gao*). For the record I am five-foot-three and my hair is auburn. I am indebted to Sara Davis, who had the same experience in Xishuangbanna, for the English transliteration of the Dai term. See Davis, *Song and Silence*, 2.

81. Interview with Hui restaurateur, Kunming, November 28, 1996.

82. Interview with Han businessman, Kunming, May 11, 1997.

6 CONCLUSION

1. Mackerras, *China's Minority Cultures*, 134–35.

2. Notar, *Displacing Desire*, chapter three; Blum, *Portraits*, chapter four; Davis, *Song and Silence*.

3. Young, *The Politics of Cultural Pluralism*, 46.

4. Gillette, *Between Mecca and Beijing*, 235–36.

5. See the discussion of Deutsch, Gellner, Hechter, Baumann, etc., in chapter one.

6. Smith, *Nationalism and Modernism*, 44.

7. Ibid.

8. Connor, "Nation-building or Nation-destroying?'" Smith, *Nationalism and Modernism*, 45–46, 199–205; Chatterjee, *The Nation and its Fragments*; and many others.

9. See the discussion in chapter one of Gupta and Ferguson, 1998; Ortner, 1999; Dirks, 1994; and Duara, 1988.

10. This type of discourse is often used in discussions about the United States. On the immigrant, mainly Latino threat to American culture and civilization, see Pat Buchanan, *The Death of the West*, and Samuel Huntington, *Who Are We?*

11. Sheila Tefft, "Ethnicity Stirs in a China set on Wealth," *Christian Science Monitor*, June 27, 1995.

12. O'Brien and Li, "Suing the Local State," 92–94. See also O'Brien and Li, *Rightful Resistance in Rural China*, and the collection of essays in Diamant, Lubman, and O'Brien, eds., *Engaging the Law*.

13. Woo, "Law and the Gendered Citizen," 322.

14. Chan Siu-sin, "Civil groups given state funding for relief operations; move signals government shift to outsourcing, say NGOs," *South China Morning Post*, March 20, 2006 (Lexis-Nexis, accessed January 15, 2007).

15. Zhang Liwei, "Fangtan: Zhongguo tese gongmin shehui de xingqi" (Discussion: The Rise of civil society with Chinese characteristics), *21 shiji jingji baodao* (Twenty-first cen-

tury economic report), December 5, 2005, http://www.nanfangdaily.com.cn/southnews/ sjjj/chanjing/200512050748.asp (accessed August 8, 2006).

16. Tsai, "Cadres, Temple and Lineage Institutions"; Zhang and Baum, "Report from the field"; Saich, "Negotiating the State"; Thurston, "China's New NGOs."

17. Woo, "Law and the Gendered Citizen," 324–28.

18. Tsai, "Cadres, Temple and Lineage Institutions." See also Weller, *Alternate Civilities.*

19. See the roundtable presentations from "Proceedings of Building a 'Harmonious Society' in China: Non-governmental and Faith-based Organizations as Agents of Social Change and Stability," Center for Strategic and International Studies, in cooperation with the Pew Forum on Religion & Public Life. Washington D.C., September 26, 2005, http://www.csis.org/media/csis/events/050926_agenda.pdf (accessed September 3, 2007).

20. Shue, "State Power and the Philanthropic Impulse."

21. Thornton, "The New Cybersects"; Perry, "Challenging the Mandate of Heaven."

22. Mayfair Yang, "Putting Global Capitalism in its Place."

23. Madsen, "Religious Organizations and Local Self Rule."

24. Atwill, *The Chinese Sultanate.*

25. Interview with Hui scholar, Kunming, January 25, 1997.

26. Chan Siu-sin, "Buddhism held up as healer of social divisions; teachings are close to Chinese outlook, says religious official," *South China Morning Post*, April 11, 2006 (Lexis-Nexis, accessed February 22, 2007).

27. Duara, *Rescuing History*, 10.

BIBLIOGRAPHY

Allès, Élisabeth, Leïla Cherif-Chebbi, and Constance-Hélène Halfon. 2003. "Chinese Islam: Unity and Fragmentation." *Religion, State & Society* 31 (1): 8–35.

Anderson, Benedict R. 1991. *Imagined Communities: Reflections on the Origin and Spread of Nationalism.* London: Verso.

Armijo-Hussein, Jacqueline M. 1997. "Sayyid 'Ajall Shams al-Din: A Muslim from Central Asia, Serving the Mongols in China, and Bringing 'Civilization' to Yunnan." PhD diss., Harvard University.

———. 1999. "Resurgence of Islamic Education in China." *ISIM Newsletter* 4: 12.

———. 2006. "Islamic Education in China." *Harvard Asia Quarterly* (Winter). http://www.asiaquarterly.com/content/view/166/ (accessed May 27, 2007).

Armstrong, Karen. 2000. *The Battle for God.* New York: Alfred A. Knopf.

Ashiwa, Yoshiko, and David L. Wank. 2006. "The Politics of a Reviving Buddhist temple: State, Association, and Temple in Southeast China." *Journal of Asian Studies* 65 (2): 337–59.

Atwill, David G. 1997. "Islam in the World of Yunnan: Muslim Yunnanese in Nineteenth Century Yunnan." *Journal of Muslim Minority Affairs* 17 (1): 9–30.

———. 2003. "Blinkered Visions: Islamic Identity, Hui Ethnicity, and the Panthay Rebellion in Southwest China, 1856–1873." *Journal of Asian Studies* 62 (4): 1079–108.

———. 2006. *The Chinese Sultanate: Islam, Ethnicity, and the Panthay Rebellion in Southwest China, 1856–1873.* Palo Alto, CA: Stanford University Press.

Bai Zhensheng. 1994. "Minzu xiandaihua yu jinji xisu" (Nationality modernization and taboo). In Song Shuhua, ed., *Minzu xue yu xiandaihua* (Modernization and the study of nationalities), 60–76. Beijing: Zhongyang Minzu Daxue Chubanshe.

Baizu Jianshi Bianzuan Weiyuanhui (Bai History Compilation Group). 1988. *Baizu jianshi* (Brief history of the Bai). Kunming: Yunnan Renmin Chubanshe.

Bakhtin, M. M. 1968. *Rabelais and His World*. Trans. H. Iswolsky. Cambridge: MIT Press.

Barmé, Geremie. 1995. "To Screw Foreigners is Patriotic: China's Avant-garde Nationalists." *The China Journal* 34: 209–34.

Barnett, A. Doak. 1993. *China's Far West: Four Decades of Change*. Boulder, CO: Westview Press.

Barth, Fredrik. 1969. *Ethnic Groups and Boundaries: The Social Organization of Culture Difference*. Boston, MA: Little Brown.

Bauman, Zygmunt. 1993. *Postmodern Ethics*. London, UK: Routledge.

Bentley, G. Carter. 1987. "Ethnicity and Practice." *Comparative Studies in Society and History* 29 (1): 24–55.

Bhabha, Homi K. 1990. *Nation and Narration*. London: Routledge.

———. 1996. "Culture's In-between." In *Questions of Cultural Identity*, ed. Stuart Hall and Paul du Gay, 53–60. London and Thousand Oaks, CA: Sage.

Bilik, Naran. 1998. "Language Education, Intellectuals, and Symbolic Representation: Being an Urban Mongolian in a New Configuration of Social Evolution." In *Nationalism and Ethnoregional Identities*, ed. Safran, 1998, 47–67.

Blum, Susan D. 2000. "China's Many Faces: Ethnic, Cultural, and Religious Pluralism." In *China Beyond the Headlines*, ed. Timothy B. Weston and Lionel Jensen, 69–95. Lanham, MD: Rowman and Littlefield.

———. 2001. *Portraits of "Primitives": Ordering Human Kinds in the Chinese Nation*. Lanham, MD: Rowman and Littlefield.

Blum, Susan D., and Lionel M. Jensen, eds. 2002. *China Off Center: Mapping the Margins of the Middle Kingdom*. Honolulu: University of Hawai'i Press.

Bo, Chen. 2003. "A Multicultural Interpretation of an Ethnic Muslim Minority: The Case of the Hui Tibetan in Lhasa." *Journal of Muslim Minority Affairs* 23 (1): 41–61.

Bovingdon, Gardner. 2002. "The Not-so-Silent Majority: Uyghur Resistance to Han Rule in Xinjiang." *Modern China* 28 (1): 39–78.

———. 2004. "Heteronomy and Its Discontents." In Rossabi, ed., 2004, 117–54.

Brook, Timothy, and Andre Schmid. 2000. "Introduction: Nations and Identities in Asia." In *Nation Work: Asian Elites and National Identities*, ed. Brook and Schmid, 1–16. Ann Arbor: University of Michigan Press.

Brubaker, Rogers. 1992. *Citizenship and Nationhood in France and Germany*. Cambridge, MA: Harvard University Press.

Buchanan, Patrick. 2002. *The Death of the West: How Dying Populations and Immigrant Invasions Imperil Our Country and Civilization*. New York: St. Martin's Press.

Burchell, G., Gordon, C., and Miller, P., eds. 1991. *The Foucault Effect: Studies in Governmentality, with Two Lectures by and an Interview with Michel Foucault*. Chicago: University of Chicago Press.

Chan, Anita, and Jonathan Unger. 1995. "China, Corporatism and the East Asian Model." *The Australian Journal of Chinese Affairs* 33: 29–53.

Chatterjee, Partha. 1986. *Nationalist Thought and the Colonial World*. Minneapolis: University of Minnesota Press.

———. 1993. *The Nation and Its Fragments: Colonial and Post-colonial Histories.* Princeton: Princeton University Press.

Chen, Nancy. 1995. "Urban Spaces and Experiences of *Qigong.*" In *Urban spaces in Contemporary China: The Potential for Autonomy and Community in Post-Mao China*, ed. Deborah S. Davis, Richard Kraus, Barry Naughton, and Elizabeth J. Perry, 347–61. Cambridge: Cambridge University Press.

———. 2003. "Healing Sects and Anti-cult Campaigns." *China Quarterly* 174 (June): 505–20.

Chen Runpu. 1997. "Yan Xiecheng." In Yunnan Historical Materials Compilation Group, *Yunnan laozihao* (Businesses of old Yunnan), 187–205. Kunming: Yunnan Renmin Chubanshe.

Chen Yung-fa. 1986. *Making Revolution: The Communist Movement in Eastern and Central China, 1937–1945.* Berkeley: University of California Press.

China Development Brief. "Law and Rights Project Digest," January 1, 2002. http://www.chinadevelopmentbrief.com/node/170 (accessed February 12, 2007).

China National Bureau of Statistics. 2006. "2005 nian quanguo baifenzhi yi renkou chouyang diaocha zhuyao shuju gongbao" (Primary findings of the 2005 one percent sample national population survey). March 16, 2006. http://www.stats.gov.cn/tjgb/rkpcgb/qgrkpcgb/t20060316_402310923.htm (accessed Sept 5, 2007).

China Sangha Metta. 2007. "2007 Foguang Zhi Jia gongzuo jihua" (2007 work plan of Foguang Zhi Jia), *China Sangha Metta*, April 4, 2007. http://www.chinasanghametta.org/article/news_view.asp?newsid=573 (accessed May 15, 2007).

Chow, Rey. 1998. "Introduction: On Chineseness as a Theoretical Problem." *boundary 2* 25 (3): 1–24.

Chuah, Osman. 2004. "Muslims in China: The Social and Economic Situation of the Hui Chinese." *Journal of Muslim Affairs* 24 (1): 155–62.

Citrin, Jack, David O. Sears, Cara Wong, and Chris Muste. 2001. "Multiculturalism in American Public Opinion." *British Journal of Political Science* 31: 247–75.

Cohen, Myron L. 1994. "Being Chinese: The Peripheralization of Traditional Identity." In *The Living Tree: The Changing Meaning of Being Chinese Today*, ed. Wei-ming Tu, 88–108. Palo Alto, CA: Stanford University Press.

Cohen, Paul T. 2000. "A Buddha Kingdom in the Golden Triangle: Buddhist Revivalism and the Charismatic Monk Khruba Bunchum." *The Australian Journal of Anthropology* 11 (2): 141–54.

Connor, Walker. 1972. "Nation-Building or Nation-Destroying?" *World Politics* 24 (3): 319–55.

———. 1984. *The National Question in Marxist-Leninist Theory and Strategy.* Princeton: Princeton University Press.

Crossley, Pamela K. 1999. *A Translucent Mirror: History and Identity in Qing Imperial Ideology.* Berkeley: University of California Press.

Daizu Jianshi Compilation Group. 1985. *Daizu jianshi* (Brief history of the Dai). Kunming: Yunnan Renmin Chubanshe.

Dali Baizu Zizhizhou Difangzhi Bianzuan Weiyuanhui (Dali Bai Autonomous Prefecture Editorial Committee). 1998, 1999, 2003. *Dali zhou nianjian* (Yearbook of Dali Prefecture). Kunming: Yunnan Keji Chubanshe.

Dali Shizhi Bianzuan Weiyuanhui (Dai City Almanac Compilation Committee). 1998. *Dali Shizhi* (Annals of Dali municipality). Beijing: Zhonghua Shuju.

Dangdai Zhongguo Congshu Bianjibu (Contemporary China Series Editorial Group). 1991. *Dangdai Zhongguo de Yunnan* (Contemporary China: Yunnan). Beijing: Dangdai Zhongguo Chubanshe.

Dao Meiying. 1995. "Cong gongzhu dao gongpu" (From princess to public servant). In Jinghong Committee of the China Peoples' Political Consultative Conference, *Jinghong wenshi ziliao* (Materials on the history and culture of Jinghong), 133–40. Jinghong: Xishuangbanna Prefecture Press.

Dao Shexun. 1987. "Baliyu dui Daiyu de yingxiang" (The influence of Sanskrit on the Dai language). In *Minzu yanjiu wenji* (Collected writings on nationalities research), ed. Ma Zhuo, 291–311. Kunming: Yunnan Minzu Chubanshe.

———. 1993. "Wo zouguo de daolu" (The road I've travelled). In *Yunnan minzu gongzuo huiyi lu* (Recollections of nationality work in Yunnan), ed. Wang Lianfang, 320–29. Kunming: Yunnan Renmin Chubanshe.

Davis, Sara L. M. 2005. *Song and Silence: Ethnic Revival on China's Southwest Borders.* New York: Columbia University Press.

Dean, Kenneth. 1997. "Ritual and Space: Civil Society or Popular Religion?" In *Civil Society in China*, ed. Timothy Brook and B. Michael Frolic, 172–94. Armonk, NY: M. E. Sharpe.

Deleuze, Gilles, and Félix Guattari. 1983. *Anti-Oedipus: Capitalism and Schizophrenia.* Trans. Robert Hurley, Mark Seem, and Helen R. Lane. Minneapolis: University of Minnesota Press.

Deutsch, Karl. 1953. *Nationalism and Social Communication.* Cambridge, MA: The MIT Press.

Diamant, Neil J., Stanley B. Lubman, and Kevin J. O'Brien, eds. 2005. *Engaging the Law in China: State, Society, and Possibilities for Justice.* Palo Alto, CA: Stanford University Press, 2005.

Diamond, Norma. 1993. "Ethnicity and the State: The Hua Miao of Southwest China." In *Ethnicity and the State*, ed. Judith B. Toland, 55–78. New Brunswick, NJ: Transaction Publishers.

———. 1995. "Defining the Miao: Ming, Qing, and Contemporary Views." In *Cultural Encounters On China's Ethnic Frontiers*, ed. Stevan Harrell, 92–116. Seattle: University of Washington Press.

Dillon, Michael. 1998. *China's Muslim Hui Community: Migration, Settlement And Sects.* Richmond, Surrey, UK: Curzon.

Ding Hong. 1994. "Lunshi Huizu jiaoyu zai Huizu shehui biange zhong de zuoyong" (The uses of Hui religion in a changing Hui society). In *Minzuxue yu xiandaihua* (Modernization and the study of nationalities), ed. Song Shuhua, 193–207. Beijing: Zhongyang Minzu Daxue Chubanshe.

Dirks, Nicholas. 1994. "Ritual and Resistance: Subversion as a Social Fact." In *Culture/Power/History: A Reader In Contemporary Social Theory*, ed. Nicholas B. Dirks, Geoff Eley, and Sherry B. Ortner, 483–503. Princeton: Princeton University Press.

Dirlik, Arif. 1999. "Bringing History Back In: Of Diasporas, Hybridities, Places and Histories." *Review of Education, Pedagogy & Cultural Studies* 21 (2): 95–131.

———. 2002. "Modernity as History: Post-Revolutionary China, Globalization and the Question Of Modernity." *Social History* 27 (1): 16–39.

Dittmer, Lowell, and Samuel S. Kim, eds. 1993. *China's Quest For National Identity*. Ithaca, NY: Cornell University Press.

Dong Jianzhong. 1992. "Renzhen zongjie Baizu de lishi yu xianzhuang tuixing Baiwen, chenxing Baizu" (Conscientious summary of Bai history and the current state of affairs of Bai language implementation). *Dali Wenhua Xuebao* 2: 160–61.

Dong Mianhan. 1999. "Baizu yinyue dui Zhongguo gudai yinyue de gongxian" (Bai contributions to the music of ancient China). *Zhongyang Minzu Daxue Xuebao (Journal of the Central Nationalities University)* 3: 81–83.

Dong Zijian. 1987. "'Minzu jingji' shi yige xinxing de xueke" ('Nationalities economy' as a new discipline). In Nationalities Research Editorial Group, *Minzu Yanjiu Wenji* (Collected writings on nationalities research), 53–67. Kunming: Yunnan Minzu Chubanshe.

Dreyer, June Teufel. 1976. *China's Forty Millions: Minority Nationalities And National Integration in the People's Republic of China*. Cambridge, MA: Harvard University Press.

Du Fachun. 1995. "Gaige kaifang, shichang jingji yu minzu zongjiao guanxi" (The relationship between reforms, the market economy, and nationality religion). *Zhongyang Minzu Daxue Xuebao* 3: 6–12.

Du Kun. 1997. *Xizhou yijiu* (Remembering Xizhou). Kunming: Yunnan Renmin Chubanshe.

Duan Shoutao. 1992. "Dali Ma, Mabang, Lumahui" (The horse and mule caravans of Dali). *Dali Wenhua Xuebao* (Journal of Dali culture) 2: 56–61.

Duara, Prasenjit. 1988. *Culture, Power, and the State: Rural North China, 1900–1942*. Palo Alto, CA: Stanford University Press.

———. 1993. "De-constructing the Chinese Nation." *Australian Journal of Chinese Affairs* 30: 1–26.

———. 1995. *Rescuing History from the Nation: Questioning Narratives of Modern China*. Chicago: University of Chicago Press.

Eagleton, Terry. 2000. *The Idea of Culture*. Malden, MA: Blackwell Publishers.

Edin, Maria. 2003. "State Capacity and Local Agent Control in China: CCP Cadre Management from a Township Perspective." *China Quarterly* 173 (1): 35–52.

Eng, Ian. 2003. "Together-in-Difference: Against Diaspora, Into Hybridity." *Asian Studies Review* 27 (2): 141–54.

Erikson, Erik H. 1962. *Young Man Luther: A Study in Psychoanalysis and History*. New York: Norton.

Eryuan Xianzhi Bianzuan Weiyuanhui (Eryuan County Compilation Committee). 1996. *Eryuan xianzhi* (Annals of Eryuan County). Kunming: Yunnan Renmin Chubanshe.

Evans, Grant. 2000. "Tai-ization: Ethnic Change in Northern Indo-China." In *Civility and Savagery: Social Identity in Tai states*, ed. Andrew Turton. Richmond, Surrey, UK: Curzon.

Fei, Hsiao-tung. 1979. *On the Social Transformation of China's Minority Nationalities*. HSDP-SCA series. Tokyo: United Nations University.

———. 1981. *Toward a People's Anthropology*. Beijing: New World Press.

Fichte, Johann Gottlieb. 1979. *Addresses to the German Nation*. Westport, CT: Greenwood Press.

Fitzgerald, C. P. 1973. *The Tower of Five Glories: A Study of the Min Chia of Ta Li. Yunnan.* Westport, CT: Hyperion Press.

Fogel, Joshua A., and Peter Zarrow. 1997. *Imagining the People: Chinese Intellectuals and the Concept of Citizenship, 1890–1920*. Armonk, NY: M. E. Sharpe.

Foster, Kenneth. 2001. "Associations in the Embrace of an Authoritarian State: State Domination of Society?" *Studies in Comparative International Development* 35 (4): 84–109.

Foucault, Michel. 1978. *The History of Sexuality*. New York: Pantheon Books.

Frolic, B. Michael. 1997. "State-led Civil Society." In *Civil Society in China*, ed. Timothy Brook and B. Michael Frolic, 46–67. Armonk, NY: M. E. Sharpe.

Friedman, Edward. 1995. *National Identity and Democratic Prospects in Socialist China*. Armonk, NY: M. E. Sharpe.

Gao Fayuan, ed. 1992. *Yunnan Huizu xiangqing diaocha* (Research on rural Hui society in Yunnan). Kunming: Yunnan Minzu Chubanshe.

Gellner, Ernest. 1983. *Nations and Nationalism*. Ithaca: Cornell University Press.

Gergen, Kenneth J. *The Saturated Self: Dilemmas of Identity in Contemporary life*. New York: Basic Books.

Giersch, C. Pat. 2001. "'A Motley Throng': Social Change on Southwest China's Early Modern Frontier, 1700–1880." *The Journal of Asian Studies* 60 (1): 67–94.

———. 2006. *Asian Borderlands*. Cambridge, MA: Harvard University Press.

Gillette, Maris. 2000. *Between Mecca and Beijing: Modernization and Consumption Among Urban Chinese Muslims*. Palo Alto, CA: Stanford University Press.

Gilroy, Paul. 1993. *The Black Atlantic: Modernity and Double Consciousness*. Cambridge, MA: Harvard University Press.

Gladney, Dru. 1991. *Muslim Chinese: Ethnic Nationalism in the People's Republic*. Cambridge MA: Council on East Asian Studies, Harvard University.

———. 1994. "Representing Nationality in China: Refiguring Majority/Minority Identities." *Journal of Asian Studies* 53 (1): 92–123.

———. 2003. "Islam in China: Accommodation or Separatism?" *China Quarterly* 174: 451–67.

———. 2004. *Dislocating China: Muslims, Minorities, and Other Subaltern Subjects*. Chicago: University of Chicago Press.

Goodman, Bryna. 1995. *Native Place, City, and Nation: Regional Identities and Networks in Shanghai*. Berkeley: University of California Press.

Greenfeld, Liah. 1992. *Nationalism: Five Roads to Modernity*. Cambridge, MA: Harvard University Press.

Gui Limei. 2001. "Cong duo xueke jiaodu taosu Huizu chuantong wenhua yu Huizu fazhan de libi" (Benefits and disadvantages of traditional culture in the development of the Hui people). In Yunnan Huizu Yanjiu Weiyuanhui (Yunnan Hui Studies Association), ed., 2001, 157–64.

Gupta, Akhil. 1998. *Postcolonial Developments: Agriculture in the Making of Modern India*. Durham, NC: Duke University Press.

Gupta, Akhil, and James Ferguson, eds. 1997. *Culture, Power, Place: Explorations in Critical Anthropology*. Durham, NC: Duke University Press.

Hansen, Mette Halskov. 1999. *Lessons in Being Chinese*. Seattle: University of Washington Press.

———. 2004. "The Challenge of Sipsong Panna in the Southwest: Development, Resources, and Power in a Multiethnic China." In Rossabi, ed., 2004, 53–83.

Harrell, Stevan. 1990. "Ethnicity, Local Interests, and the State: Yi Communities in Southwest China." *Comparative Studies in Society and History* 32 (3): 515–48.

———. 1995. "Introduction: Civilizing Projects and the Reaction to Them." In *Cultural Encounters on China's Ethnic Frontiers*, ed. Stevan Harrell, 3–36. Seattle: University of Washington Press.

———. 2001. *Ways of Being Ethnic in Southwest China*. Seattle: University of Washington Press.

———. 2007. "L'état, c'est nous, or We Have Met the Oppressor and He Is Us: The Predicament of Minority Cadres in the PRC." In *The Chinese State at the Borders*, ed. Diana Lary, 221–39. Vancouver, BC: UBC Press.

He Limin. 1995. "Chongzu minzu wenhua, zhenxing Naxi minzu jingji" (Reestablish nationality culture, vigorously develop the national economy of the Naxi). *Minzu xue* (Ethnology) 1 (2): 36–39.

He Liyi, with Claire Anne Chik. 1993. *Mr. China's Son: A Villager's Life*. Boulder, CO: Westview Press.

Heberer, Thomas. 1989. *China and Its National Minorities: Autonomy or Assimilation?* Armonk, NY: M. E. Sharpe.

Hechter, Michael. 1975. *Internal Colonialism: The Celtic Fringe in British National Development, 1536–1966*. Berkeley: University of California Press.

———. 2000. *Containing Nationalism*. New York: Oxford University Press.

Herman, John E. 1997. "Empire in the Southwest: Early Qing Reforms to the Native Chieftain System." *Journal of Asian Studies* 56: 47–73.

Hillman, Ben. 2003. "Paradise Under Construction: Minorities, Myths and Modernity in Northwest Yunnan." *Asian Ethnicity* 4 (2): 175–88.

Hirschman, Albert O. 1970. *Exit, Voice, and Loyalty: Responses to Decline in Firms, Organizations, and States*. Cambridge, MA: Harvard University Press.

Hobsbawm, Eric J. 1990. *Nations and Nationalism since 1780: Programme, Myth, Reality*. Cambridge: Cambridge University Press.

Hoddie, Matthew. 1998. "Ethnic Identity Change in the People's Republic of China: An Explanation Using Data from the 1982 and 1990 Census Enumerations." In Safran, ed., 1998, 119–41.

Honig, Emily. 1992. *Creating Chinese Ethnicity: Subei People in Shanghai, 1850–1980*. New Haven, CT: Yale University Press.

Horowitz, Donald O. 1971. "Three Dimensions of Ethnic Politics." *World Politics* 23 (2): 232–44.

———. 1985. *Ethnic Groups in Conflict*. Berkeley: University of California Press.

Hsieh Shih-chung. 1995. "On the Dynamics of Tai/Dai-Lüe Ethnicity: An Ethnohistorical Analysis." In *Cultural Encounters on China's Ethnic Frontiers*, ed. Stevan Harrell, 301–28. Seattle: University of Washington Press.

Hsu Cho-yun. 1994. "A Reflection on Marginality." In *The Living Tree: The Changing Meaning of Being Chinese Today*, ed. Wei-ming Tu, 239–41. Palo Alto, CA: Stanford University Press.

Hsu, Francis L. K. 1948. *Under the Ancestors' Shadow: Kinship, Personality, and Social Mobility in China*. New York: Columbia University Press.

Hu Hongzhang. 1993. "Huiyi Zhongyang Fangwen Tuan Yunnan fen tuan" (Recollections of the Yunnan branch of the Central Investigative Group). In *Yunnan minzu gongzuo huiyi lü* (Recollections of nationality work in Yunnan), ed. Wang Lianfang, 126–42. Kunming: Yunnan Renmin Chubanshe.

Hu Xuefeng. 2000. "Jianlun qingzhensi zai Huizu wenhua chuanchengzhong de zuoyong" (The role of mosques in the transmission of Hui culture). *Huizu yanjiu* (Hui studies) 38 (2): 47–49.

Huang Huikun. 1987. "Chan-Dai gudai kao" (Archeology of the ancient Shan-Tai). In Nationalities Research Editorial Group, *Minzu yanjiu wenji* (Collected writings on nationalities research), 136–57. Kunming: Yunnan Minzu Chubanshe.

———. 1992. *Cong Yueren dao Tairen* (From Yues to Tais). Kunming: Yunnan Minzu Chubanshe.

———. 2001. "Xishuangbanna Manjinglan lüyou xincun zong cehua" (Overall plan of Xishuangbanna Manjinglan new tourism village). *Sixiang Zhanxian* 27 (5): 53–62.

Hunt, Lynn A. 1984. *Politics, Culture, and Class in the French Revolution*. Berkeley: University of California Press.

Huntington, Samuel P. 2005. *Who Are We? The Challenges to America's National Identity*. New York: Simon & Schuster.

Hyde, Sandra T. 2000. "Selling Sex and Side-stepping the State: Prostitutes, Condoms and HIV/AIDS Prevention in Southwest China." *East Asia: An International Quarterly* 18 (4): 108–36.

———. 2003. "When Riding a Tiger It Is Difficult to Dismount." *The Yale-China Health Journal* 2: 71–82.

———. 2007. *Eating Spring Rice: The Cultural Politics of AIDS in Southwest China*. Berkeley: University of California Press.

Inkeles, Alex. 1974. *Becoming Modern: Individual Change in Six Developing Countries*. Cambridge, MA: Harvard University Press.

Israeli, Raphael. 1984. "Islam's Incompatibility with the Chinese Order." In *Islam in Asia*, ed. Raphael Israeli and Anthony H. Johns. Vol. 2. Boulder, CO: Westview Press.

———. 1997. "A New Wave of Muslim Revivalism in China." *Journal of Muslim Minority Affairs* 17 (2): 269–82.

Israeli, Raphael, and Gardner-Rush, Adam. 2000. "Sectarian Islam and Sino-Muslim Identity in China." *Muslim World* 90 (3/4): 439–57.

Jaschok, Maria, and Jingju Shui. 2000. *The History of Women's Mosques in Chinese Islam*. Richmond, Surrey, UK: Curzon.

Jin Shaping. 1991. "Yunnan Huizu zongjiao zhidu tanxi" (Analysis of the religious system of the Yunnan Hui). *Huizu yanjiu* 2 (2): 13–20.

Jing Dexin. 1991. *Du Wenxiu Qiyi* (The Du Wenxiu uprising). Kunming: Yunnan Minzu Chubanshe.

Jinghong Historical Materials Committee. 1995. *Jinghong wenshi ziliao*. Jinghong: Xishuangbanna Prefecture Press.

Kaup, Katherine Palmer. 2000. *Creating the Zhuang: Ethnic Politics in China*. Boulder, CO: Lynne Rienner.

———. 2002. "Regionalism vs. Ethnic Nationalism in the People's Republic of China." *China Quarterly* 172: 863–82.

Kim Ho-dong. *Holy War in China: The Muslim Rebellion and State in Chinese Central Asia, 1864–1877*. Palo Alto, CA: Stanford University Press, 2004.

Kohn, Hans. 1961. *The Idea of Nationalism*. New York: Macmillan.

Kong Lingwen. 2001. "Huizu minjian jiaoyu de zouxiang jiqi zai shehuizhuyi chuji jieduan Huizu sanzaju pinkong diqu de zuoyong" (New trends and role of Hui religious education in poor regions). In Yunnan Huizu Yanjiu Weiyuanhui (Yunnan Hui Studies Association), ed., 2001, 241–44.

Kraus, Richard Curt. 1981. *Class Conflict in Chinese Socialism*. New York: Columbia University Press.

———. 1989. *Pianos and Politics in China: Middle-class Ambitions and the Struggle over Western Music*. Oxford: Oxford University Press.

Kryukov, M. V. 1996. "Self-determination from Marx to Mao." *Ethnic and Racial Studies* 19 (2): 352–78.

Kymlicka, Will. 1995. *Multicultural Citizenship*. Oxford: Oxford University Press.

Lang, Graeme, Selina Ching Chan, and Lars Ragvald. 2005. "Folk Temples and the Chinese Religious Economy." *Interdisciplinary Journal of Research on Religion* 1 (4): 1–29.

Langlois, John D. Jr. 1980. "Chinese Culturalism and the Yuan Analogy: Seventeenth-Century Perspectives." *Harvard Journal of Asiatic Studies* 40 (2): 355–98.

Leach, Edmund R. 1965. *Political Systems of Highland Burma*. Boston: Beacon Press.

Lee, James. 1982. "Food Supply and Population Growth in Southwest China, 1250–1850." *Journal of Asian Studies* 41 (4): 711–46.

Lee, Leo Ou-fan. 1994. "On the Margins of the Chinese Discourse: Some Personal Thoughts on the Cultural Meaning of the Periphery." In *The Living Tree: The Changing Meaning of Being Chinese Today*, ed. Wei-ming Tu, 221–38. Palo Alto, CA: Stanford University Press.

———. 2000. "The Cultural Construction of Modernity in Urban Shanghai: Some Preliminary Explorations." In *Becoming Chinese: Passages to Modernity and Beyond*, ed. Wen-hsin Yeh, 31–61. Berkeley: University of California Press.

Lefferts, Leedom. 1999. "Time Out of Time in Time: The 'Bun Bang Fay' (Rocket Festival) in Northeast Thailand." Paper presented at the annual meeting of the American Anthropological Association.

Lerner, Daniel. 1965. *The Passing of Traditional Society: Modernizing the Middle East*. New York: The Free Press.

Leslie, Donald. 1998. *The Integration of Religious Minorities in China: The Case of Chinese Muslims*. Canberra: Australian National University Press.

Levathes, Louise. 1996. *When China Ruled the Seas: The Treasure Fleet of the Dragon Throne, 1405–1433*. New York: Oxford University Press.

Levenson, Joseph R. 1968. *Confucian China and Its Modern Fate: A Trilogy*. Berkeley: University of California Press.

Li Donghong. 1997. "Baizu *benzhu* chongbai yanjiu shuping" (Review of research on Bai *benzhu* worship). *Sixiang zhanxian* 137 (5): 82–86.

Li Gui, ed. 1995. *Yunnan jindai jingjishi* (Modern Yunnan economic history). Kunming: Yunnan Minzu Chubanshe.

Li Ji. 1994. "Yunnan Bai, Naxi, Zangzu de zongjiao xinyang yu xiandaihua" (Modernization and the religion of the Yunnan Bai, Naxi, and Tibetan nationalities). In *Minzuxue yu xiandaihua* (Modernization and the study of nationalities), ed. Song Shuhua, 135–49. Beijing: Zhongyang Minzu Daxue Chubanshe.

Li Rongkun. 1996. "Yunnan Yisilanjiao shi fenqi ji tezheng" (Stages and characteristics of Islam in Yunnan). *Yunnan zongjiao yanjiu* (Research on Yunnan religion) 18 (1): 35–40.

Li Xiaoping. 2000. "The Incoherent Nation: An Exploration of Chinese 'Postnationalism.'" In *Nation Work: Asian Elites and National Identities*, ed. Timothy Brook and Andre Schmid, 191–218. Ann Arbor: University of Michigan Press.

Lin Taorong. 1994. "Shichang jingji yu Zhongguo zongjiaotu xiang tansu (Analysis of the market economy and China's religious adherents)." *Shijie zongjiao yanjiu* (Studies of world religions) 2: 100–108.

Lipman, Jonathan N. 1997. *Familiar Strangers: A History of Muslims in Northwest China*. Seattle: University of Washington Press.

Litzinger, Ralph. 2000. *Other Chinas: The Yao and the Politics of National Belonging*. Durham, NC: Duke University Press.

Liu, Lydia. 1995. *Translingual Practice: Literature, National Culture, and Translated Modernity—China, 1900–1937*. Palo Alto, CA: Stanford University Press.

Ma Bin. 2001. "Guanyu Xi'an huifang jiaoyu xiankuang de sikao" (Thoughts on the educational situation in the Hui district of Xi'an). In Yunnan Huizu Yanjiu Weiyuanhui (Yunnan Hui Studies Association), ed., 2001, 201–04.

Ma Hengfeng. 1990. "Guanyu Ma Dexin xin pingjia wenti de zhenglun yu sikao" (On the debate concerning the reappraisal of Ma Dexin). *Yunnan zongjiao yanjiu* (Research on Yunnan religion) 8 (1): 48–52.

Ma Shiming. 2001. "Dui jingtang jiaoyu gaige de sikao" (Thoughts on the reform of religious education). In Yunnan Huizu Yanjiu Weiyuanhui (Yunnan Hui Studies Association), ed., 2001, 282–85.

Ma Tengfei. 1996. "Qing dai Yunnan Yisilanjiao gaikuang" (Situation of Yunnan Islam in the Qing dynasty). *Yunnan zongjiao yanjiu* (Research on Yunnan religion) 18 (1): 41–46.

Ma Weiliang. 1999. "Yunnan Daizu, Baizu, Zangzu he xiao liangshan Yizu diqu de Huizu" (The Hui of Dai, Bai, Tibetan and Liangshan Yi areas). In *Yunnan Huizu lishi yu wenhua yanjiu* (Research on the culture and history of the Yunnan Hui), ed. Ma Weiliang, 101–27. Kunming: Yunnan University Press.

———. 2001. "Yisilan wenhua yu shehui zhuyi jingshen wenming jianshe" (Islam and the construction of socialist spiritual civilization). In Yunnan Huizu Yanjiu Weiyuanhui (Yunnan Hui Studies Association), ed., 2001, 64–70.

Ma Xiongfu, ed. 1994. *Huizu zhishi cidian* (Dictionary of knowledge about the Hui). Changji Hui Autonomous Prefecture: Xinjiang Renmin Chubanshe.

Ma Zhanlun. 1997. *Yunnan Huizu Miaozu bai shehui jingji diaocha* (Social and economic research on the Yunnan Hui and Miao). Kunming: Yunnan Nationalities Press.

Ma Zhaoxiong. 2000. *Weishan Huizu jianshi* (Brief history of the Weishan Hui). Kunming: Yunnan Minzu Chubanshe.

Ma Zhuo and Chen Qi, eds. 1994. *Yunnan minzu gongzuo sishinian* (Forty years of nationality work in Yunnan). Kunming: Yunnan Minzu Chubanshe.

Mackerras, Colin. 1988. "Aspects of Bai Culture." *Modern China* 14 (1): 51–84.

———. 1994. *China's Minorities: Integration and Modernization in the Twentieth Century.* Hong Kong: Oxford University Press.

———. 1995. *China's Minority Cultures: Identities and Integration Since 1912.* New York: St. Martin's Press.

———. 1998. "Han-Muslim and Intra-Muslim Social Relations in Northwestern China." In Safran, ed., 1998, 28–46.

Madsen, Richard. 1984. *Morality and Power in a Chinese Village.* Berkeley: University of California Press.

———. 1998. *China's Catholics.* Berkeley: University of California Press.

———. 2004. "Religious Organizations and Local Self Rule in Rural China." Paper presented at the International Conference on Grassroots Democracy and Local Governance in China during the Reform Era, National Chengchi University, Taiwan.

McCarthy, Susan K. 2000. "Ethno-religious Mobilisation and Citizenship Discourse in the People's Republic of China." *Asian Ethnicity* 1 (2): 107–16.

———. 2004. "Gods of Wealth, Temples of Prosperity: Party-state Participation in the Minority Cultural Revival." *China: An International Journal* 2 (1): 28–52.

———. 2005. "If Allah Wills It: Integration, Isolation, and Muslim Authenticity in Yunnan Province in China." *Religion, State & Society* 33 (2): 121–36.

McKhann, Charles F. 1995. "The Naxi and the Nationalities Question." In *Cultural Encounters on China's Ethnic Frontiers,* ed. Stevan Harrell, 39–62. Seattle: University of Washington Press.

Menghai Xian Difangzhi Bianzuan Weiyuanhui (Menghai County Almanac Compilation Committee). 1997. *Menghai xianzhi* (Annals of Menghai County). Kunming: Yunnan Renmin Chubanshe.

Mengla Xian Difangzhi Bianzuan Weiyuanhui (Mengla County Almanac Compilation Committee. 1994. *Mengla xianzhi* (Annals of Mengla County). Kunming: Yunnan Renmin Chubanshe.

Mi Yunguang. 1995. "Shangzuobu Fojiao yu Daizu jiaoyu de guanxi" (Observations on correct handling of the relationship between Theravada Buddhism and Dai education). In *Yunnan minzu jiaoyu lunwenji* (Theses on nationality education in Yunnan), ed. Hai Song, 119–21. Kunming: Yunnan Minzu Chubanshe.

Miller, Toby. 2001. "Introducing . . . Cultural Citizenship." *Social Text* 19 (4): 1–5.

Moerman, Michael. 1965. "Ethnic Identification in a Complex Civilization: Who Are the Lüe?" *American Anthropologist* 67 (5): 1215–30.

———. 1967. "A Minority and Its Government: The Thai-Lüe of Northern Thailand." In *Southeast Asian Tribes, Minorities, and Nations*, ed. Peter Kunstadter, 401–24. Princeton: Princeton University Press.

Moseley, George V. H. 1966. *The Party and the National Question in China*. Cambridge: MIT Press.

———. 1973. *The Consolidation of the South China Frontier*. Berkeley: University of California Press.

Moser, Leo. 1985. *The Chinese Mosaic: The Peoples and Provinces of China*. Boulder, CO: Westview Press.

Mote, Frederick W., and Denis Twitchett, eds. 1978. *The Cambridge History of China: The Ming Dynasty, 1368–1644*. Vol. 9. Cambridge: Cambridge University Press.

Mueggler, Erik. 2001. *The Age of Wild Ghosts: Memory, Violence and Place in Southwest China*. Berkeley: University of California Press.

Na Wenhui. 1989. *Yunnan Huizu shi* (History of the Yunnan Hui). Kunming: Yunnan Renmin Chubanshe.

———. 2001. "Miandui 21 shiji—yunnan huizu diqu de jingji fazhan yu wenhua jiaoyu (The economic development and cultural education of the Yunnan Hui in the twenty-first century)." In Yunnan Huizu Yanjiu Weiyuanhui (Yunnan Hui Studies Association), ed., 2001, 211–15.

National Bureau of Statistics of China. 2006. "2005 nian quanguo 1% renkou chouyang diaocha zhuyao shuju gongbao" (Report on primary findings of the 2005 national one percent sample population survey)," March 16, 2006. http://www.stats.gov.cn/tjgb/rkpcgb/qgrkpcgb/t20060316_402310923.htm (accessed Sept 5, 2007).

Notar, Beth E. 1999. "Wild Histories: Popular Culture, Place and the Past in Southwest China." PhD diss., University of Michigan.

———. 2006. *Displacing Desire: Travel and Popular Culture in China*. Honolulu: University of Hawai'i Press.

———. 2006. "Authenticity Anxiety and Counterfeit Confidence." *Modern China* 32 (1): 64–98.

Nu Lunding. 2002. "Mingji lishi; zhongshi jiaoyu" (Always bear in mind history, attach importance to education). *Dali Muzhuan* (Journal of the Dali Muslim Culture Vocational College) 1:49–50.

O'Brien, Kevin J. 1996. "Rightful Resistance." *World Politics* 49: 31–55.

———. 2001. "Villagers, Elections and Citizenship in Contemporary China." *Modern China* 27 (4): 407–35.

O'Brien, Kevin J., and Lianjiang Li. 1995. "The Politics of Lodging Complaints in Rural China." *China Quarterly* 143: 756–83.

———. 2004. "Suing the Local State: Administrative Litigation in Rural China." *The China Journal* 51 (January): 75–96.

———. 2006. *Rightful Resistance in Rural China*. Cambridge: Cambridge University Press.

Ong, Aihwa. 1997. "Cultural Citizenship as Subject-Making." *Current Anthropology* 37 (5): 737–51.

Ortner, Sherry B. 1999. "Thick Resistance: Death and the Cultural Construction of Agency in Himalayan Mountaineering." In *The Fate of "Culture": Geertz and Beyond*, ed. Sherry B. Ortner, 136–63. Berkeley: University of California Press.

Pang, Keng-fong. 1998. "Unforgiven and Remembered: The Impact of Ethnic Conflicts in Everyday Muslim-Han Social Relations on Hainan Island." In Safran, ed., 1998, 142–62.

Pearson, Margaret. 1994. "The Janus Face of Business Associations in Foreign Enterprises." *The Australian Journal of Chinese Affairs* 33: 25–38.

Perry, Elizabeth J. 1980. *Rebels and Revolutionaries in North China, 1845–1945*. Palo Alto, CA: Stanford University Press.

———. 1985. "Rural Violence in Socialist China." *The China Quarterly* 103: 414–40.

———. 1993. *Shanghai on Strike: The Politics of Chinese Labor*. Vol. 1. Palo Alto, CA: Stanford University Press.

———. 1999. "Crime, Corruption, and Contention." In *The Paradox of China's Post-Mao Reforms*, ed. Merle Goldman and Roderick MacFarquhar, 308–29. Cambridge, MA: Harvard University Press.

———. 2001. "Challenging the Mandate of Heaven: Popular Protest in Modern China." *Critical Asian Studies* 33 (2): 163–80.

World Bank. 2001. *China: Overcoming Rural Poverty*. Washington, D.C.: World Bank.

Pye, Lucien W. 1993. "How China's Nationalism was Shanghaied." *The Australian Journal of Chinese Affairs* 29: 107–33.

Ravetz, J. R. 1991. "Prospects for an Islamic Science." *Futures: The Journal of Policy, Planning and Futures Studies* 23 (3): 262–72.

Rosaldo, Renato. 1994. "Cultural Citizenship and Educational Democracy." *Cultural Anthropology* 9 (3): 401–11.

Rossabi, Morris. 1988. *Kubilai Khan: His Life and Times*. Berkeley: University of California Press.

Rossabi, Morris, ed. 2004. *Governing China's Multiethnic Frontiers*. Seattle: University of Washington Press.

Rothschild, Joseph. 1981. *Ethnopolitics*. New York: Columbia University Press.

Saich, Anthony. 2000. "Negotiating the State: The Development of Social Organizations in China." *China Quarterly* 61: 124–41.

Said, Edward. 1978. *Orientalism*. New York: Random House.

Safran, William, ed. 1998. *Nationalism and Ethnoregional Identities in China*. Portland, OR: Frank Cass.

Schein, Louisa. 1997. "Gender and Internal Orientalism in China." *Modern China* 23 (1): 69–98.

———. 2000. *Minority Rules: The Miao and the Feminine in China's Cultural Politics*. Durham, NC: Duke University Press.

Scott, James C. 1990. *Domination and the Arts of Resistance*. New Haven: Yale University Press.

Selden, Mark. 1993. *The Political Economy of Chinese Development.* Armonk, NY: M. E. Sharpe.

Sethakul, Ratanaporn. "Tai Lüe of Sipsongpanna and Müang Nan in the Nineteenth Century." In *Civility and Savagery: Social Identity in Tai States,* ed. Andrew Turton, 319–29. Richmond, Surrey, UK: Curzon.

Shadian District Party Committee and Government. 1996. *Shadian de zuotian, jintian* (Shadian, yesterday and today). Kunming: Yunnan Renmin Chubanshe.

Shih Chih-yu. 2000. "Between the Mosque and the State: The Identity Strategies of the Litang Muslims." *Religion, State & Society* 28 (2): 197–211.

———. 2002. "Ethnic Economy of Citizenship in China: Four Approaches to Identity Formation." In *Changing Meanings of Citizenship in Modern China,* ed. Merle Goldman and Elizabeth J. Perry, 232–54. Cambridge, MA: Harvard University Press.

Shue, Vivienne. 1988. *The Reach of the State: Sketches of the Chinese Body Politic.* Palo Alto, CA: Stanford University Press.

———. 1998. "State Power and the Philanthropic Impulse in China Today." In *Philanthropy in the World's Traditions,* ed. Warren Ilchman, Stanley Katz, and Edward Queen, 332–54. Bloomington: Indiana University Press.

Siu, Helen F. 1990. "Recycling Tradition: Culture, History, and Political Economy in the Chrysanthemum Festivals of South China." *Comparative Studies in Society and History* 32 (4): 765–94.

Smith, Anthony D. 1986. *The Ethnic Origins of Nations.* London: Basil Blackwell.

———. 1998. *Nationalism and Modernism.* London: Routledge.

Snow, David A., and Robert D. Benford. 1992. "Master Frames and Cycles of Protest." In *Frontiers in Social Movement Theory,* ed. Aldon D. Morris and Carol McClurg Mueller, 133–55. New Haven: Yale University Press.

Solinger, Dorothy J. 1977. *Regional Government and Political Integration in Southwest China, 1949–1954.* Berkeley: University of California Press.

———. 1999. *Contesting Citizenship in Urban China: Peasant Migrants, the State, and the Logic of the Market.* Berkeley: University of California Press.

Somers, Margaret R. 1993. "Citizenship and the Place of the Public Sphere: Law, Community, and Political Culture in the Transition to Democracy." *American Sociological Review* 58 (5): 587–620.

Spivak, Gayatri Chakravorty. 1988. "Can the Subaltern Speak?" In *Colonial Discourse and Post-Colonial Theory,* ed. Patrick Williams and Laura Chrisman, 66–111. Hemel Hempstead: Harvester Wheatsheaf.

Strand, David. 2000. "'A High Place Is No Better Than a Low Place': The City in the Making of Modern China." In *Becoming Chinese: Passages to Modernity and Beyond,* ed. Wen-hsin Yeh, 98–136. Berkeley: University of California Press.

Sturgeon, Janet C. 2005. *Border Landscapes: The Politics of Akha Land Use in China and Thailand.* Seattle: University of Washington Press.

Swain, Margaret B. 1990. "Commoditizing Ethnicity in Southwest China." *Cultural Survival Quarterly* 14 (1): 26–29.

Tan Leshan. 1986. "Xishuangbanna Daizu shehui de bianqian yu dangqian mianlin de wenti" (Past and current problems facing Xishuangbanna Dai society). In *Yunnan duominzu tese de shehui zhuyi xiandaihua wenti yanjiu* (Problems of socialist modernization among Yunnan minorities), ed. Xiao Qi, 278–81. Kunming: Yunnan Renmin Chubanshe.

Tapp, Nicholas. 2000. "Ritual Relations and Identity: Hmong and Others." In *Civility and Savagery: Social Identity in Tai States*, ed. Andrew Turton, 84–103. Richmond, Surrey, UK: Curzon.

Thornton, Patricia M. 2003. "The New Cybersects: Resistance and Repression in the Reform Era." In *Chinese Society: Change, Conflict and Resistance*, ed. Elizabeth J. Perry and Mark Selden, 247–70. 2d ed. London; New York: RoutledgeCurzon.

Thurston, Anne F. 2004. "China's New NGOs and the Rise of Social Entrepreneurship: Their Effect on Civil Society and Local Level Leadership." Paper presented at the International Conference on Grassroots Democracy and Local Governance in China during the Reform Era, National Chengchi University. http://140.109.171.199/1010meeting/1-1 .pdf (accessed Sept. 5, 2006).

Tonghai Xianzhi Gongzuo Weiyuanhui. 1992. *Tonghai xianzhi* (Annals of Tonghai county). Kunming: Yunnan Renmin Chubanshe.

Townsend, James. 1992. "Chinese Nationalism." *The Australian Journal of Chinese Affairs* 27: 97–130.

Trevor-Roper, Hugh. 1992. "The Invention of Tradition: The Highland Tradition of Scotland." In *The Invention of Tradition*, ed. E. J. Hobsbawm and Terence O. Ranger, 15–41. Cambridge: Cambridge University Press.

Tsai, Lily Lee. 2002. "Cadres, Temple and Lineage Institutions, and Governance in Rural China." *The China Journal* 48: 1–27.

Tu, Wei-ming. 1994. "Cultural China: The Periphery as the Center." In *The Living Tree: The Changing Meaning of Being Chinese Today*, ed. Tu Wei-ming, 1–34. Palo Alto, CA: Stanford University Press.

Twitchett, Denis C., ed. 1978. *The Cambridge History of China: Alien Regimes and Border States, 907–1368*. Vol. 7. Cambridge: Cambridge University Press.

Unger, Jonathan. 1996. "Bridges: Private Business, the Chinese Government and the Rise of New Associations." *China Quarterly* 147: 795–819.

United States Congressional-Executive Commission on China. 2004. *Practicing Islam in Today's China: Differing Realities for the Uighurs and the Hui*. 108th Cong., 2d session. Washington: GPO, 2004.

Wakeman, Frederic Jr. 1993. "The Civil Society and Public Sphere Debate: Western Reflections on Chinese Political Culture." *Modern China* 19 (April): 108–38.

———. 2000. "*Hanjian* (Traitor)! Collaboration and Retribution in Wartime Shanghai." In *Becoming Chinese: Passages to Modernity and Beyond*, ed. Wen-hsin Yeh, 298–341. Berkeley: University of California Press.

Wan Guanghua and Zhou Zhangyue. 2004. "Income Inequality in China." *United Nations University-World Institute for Development Economics Research Paper* 51. http://www .wider.unu.edu/publications/rps/rps2004/rp2004-051.pdf (accessed August 3, 2005).

Wang Hui. 2000. "Zhang Taiyan's Concept of the Individual and Modern Chinese Identity." In *Becoming Chinese: Passages to Modernity and Beyond*, ed. Wen-hsin Yeh, 231–59. Berkeley: University of California Press.

Wang Hui, and Rebecca Karl. 1998. "Contemporary Chinese Thought and the Question of Modernity." *Social Text* 55: 9–44.

Wang Jianping. 1996. *Concord and Conflict: The Hui Communities of Yunnan.* Stockholm: Almqvist & Wiksell.

Wang Yunfang. 1985. "Kunming diqu qingzhensi diaocha" (Research on Kunming area mosques). In Yunnan Sheng Buanzuan Weiyuanhui (Yunnan Provincial Compilation Committee), *Yunnan Huizu shehui lishi diaocha zhi yi* (Research on the social history of the Yunnan Hui), 97–99. Kunming: Yunnan Minzu Chubanshe.

Wang Zhusheng, and Yang Hui. 1987. "Guanyu Minzu Jingji de jige lilun wenti" (Several questions concerning nationalities economy). In Nationalities Research Editorial Group, *Minzu yanjiu wenji* (Collected writings on nationalities research), 68–77. Kunming: Yunnan Minzu Chubanshe.

Wank, David L. 1995. "Civil Society in Communist China? Private Business and Political Alliance, 1989." In *Civil Society: Theory, History, Comparison*, ed. John A. Hall, 56–79. Cambridge: Polity Press.

———. 1995. "Private Business, Bureaucracy, and Political Alliance in a Chinese City." *Australian Journal of Chinese Affairs* 33: 55–71.

———. 1998. "Political Sociology and Contemporary China: State-Society Images in American China Studies." *Journal of Contemporary China* 7 (18): 205–27.

Weber, Max. 1968. "On the Nature of Charismatic Authority and Its Routinization." In *On Charisma and Institution Building*, ed. S. N. Eisenstadt, 48–65. Chicago: University of Chicago Press.

Weishan Yizu Huizu Zizhixian Bianzuan Weiyuanhui (Weishan Yi-Hui Autonomous County Compilation Committee), ed. 1992. *Weishan Yizu Huizu zizhixian minzu zongjiao zhi* (Annals of Weishan minorities and religion). Kunming: Yunnan Renmin Chubanshe.

———. 1993. *Weishan xianzhi* (Annals of Weishan Yi-Hui Autonomous County). Kunming: Yunnan Renmin Chubanshe.

———. 1999. *Weishan nianjian* (Weishan yearbook). Mangshi: Dehong Minzu Chubanshe.

Weller, Robert P. 1999. *Alternate Civilities: Democracy and Culture in China and Taiwan.* Boulder, CO: Westview Press.

White, Gordon, Jude Howell, and Hsiao-yuan Shang, eds. 1996. *In Search of Civil Society.* Oxford: Oxford University Press.

White, Sydney D. 1998. "State Discourses, Minority Policies, and the Politics of Identity in the Lijiang Naxi People's Autonomous County." In Safran, ed., 1998, 9–27.

Wong, R. Bin. 1999. "Citizenship in Chinese History." In *Extending Citizenship, Reconfiguring States*, ed. Michael Hanagan and Charles Tilly, 97–122. Lanham, MD: Rowman & Littlefield.

———. 2000. "Two Kinds of Nation, What Kind of State?" In *Nation Work: Asian Elites and National Identities*, ed. Timothy Brook and Andre Schmid, 109–24. Ann Arbor: University of Michigan Press.

Woo, Margaret Y. K. 2002. "Law and the Gendered Citizen." In *Changing Meanings of Citizenship in Modern China*, ed. Merle Goldman and Elizabeth J. Perry, 308–29. Contemporary China Series. Cambridge, MA: Harvard University Press.

Wu, David Y. H. 1990. "Chinese Minority Policy and the Meaning of Minority Culture: The Example of the Bai in Yunnan, China." *Human Organization* 49 (1): 1–13.

———. 1994. "The Construction of Chinese and non-Chinese Identities." In *The Living Tree: The Changing Meaning of Being Chinese Today*, ed. Tu Wei-ming, 148–67. Palo Alto, CA: Stanford University Press.

Wu Guodong. 1992. *Baizu yinyuezhi* (Annals of Bai music). Beijing: Wenhua Yishu Chubanshe.

Wu Xude. 1986. "Yisilanjiao yu dangdai guoji zhengzhi" (Islam and contemporary international politics). In *Zongjiao lungao* (Essays on religion), 36–81. Kunming: Yunnan Renmin Chubanshe.

Xiao Qi, ed. 1986. *Yunnan duominzu tese de shehui zhuyi xiandaihua wenti yanjiu* (Special problems of socialist modernization in multiethnic Yunnan). Kunming: Yunnan Renmin Chubanshe.

Xie Jingqiu. 1999. *Yunnan jingnei de shaoshu minzu* (Minorities of the Yunnan interior). Beijing: Minzu Chubanshe.

Xiong Xiyuan. 1994. *Minzu xinli yu minzu yishi* (Nationality psychology and nationality consciousness). Kunming: Yunnan University Press.

Xishuangbanna Guotu Jingji Bianzhi Weiyuanhui (Xishuangbanna Ministry of Land and Resources Editorial Committee). 1990. *Xishuangbanna guotu jingji kaocha baogao* (Economic report of the Ministry of Land and Resources of Xishuangbanna). Kunming: Yunnan Renmin Chubanshe.

Xishuangbanna Nianjian Bianzhi Weiyuanhui (Xishuangbanna Yearbook Editorial Committee), ed. 1997. *Xishuangbanna nianjian* (Xishuangbanna yearbook). Kunming: Yunnan Keji Chubanshe.

Xu Ben. 1998. "'From Modernity to Chineseness': The Rise of Nativist Cultural Theory in Post-1989 China." *Positions* 6 (1): 203–37.

Xu Jian. 1999. "Body, Discourse, and the Cultural Politics of Contemporary Chinese Qigong." *Journal of Asian Studies* 58 (4): 961–99.

Yang Dali. 1997. *Beyond Beijing: Liberalization and the Regions of China*. London: Routledge.

Yang Jingchu. 1994. "Shehui zhuyi shichang jingji yu minzu guanxi de jige wenti" (Several questions concerning the socialist market economy and nationality relations). *Minzu yanjiu* (Research on nationalities) 5: 1–9.

Yang, Mayfair Mei-hui. 2000. "Putting Global Capitalism in Its Place: Economic Hybridity, Bataille, and Ritual Expenditure." *Current Anthropology* 41 (4): 477–509.

Yang Qichang. 1995. "Chonghuan Naxizu kaikuo jingshang de minzu jingsheng" (Reawake the original commercial spirit of the Naxi nationality)." *Minzu Xue* (Ethnology) 1 (2): 40–45.

Yang Xuandian, ed. 1988. *Xizhou zhi* (Annals of Xizhou). Dali: Dali Shi Yinshuachang.

Yang Xuyun. 1994. "Yongping xian Qutong Huizu xiang funü wenti diaocha" (Investigation of the situation of women in Qutong Hui Township, Yongping County). *Minzu Xue* (Ethnography) 1 (2): 75–78.

Yang Yingxin. 1992. "Baizu wenzi keyi zouchao fangyan biaoyin wenzi de daolu" (Representing local dialects in the Bai script). *Dali wenhua xuebao* (Journal of Dali culture) 2: 83–85.

Yang Zhengye. 1994. *Benzhu wenhua* (Benzhu culture). Kunming: Yunnan Renmin Chu-banshe.

Young, Crawford. 1976. *The Politics of Cultural Pluralism*. Madison: University of Wisconsin Press.

Yunnan Huizu Yanjiu Weiyuanhui (Yunnan Hui Studies Association), ed. 2001. *Quanguo di shiyi ci Huizu shi taolunhui gai quanguo Huizu xuehui chengli dahui lunwenji (Proceedings of the 11th National Conference of Hui Studies and the Establishment Ceremony of China Hui Studies Association in Kunming)*. Vol. 1. Kunming: Yunnan University Press.

Yunnan Jingji Nianjian Bianzhibu (Yunnan Economic Yearbook Editorial Group). Multiple years. *Yunnan jingji nianjian* (Yunnan economic yearbook). Kunming: Yunnan Renmin Chubanshe.

Yunnan Nianjian Bianzhi Weiyuanhui (Yunnan Yearbook Editorial Committee). Multiple years. *Yunnan nianjian* (Yunnan yearbook). Kunming: Yunnan Nianjian Zazhishi Chubanshe.

Yunnan Sheng Bianji Weiyuanhui (Yunnan Provincial Compilation Committee). 1983. *Daizu shehui lishi diaocha* (Research on the social history of the Daï). Vols. 1–10. Kunming: Yunnan Minzu Chubanshe.

———. 1983. *Xishuangbanna Daizu shehui zonghe diaocha* (Synthesis of research on Xishuangbanna Dai society). Vols. 1, 2. Kunming: Yunnan Minzu Chubanshe.

———. 1985. *Yunnan Huizu shehui lishi diaocha* (Research on the social history of the Yunnan Hui). Vols. 1–3. Kunming: Yunnan Minzu Chubanshe.

———. 1988. *Baizu shehui lishi diaocha* (Research on the social history of the Bai). Vols. 2–4. Kunming: Yunnan Binzu Chubanshe.

Yunnan Sheng Difangzhi Bianzuan Weiyuanhui (Yunnan Provincial Local Records Compilation Committee). 1995. *Yunnan shengzhi: Jiaoyu zhi* (Annals of Yunnan Province: Education). Kunming: Yunnan Renmin Chubanshe.

———. 1995. *Yunnan shengzhi: Zongjiao zhi* (Annals of Yunnan Province: Religion). Kunming: Yünnan Renmin Chubanshe.

Yunnan Sheng Renkou Pucha Bangongshi (Yunnan Provincial Population Census Office). 1992. *Yunnan sheng 1990 nian renkou pucha ziliao* (Data on the 1990 Yunnan provincial census). Beijing: Zhongguo Tongji Chubanshe.

———. 2002. *Yunnan sheng 2000 nian renkou pucha ziliao* (Data on the 2000 Yunnan provincial census). Kunming: Yunnan Keji Chubanshe.

Yunnan Sheng Tongji Jubian (Statistical Bureau of Yunnan Province). Multiple years. *Yunnan tongji nianjian* (Yunnan statistical yearbook). Beijing: Zhongguo Tongji Chubanshe.

Zanasi, Margherita. 2000. "Chen Gongbo and the Construction of a Modern Nation." In *Nation Work: Asian Elites and National Identities*, ed. Timothy Brook and Andre Schmid, 125–58. Ann Arbor: University of Michigan Press.

Zarrow, Peter. 1997. "Introduction: Citizenship in China and the West." In *Imagining the People: Chinese Intellectuals and the Concept of Citizenship, 1890–1920*, ed. Joshua Fogel and Petter Zarrow. Armonk, NY: M. E. Sharpe.

Zhang Wenbo. 1992. "Jianchuan Xizhong Bai Han shuangyuwen jiaoxue shixian qingkuang de diaocha" (Investigation of the Jianchuan Xizhong Bai-Han bilingual education experiment). *Keji jiaoyu* (Science and technology education) 2: 34–40.

———. 1992. "Zhang Zizhai, Ma Zhuo deng tongzhi tan tuixing Baizu wenzi wenti" (Comrades Zhang Zizhai and Ma Zhuo on problems regarding the implementation of the Bai script). *Dali wenhua xuebao* (Journal of Dali culture) 2: 34–48.

———. 1995. "Bai Han shuangyu jiaoxue yanjiu" (Research on Bai-Han bilingual education). In Minzu Jiaoyu Bianjizu (Nationalities Education Editorial Group), *Yunnan shaoshu minzu shuangyu jiaoxue yanjiu* (Research on Yunnan minority bilingual education), 239–60. Kunming: Yunnan Minzu Chubanshe.

Zhang, Xin, and Richard Baum. 2004. "Report from the Field: Civil Society and the Anatomy of a Rural NGO." *The China Journal* 52: 97–113.

Zhang Xudong. 1997. *Chinese Modernism in the Era of Reforms*. Durham, NC: Duke University Press.

Zhang Yongqing. 1994. "Yisilanjiao de shichang guan yu xibei musilin juju diqu de shichang jianshe" (The Islamic view of markets and the establishment of markets in Muslim communities of the Northwest). *Minzu yanjiu* (Nationalities research) 2: 23–31.

Zhang Yongqing, Ma Ping, and Liu Tianming. 1994. *Yisilanjiao yu jingji* (Islam and economics). Yinchuan: Ningxia Renmin Chubanshe.

Zhao Chunzhou. 1995. "Banna xiangjiao shiye de kaikuozhe Qian Fangzhou" (Qian Fangzhou, developer of the rubber industry in Banna). In Jinghong Committee of the CPPCC, *Jinghong wenshi ziliao* (Materials on the history and culture of Jinghong), vol. 2, 133–40. Jinghong: Xishuangbanna Prefecture Press.

Zhao Cunxin. 1991. "Cong guizu dao gongpu" (From aristocrat to public servant). In Minzu Tuanjie Bianzhibu (Nationalities Unity Editorial Group), *Zhongguo de zizhizhou zhouzhang* (Leading officials of China's autonomous prefectures), 45–56. Beijing: Jinri Zhongguo Chubanshe.

———. 1995. "Zai Cheli xian gongzuo de huiyi" (Recollections on work in Cheli county). In Jinghong Committee of the CPPCC, *Jinghong wenshi ziliao* (Materials on the history and culture of Jinghong), 125–32. Vol. 2. Jinghong: Xishuangbanna Prefecture Press.

Zhao Suisheng. 2004. *A Nation-State By Construction: Dynamics of Modern Chinese Nationalism*. Palo Alto, CA: Stanford University Press.

Zhong Gong Xishuangbanna Zhouwei, Dangshi Zhengji Yanjiu Shibian (Xishuangbanna Party Committee Office of Party History Records Research). 2000. *Xishuangbanna wushi nian, 1950–2000* (Xishuangbanna fifty years, 1950–2000). Xishuangbanna: Dangshi Zhengji Yanjiu Shibian.

Zhongguo Jiaoyu Nianjian Bianzhi Weiyuanhui (China Education Yearbook Editorial Committee). 1998. *Zhongguo jiaoyu nianjian* (China education yearbook). Beijing: Zhongguo Jiaoyu Chubanshe.

Zhongguo Shaoshu Minzu Jiaoyu Bianzhi Weiyuanhui (China Minority Education Editorial Group). 1998. *Zhongguo shaoshu minzu jiaoyu shi* (History of minority education in China). Kunming: Yunnan Jiaoyu Chubanshe.

Zhongguo Tongji Nianjian Bianzhi Weiyuanhui (China Statistical Yearbook Editorial Committee). Multiple years. *Zhongguo tongji nianjian* (China statistical yearbook). Beijing: Zhongguo Tongji Chubanshe.

INDEX

acculturation, 62–63, 155–56. *See also* assimilation

activism, cultural, 6, 15, 18; associations for, 93; and cultural entrepreneurs, 111; as critique, 72, 92–94, 99, 128, 173; expressing Chinese identity, 32, 40, 47–48, 99, 101–2, 169, 173; as resistance, 34, 37, 39–40, 131, 161, 166, 169

ahong, 136–37, 145, 164, 179

AIDS, 18, 95–98

Anderson, Benedict, 116, 164

Arabic: as Hui "mother tongue," 124, 151; in Islamic education, 134, 136, 143, 149–51, 153–59; mosque architectural styles, 141, 143–47; translations into Chinese, 69. *See also* Islamic education; mosques

Armstrong, Karen, 160

Asian Development Bank, 83

assimilation: of minorities, 10, 12–13, 15, 62, 152, 166; and the nation, 23, 25–27; policies of, 43, 53, as sinicization or *Hanhua*, 46, 66. *See also* acculturation

authenticity, 7–8, 12, 62, 86, 172; contested, 87–88, 92–93, 117, 155–57; minorities as repositories of, 35, 46–47, 130

autonomy. *See* minority autonomy

backwardness: Bai, 7, 105, 120, 124, 170; cultural revival as response to, 9, 40, 48, 120–21, 126; Dai, 47, 53, 81–82, 99, 105; exacerbated by Maoist policies, 81–82; Hui, 159; and minority stereotypes, 7, 9, 45–47, 99, 130

Bai: ambiguous identity of, 14, 15, 59–63, 101–3; bilingual education, 101, 118, 120–29; Chineseness, viii, 14, 59, 62–64, 101, 112; cultural syncretism, 60–62, 101–3, 109–12; economic conditions, 7, 63, 104–5, 121; education and literacy rates, 118–20; language, 14, 59, 62, 101–3, 118, 120–28; Maoist policies toward, 63–64, 113–17; as *minjia*, 14, 59, 102, 170; music, 107–17; Nanzhao origins, 62–63, 108–12; nostalgia, 101; as relatively advanced,